THE TRIAL OF
LEONARD PELTIER

THE TRIAL OF LEONARD PELTIER

by Jim Messerschmidt

Foreword by
William Kunstler

south end press   boston ma

TO HELP LEONARD PELTIER FIGHT FOR JUSTICE

Send inquiries about how you can help and donations to:
    Leonard Peltier Defense Committee
    P.O. Box 583
    Lawrence, KS 66044

Send letters of support directly to Leonard:
    Leonard Peltier #89637-132
    United States Penitentiary
    P.O. Box 1000
    Leavenworth, KS 66048-3333

Copyright © 1983 by Jim Messerschmidt

Any properly footnoted quotation of up to 500 sequential words may be used without permission, as long as the total number of words quoted does not exceed 2,000. For longer quotations or for a greater number of total words, please write for permission to South End Press.

Cover design by Todd Jailer
Cover graphic by Robert Warrior
Typeset by Trade Composition and South End Press
Produced by the South End Press collective
Printed in the U.S.A. on acid-free, recycled paper.

Library of Congress Number: 82-061152
ISBN: 0-89608-163-x (paper)
ISBN: 0-89608-164-8 (cloth)

South End Press, 116 Saint Botolph Street, Boston, MA 02115
97 96 95 94   6 7 8 9

THIS BOOK IS WRITTEN FOR LEONARD
WHO REMAINS A POLITICAL PRISONER
ON HIS OWN LAND. I DEDICATE THE
BOOK TO ERIK AND THE FUTURE OF
HIS GENERATION.

Leonard Peltier
Courtesy of the Leonard Peltier Defense Committee

FOREWORD
William Kunstler*

Having tried the case of one of Leonard Peltier's co-defendants, twice argued Mr. Peltier's appeals from his convictions of the murders of two FBI agents on the Pine Ridge (SD) Indian Reservation, and presently handling his motion for a new trial, I can hardly be ranked as a disinterested witness. Accordingly, I must confess, at the outset, that not only do I believe that he was unjustly tried, convicted and sentenced, but that his travails were the result of FBI misconduct of such magnitude that any fair-minded society would have lost no time in condemning it out of hand. The fact that it took a book like this one to give Mr. Peltier's ordeal a wider audience than his small but devoted band of relatives, friends and supporters is undoubtedly the best evidence that we do not live in such an environment.

I do not believe that a foreword should be either a review or rehash of a book. This is particularly true in this case where very little space is devoted to the trial of Robert Robideau and Darrelle Dean Butler who, along with a youth named Jimmy Eagle, were indicted for the same crimes as was Mr. Peltier. Tried in Cedar Rapids, Iowa, before a different judge, Butler and Robideau were both acquitted, following which the charges against Eagle were dropped by the Government so that in its own words, "the full prosecutive weight of the Federal Government could be directed against Leonard Peltier."

*Kunstler is Vice-President and volunteer staff attorney, Center for Constitutional Rights.

i

The tragic fact of the matter is, had Peltier been tried along with Butler and Robideau, he would surely also have been acquitted. His flight to Canada and the long extradition proceedings which followed it eventually resulted in a separate trial for him in Fargo, ND, hardly a sympathetic locality insofar as militant Native Americans are concerned, before a judge who apparently shared his neighbors' antipathies in this area. One of the most telling portions of Dr. Messerschmidt's book is his side-by-side comparison of the diametrically opposite rulings of the Cedar Rapids and Fargo judges on the same issues. In virtually every instance, the latter resolved contested legal questions against the defendant, in sharp contrast to their disposition in Iowa. For example, where the Cedar Rapids judge had excluded particularly gruesome autopsy photographs of the dead agents, his Fargo counterpart quickly waved them into evidence.

It is obvious that the Government, having lost the Robideau-Butler trial, lobbied mightily for a change of locale and presiding judge for that of Mr. Peltier. With three of the four defendants originally accused of the crimes out of the picture, it was determined to obtain at least one conviction. In short, it was given a second chance to win and it did everything in its power to alter those circumstances which, in its opinion, had materially contributed to the Cedar Rapids acquittals. That it succeeded is graphic evidence of the insidious nature of governmental judge- and venue-shopping in political cases. Witness the selection of Harrisburg, PA, for the 1972 trial of Phillip Berrigan and his six Catholic anti-war activists accused of a conspiracy to kidnap Henry Kissinger, and Pensacola, FL, the original site of the trial of eight Vietnam Veterans Against the War (VVAW) for disruption of the 1972 Republican National Convention in Miami, to name but two better known examples.

Recently acquired FBI files, obtained by Peltier's counsel through the Freedom of Information Act (FOIA), now clearly reveal that the Government, bitterly dissatisfied with the conduct of the Cedar Rapids judge in the Robideau-Butler trial, somehow engineered a change of venue to Fargo. Once the transfer had taken place, its minions lost no time in furnishing derogatory material about the defendant and the American Indian Movement (AIM) to the new judge. In addition, the latter and the FBI began to work closely together on a number of matters, including "a technical security survey" of the judge's chambers, inspired by official innuendoes that defense counsel might be eavesdropping in that area.

Moreover, the FBI files indicated a clear collaboration between the

Government and the South Dakota federal judge who had supervised the grand jury investigation of the case. Among other things, this judge stated that he would be willing to accede to the prosecutor's request to move the grand jury from more liberal Sioux Falls to Rapid City, providing that he was furnished with "a 'game plan' that would insure there would not be any problems with people either refusing to answer subpoenas or refusing to testify once they were before the FGJ [Federal Grand Jury]." Additionally, the judge was meeting regularly with governmental representatives and, on at least one occasion, invited an FBI agent "to see him [about the case] when he was in Rapid City."

There is now pending before the Fargo judge a motion for a new trial based on other FOIA-obtained documents which conclusively prove that crucial evidence which would have destroyed or seriously compromised the case against Peltier was not disclosed to the defense by the Government as required by law. For example, a high velocity shell casing allegedly found in the trunk of one of the fatally wounded agents' cars, which was characterized by the prosecutor as "the most important piece of evidence in this case," was connected at trial by an FBI firearms expert to an automatic weapon attributed to Peltier. However, the defense was never informed that the comparison tests conducted on the casing and the weapon in question had proved negative.

This non-disclosure, as well as at least five others of comparable significance, formed the basis of the new trial motion. Shortly after the filing of this motion, another one was made to disqualify the Fargo judge on the ground that he had collaborated closely with the prosecution before and during Peltier's trial. At this writing, no action on either application has been taken, but I am certain that, granted an evidentiary hearing, the defense will be able to demonstrate that Peltier's conviction was obtained by gross and pervasive governmental misconduct.

It is not expected that there will be a definitive conclusion to the Peltier case before this compassionate and well-informed study, not only of this matter but of the FBI vendetta against Native American activists, is published. Hopefully, it will open the eyes of many non-Indians as to the extent of official criminality against AIM and its members, a state of affairs which led one federal judge, in one of the Wounded Knee leadership cases, to dismiss a prosecution on the ground that "the waters of justice have been polluted." At the very least, it should help to mobilize support for the release of a major victim of the white man's politically motivated criminal justice system.

PREFACE
The "Trial" of Leonard Peltier
Ward Churchill

"War," wrote von Clauswitz in his famous treastise, *On War*, "is policy continued by other means." It seems appropriate, when considering the 20th century relationship of the United States and American Indian peoples, to observe that the Clauswitz dictum of military purpose may rightly be inverted upon occasion: Policy has become the continuation of war "by other means."

Article I of the United States Constitution posits the principle that the federal government alone possesses treaty making powers; no state or local government is so entitled. The same article further states that federal level treaty making occurs between the United States and *other sovereign nations*. Hence, the terms and conditions of the various treaties into which the U.S. has chosen to enter over the years assume a special juridicial status within American legal life. They assume a theoretical force and validity on a par with that of the constitution itself, according to Article VI.

For subordinate legislation or governmental action to challenge the terms and conditions of a standing treaty is clearly illegal on the basis of constitutionality alone. This, however, is a consideration bearing solely upon the *internal* legal circumstances of the United States. A treaty, first and foremost, is a document representing an *international* agreement, an arrangement between sovereigns, and is thus subject to international understandings of law and extralegal activities on the part of governments. This is an arena within which the internal actions and legislation of the U.S. have seldom been scrutinized.

At the international level, it is commonly held that the unilateral violation of a treaty is illegal. When the violation involves the usurpation of the territory or sovereignty (usually, both) of another nation, it constitutes an act of *war*. This principle holds true whether or not such a seizure involves the use of outright military force—as is generally the case—or occurs through some less overt, more indirect means. The latter is different only in technique.

The indirect method of waging war, while potentially as effective as more direct means (under certain conditions) is considerably less obvious. It is the propagandist/polemicist's dream: Instead of discussing the reasons behind the war, what's at stake for the forces involved, people argue over whether or not the war actually exists. Meanwhile, the aggressor is able to pursue strategic goals and objectives at leisure.

It is within this netherworld of international aggression that the U.S. is, and has long been, engaged with the American Indian. This is not a new or sudden situation, but has evolved over the past century and a half. Its overt formulation emerged at least as early as Chief Justice (of the U.S. Supreme Court) John Marshall's 1831 pronouncement that the various North American Indian tribes, rather than possessing fully sovereign status in the manner of foreign nations, constituted "domestic, dependent nations" within the corpus of an expanding American empire.

Marshall has long been regarded as a "friend to the Indian," primarily because of his firm (if wholly theoretical) opposition to the Jackson administration's blatantly genocidal dispossession/relocation of the so-called Five Civilized Tribes from the Southeast. Yet, it is difficult to imagine a more presumptuous, indeed arrogantly aggressive conclusion than his statement that the tribes were somehow "dependent" upon the U.S.—this at a time when American penetration beyond the Mississippi was little more than a pipe-dream shared by some land speculators and politically ambitious visionaries.

Similarly, to proclaim the "domestic" inclusion of peoples to whom U.S. citizenship would be formally denied for nearly a century, who autonomously occupied territories over which the U.S. could not then pretend to hold sway, and who—without doubt—had never so much as heard of the American republic, is to advance what is at best an absurdity as an anchor of jurisprudence. At worst, the Marshall formulation was intended as exactly what it became: A legalistic obfuscation designed to rationalize and disguise a policy of systematic expropriation and colonization of peoples indigenous to the area now known as the United States of America.

That Marshall's position flew in the face of international circumstance seems undeniable. Equally undeniable is the fact that the peoples he was concerned with possessed binding treaties with the government he represented, a government bound by its own constitution to make treaties *only* with other sovereign entities. This cannot be hedged: The United States government was never empowered to enter into treaty relationships with quasi-sovereign "domestic dependent nations" (whatever these may be) any more than with the city of Boston or the state of Kentucky.

It might be, and has been, argued that this last is evidence of initial confusion on the part of the federal government which, while regrettable, was remedied by the Marshall formulation. Such a view allows all treaties entered into with the tribes between 1791 and 1831 to have been mistakes, errors creating "special circumstances," but not necessarily imparting actual sovereignty to the Indian nations.

Such a doctrine might be consistently arguable were it not for the fact that the government (including Marshall and the Supreme Court) *continued* to enter into treaty relationships with the tribes for another half century and more, until 1868. Further contestation concerning the formal recognition of the tribal/national sovereignty possessed by the American Indian was and is rendered moot. It is clear that the ratification of treaties with the Indians implies a sovereignty equivalent to that of England or France in relation to the United States.

Equally clearly, however, the United States has never chosen to acknowledge this reality—at least not since 1831. A doctrine has been in effect whereby Indian sovereignty has been reinforced for purposes of treaty making and simultaneously diminished through exercise of Marshall's "domestic, dependent" invention. That the two principles are mutually exclusive in their implications did not seem to particularly concern American leadership during the period of the consolidation of U.S. territory—or thereafter, for that matter.

The juxtaposition of totally contradictory processes was, and, to a certain extent, remains, advantageous to Washington. Viewed as an opportunistic vehicle for U.S. expansion, it may be schematized as follows: Troops would be used, in combination with other sanctioned governmental formations, as a means to gain tribal willingness to negotiate with Washington. A treaty would then be entered into between the two sides whereby the Indians inevitably ceded portions of their territory to the U.S. in exchange for the latter's guarantee of the integrity of residual ("reserved") Indian lands. The Indians, as a rule, stipulated that they retain governmental and legal hegemony within their reserved areas, while Washington demanded control over commerce and intergovernmental relations. With much ballyhoo, such agreements were customarily promoted as having marked the successful conclusion of another in a long sequence of "Indian Wars."*

Interestingly, it was precisely at the moment when the treaty was signed, at the very instant when the U.S. solemnly pledged to insure the territoriality and sovereignty of the tribes, that they truly became domestic and dependent by Washington's standards. Even the latter could not seriously extend the facade that tribes with which no documentary understandings existed were other than fully autonomous nations in practice. The treaties, then, were all along consciously employed as the inverse of their constitutionally and internationally defined purpose.

They were a tactic, integral to the policy of expansion and conquest. Each treaty secured tribal agreement and consent to the passage of title to vast tracts of land to the U.S. while simultaneously providing the basis for absolute U.S. hegemony of the remaining, tribally reserved areas. Moreover, should any tribe care to resist once the intentions became clear, each treaty had insured that the U.S. would retain its military advantage by virtue of having eliminated Indian mobility and open land. It was a virtually seamless process.

Mockingly described by Vine Deloria, Jr., in its own vernacular as being "of utmost good faith," U.S. treaty making with the Indian was an exercise in cynical manipulation. Each treaty was *conceptually* broken before being drawn up. Each marked the transformation of warfare against the Indian from overt to covert status. None marked the conclusion, literally or figuratively, of the systematic erosion of Indian landbase and Indian sovereignty at the hands of Washington policy-makers.

---

*The term is revealing in itself. There is *no* historical record of any war between the tribes and the U.S. which was initiated by the Indians. Each known outbreak of open warfare was predicated upon documentable invasion of defined (or definable) Indian lands by U.S. citizenry. The defensive nature of Indian participation in these wars is thus clear. Logically, they should thus be termed "settler's wars" or, more accurately, "wars of conquest."

Consider certain post-treaty period aspects of the performance of the U.S. government vis a vis those Indian nations, the integrity of which it had promised to safeguard, in perpetuity, as formal treaty commitments:

1) A sovereign state, a nation capable of entering into a treaty relationship with the U.S. or any other country, must—by definition—possess a mode of governance of its own. Yet, in 1934, the U.S., by legislative fiat, unilaterally constituted its preferred version of government within every reservation area of the country. This was termed the "Indian Reorganization Act," and through it traditional *Indian* leadership forms were simply declared null and void.

2) Sovereign states inherently possess the rights and mechanisms by which citizenship is defined. Yet the U.S. has unilaterally defined Indians as citizens of its own polity, subject to the rules and restrictions thereof, while denying that mechanisms such as naturalization apply to membership in the tribes. Rather, the U.S. has imposed a genetic code, called "blood quantum," through which Indian identity (rather than citizenship) is defined.

3) Any nation may be expected to possess mechanisms through which property relations, particularly those concerning land tenure, are defined. So it was/is with the tribes: Land was/is held in common. Yet the United States, in 1887, imposed the so-called Indian Allotment Act, unilaterally dissolving the basis of collective tribal ownership and imposing an Anglo-Saxon model of individuated holdings.*

4) A sovereign state, by definition, may be said to possess a structure

---

*Of the reserved tribal lands subjected to reapportionment under terms and provisions of the Allotment Act, all that was not individually assigned to tribal members was declared "surplus." A large portion was then homesteaded by non-Indians, title having "legally" passed from the tribes. It is interesting, however, that other large tracts were incorporated into federal holdings, such as national parks and forests, held—in theory at least—in common by U.S. citizens. Hence, the government demonstrably argued that collective ownership was unacceptable for Indians, but fine for non-Indians.

Such an absurdity does not seem inconsistent with the current federal practice of lumping reservation lands together with such *federally* held areas as the parks and forests, wilderness areas, military bases and Bureau of Land Management tracts. At this juncture, the process seems to to have proceeded to the point where reservations are considered only marginally "Indian," if they are truly considered that in any way at all.

of legality which—as a function of government—is extended to its citizens. Yet, beginning at least as early as *ex parte Crow Dog* in 1895, the United States has unilaterally and increasingly declared the jurisdiction of its statutory codes within the various reservation areas.

These are salient points. The list could be (and has been elsewhere) extended through volumes. But the point should be made that the federal government has historically and systematically utilized treaties and a range of other devices to consistently erode the territoriality and usurp the sovereignty of American Indian peoples. This, in effect, is what is meant by the notion that war has been carried out by other means.

Of course, the United States has not been alone in this behavior. Other nations have been guilty of using treaties and agreements with this sort of cynicism, as devices through which to gain tactical advantages in wars of territorial expansion. They too been wont to define their adversaries in terms of genetic codes rather than nationalities, of imposing strange and wonderful systems of legalism, of establishing forms of governance conducive to their own interests within the occupied areas.

France, England, Spain, Holland, Italy, Japan, the Soviet Union number among those guilty of such practices in modern times. But none perhaps so nearly coincides with the U.S. model as does the Third Reich of Germany. The *Anschluss* is surely a correlative example. So too, the Munich travesty, the tentative "understanding" with Poland, and the "Mutual Non-Aggression Pact" with the USSR. The "eugenic" codes by which the nazis defined Jewish, Slavic and other groups must surely correlate to U.S. "quantum" policies. The Nuremburg "Laws" and other pseudo-legal doctrines by which ethnic group expropriation was duly sanctified bear more than passing conceptual resemblance to the convoluted logic through which the U.S. has expropriated Indian lands. The establishment of a series of "Quisling" governments to administer occupied Europe corresponds to the U.S. reliance upon the regimes, such as those of Dick Wilson (Pine Ridge) and Peter McDonald (Navajo) in principle, if not in particulars.

Small wonder, then, that Adolf Hitler himself was known to remark upon occasion that he was drawing upon the U.S. model of "Indian Affairs" in formulating his *Lebensraumpolitik* and other nazi doctrines. The nazi expansion and genocide of the 1930s and 40s found a clear prototype in North America. The main difference was and is temporal: the nazis compressed their work into a period barely spanning a decade, rendering it crystalline in the process. The U.S. accomplishment of many of the same feats of illegality and atrocity have been strung out over two centuries, rendering it much more diffuse and difficult to pin down in clear terms.

But what of the U.S. response to nazi imitation? The answer lies in the formulation and implementation of the so-called Nuremburg Doctrine through an international tribunal assembled primarily as a result of American insistence. Both the nazi hierarchy (personally) and nazi structure (conceptually) were tried, convicted and effectively liquidated on the basis of having pursued policies of aggressive war and, concommitantly, "crimes against humanity," i.e., following the same course that has marked U.S. relations with the American Indian. In essence, the United States convicted itself along with Hermann Goering and Martin Bormann.

There is more. Imbedded in the tribunal's logic and findings at Nuremburg was the point that the nazi war of aggression did not cease with the signing of peace accords, treaties, between Germany and the occupied countries. Rather, the war continued for the duration of the nazi expropriation of territory and usurpation of sovereignty within each conquered nation. Thus, the war between Germany and France did not end with the Blitzkrieg and establishment of a puppet government at Vichy in 1940, but continued unabated until the end of the German occupation of France in 1944. The occupation and nazi diminishment of French sovereignty were in themselves considered acts of war.

Of these acts, the United States remains patently guilty relative to the Indian tribes of North America, and it is on this basis that Bruce Johanson and Roberto Maestas have referred to "the continuing Indian wars." It is also from this perspective that the present volume has been written and should be read.

Jim Messerschmidt speaks of Leonard Peltier as a political prisoner. This is entirely true in terms of war being politics "by other means." But Peltier is also, as Messerschmidt acknowledges, a prisoner of *war*, a war waged unremittingly by the U.S. against Indian people since the first instant of U.S. national existence, a war which continues unabated at the present moment, a war which seems likely to be continued until the last resources and last vestiges of Indian identity have been extinguished or the U.S. is finally defeated. It is a secret war in the manner of the U.S. engagement in Laos; it is a war of annihilation on the part of the U.S., survival on the part of the Indian. It is, in this sense, "total war."

Leonard Peltier is and has been a member of the American Indian Movement (AIM) and may thus rightly be considered as subject to purely political repression on the part of the U.S. government. First and foremost, however, he is *Akicita,* a Lakota warrior, pledged to the perpetual defense of his people against any and all transgression whether internally or externally generated. It is within this context that his story has unfolded and that he and his circumstances may be best understood.

At one level, Peltier stands for and has acted in behalf of American Indian resistance to colonization, expropriation and oppression everywhere, regardless of tribal affiliation/citizenship. More particularly, however, he must be associated with the struggle peculiar to the Lakota. He is, as Russell Means has said, "a cultural nationalist," "an Oglala Lakota patriot." Hence, the specifics of the Lakota treaty relationship to the federal government are all important in understanding "the Peltier case."

Here, the Fort Laramie Treaty of 1868 is the definitive document. It guarantees the Lakota approximately 5% of the aggregate landbase of the 48 contiguous states in perpetuity. The area in question centers upon the *Paha Sapa* (Black Hills) region, an area central to Lakota spirituality and concepts of national identity. It is land which, by treaty provision, could never pass from Lakota ownership without the expressed consent of three-quarters of all adult male Lakotas,* a formally reserved area within which the Lakota would retain full governmental/legal powers, free from federal "guidance" or control. These are the terms of the Lakota relationship to the United States, terms which remain in effect by virtue of a standing treaty.

Consent to transfer of title to Lakota lands into non-Indian domain was never secured in accordance with the treaty. The traditional Lakota leadership never agreed to alterations in the tribal governmental and legal structures. Yet, as a Lakota, Peltier was confronted with his people being formally restricted to less than 10% of their guaranteed landbase, "legal" government accruing only through Washington approved tribal administrations (as opposed to the ongoing traditional council of chiefs), tribal jurisdiction even within the residual treaty area circumscribed and subordinated to

---

*The stipulation upon male consent comes from Washington, not the tribe. It is likely not to have been contested insofar as it was considered irrelevant by the Lakota: consent to further cessions was/is not perceived as likely in any quarter, male or female, young or old.

federal law enforcement. As a patriot, he had no more choice in actively resisting such conditions than did, for example, the *Maquis* in occupied France.

Today, the French resistance fighters are considered heroic by free people everywhere. To the nazis, of course, they appeared somewhat differently. They were criminals, resisting the law of the Reich, a social problem to be eliminated through death and imprisonment. So it is with the AIM warriors, their actions cast by the government of their occupiers as merely criminal, matters to be dealt with by whatever repressive form is most effective.

The *Maquis* was countered largely by the Gestapo, the secretive political and quasi-military police of the nazi central government, in combination with the repressive apparatus allowed the Vichy regime of France itself. Similarly, the Dakota AIM organization, of which Peltier was and remains a member, has been subjected simultaneously to repression by the FBI (America's counterpart, in both form and function, to Germany's Gestapo) and by "goon squads," members of the political police allowed to puppet tribal administrations. The nature of AIM's struggle must be viewed in this light.

Messerschmidt defines the true role of the FBI/goon squad activities relative to AIM, setting the stage for his detailed examination of the assorted ploys utilized to insure Peltier's conviction as a murderer, a common criminal worthy of permanent imprisonment or worse. The government actions exposed by Messerschmidt would appear ludicrous were it not for the fact that Peltier remains in prison, subject to possible assassination as his case and cause undergo public scrutiny, a martyr to his people's struggle for sovereignty and self-determination.

Leonard Peltier is a dangerous man to the U.S. government. This is so not because he allegedly killed two federal agents on the Pine Ridge Dakota Reservation in 1975—it is likely that even the government does not believe *that*—but because he pointed to the fact that the very presence of the agents was illegal. He organized people around such issues. He spearheaded a resistance to the whole range of federal illegalities relative to the Lakota. He called things by their proper names and people began to listen. He was and is, therefore, a man whose activities, from the federal perspective, must be terminated.

The struggle of Leonard Peltier did not end with his "trial" and incarceration in a federal penitentiary. Rather, it continues both on the level of securing his personal freedom and in the broader arena of issues with which he was actively engaged prior to his arrest and "elimination."

Always central to the latter was the question of recovering Lakota treaty lands lost to white incursion and the assertion of full sovereignty over this territory. "In the spirit of Leonard Peltier" is a slogan by which such activity goes forward. For example, the Lakota, in what has come to be known as the "Lincoln Sovereignty Hearings," took the U.S. to court in 1974 to challenge federal jurisdiction over reservation areas. While they lost, they were able to force Judge Warren Urbom to articulate the government's position as being that while the Lakota were "once sovereign," the "passage of time...and federal practice... have eroded this sovereignty."

Hence, if a law is old enough and is violated consistently enough, it no longer retains force and validity. One assumes then that the Anglo-Saxon legal proscription on murder, under which Peltier was prosecuted and imprisoned, would also lack force and validity. Certainly, it is old enough and sees constant violation. But such contradiction and selectivity are the stuff of "Indian Law" in America.

Similarly, the Lakota have sued the government for non-enforcement, indeed the violation, of the 1868 treaty. In 1977, the Supreme Court came out in favor of the Lakota by maintaining that the U.S. had never gained clear title to lands expropriated from the original treaty area. The government was then assigned to make recompense for what was tacitly acknowledged to be stolen property. The government's offer was to pay the estimated worth of the land *at the time of the expropriation*, a total of less than $20 million.

In 1978, this offer was overwhelmingly rejected by Lakota referendum, and AIM advanced the slogan, "The Black Hills Are Not For Sale." Seemingly troubled by the militant ring attached to a Supreme Court ruling, the government in 1980 offered simple interest of 5% upon the original amount, covering the years since expropriation, making the grand total in excess of $120 million. This, too, was in the process of being rejected by Lakota referendum when the Supreme Court reentered the fray, taking the government off the hook. In 1982, the Court discovered that the Lakota had no choice but to accept a "reasonable" cash offer for damages done.

Of course, by this standard, a car thief apprehended in possession of stolen property would be subject only to "compensate" his/her victim—at a rate the thief deemed "fair"—and the victim would have no recourse but to accept payment while the thief retained the vehicle (legal title having passed). The equity of such a proposition is entirely indicative of overall U.S. relations with the tribes.

This flow of events has prompted an AIM takeover of a tract within the Black Hills in 1981. Nominally led by Bill and Russell Means, and acting in behalf of the tribal elders, the occupiers have announced their objective as being "the initiation of the reoccupation of the Black Hills." Operating as nearly as possible within the traditional Lakota mode of government and legality, the reoccupation remains in effect as of this writing, well over a year later.

Yellow Thunder Tiospaye (as the reoccupation area has been designated by its inhabitants) and the case of Leonard Peltier are aspects of the same struggle. The stakes involved are quite high, as Messerschmidt correctly observes in his concluding chapter. For those seriously concerned with altering the U.S. status quo, the outcome of this ongoing war between the American Indian and the American government must be a matter of utmost importance. Issues of the magnitude of U.S. territorial integrity, access to critical mineral resources and outright genocide are clearly involved.

Insofar as this book is primarily concerned with Leonard Peltier and his specific case, it is of limited though thoroughly important utility. Insofar as it offers a means for understanding the broader struggle of which Peltier is a part and which he represents, it holds an even more critical position within recent dissident literature in the U.S. In either or both events, Jim Messerschmidt is to be commended for having written this, the first comprehensive analysis of the strange case of Leonard Peltier.

Boulder, CO
September 1982

NAMES OF PEOPLE INVOLVED IN THE CASE

Gary Adams—FBI Special Agent and SWAT team member who testified to hearing Williams' radio transmission about individuals getting into a red pickup, which the agents then followed onto the Jumping Bull property. Shortly after the agents were killed, Adams observed a red pickup leave the area where the killings occurred. He was a personal friend of Ron Williams and was involved in securing statements from Brown, Anderson, and Draper.

Michael Anderson—testified for the government that he observed Peltier at the scene of the killings. Also testified under cross examination that he feared life imprisonment and beatings in jail if he did not cooperate with the FBI.

Annie Mae Aquash—AIM member whose death has raised controversy. A second autopsy revealed that she was executed, killed by a .38 caliber revolver; an FBI autopsy maintains she died of exposure.

Edgar Bear Runner—member of AIM.

Judge Paul Benson—U.S. District Judge who presided over the Peltier trial.

Dr. Robert Bloemendaal—pathologist who testified for the government and possibly perjured himself.

Norman Brown—testified for the government that he observed Peltier, after agents Coler and Williams fired on him, return fire from the treeline on them. Also testified under cross examination that the FBI scared him, and he feared for his life.

Dino Butler—indicted on 25 November 1975 for killing Special Agents Coler and Williams. Acquitted summer 1976 in Cedar Rapids, Iowa.

Jack Coler—FBI Special Agent and SWAT team member killed at Pine Ridge on 26 June 1975.

Fred Coward—FBI Special Agent and SWAT team member who testified sighting Peltier through a 2x7 power rifle scope at a distance of one-half mile. His testimony was possibly perjured.

Lynn E. Crooks—Assistant U.S. Attorney and member of the prosecution team at the Peltier trial.

Cortlandt Cunningham—FBI Special Agent, chief of the Firearms and Toolmarks Division, who signed under oath a false affidavit used in the extradition of Leonard Peltier.

Standing Deer a/k/a *Robert Hugh Wilson*—approached by federal prison administrators to "neutralize" Leonard Peltier while in prison.

Wilford Draper—testified for the government that Peltier was in the tent area prior to and after the death of the agents.

Roque Dueñas—assisted Peltier escape from Lompoc Federal Prison. Has been missing since 2 October 1981.

Jimmy Eagle—first charged with killing agents Coler and Williams in July 1975, he was indicted for murders on 25 November 1975. Charges dropped 8 September 1976.

Robert Ecoffey—BIA police officer who accompanied Coler and Williams on their search for Jimmy Eagle, 25 June 1975.

Bruce Ellison—attorney and member of the defense team at the Peltier trial. Currently an attorney for Peltier.

Bobby Garcia—assisted Leonard Peltier escape from Lompoc Federal Prison. Found dead in his cell on 13 December 1980.

James P. Hall—manager of a sporting goods shop in Fargo, ND, that specializes in the sale of firearms, scopes and reloading devices. Testified for the defense that he could not determine facial features of an acquaintance through a 2x7 power rifle scope, such as SA Coward's.

Evan Hodge—FBI Special Agent who possibly perjured himself regarding types of tests performed on the AR-15 found in Wichita, KS.

Dean Hughes—FBI Special Agent and SWAT team leader who testified to hearing Williams say over the radio, "I am hit."

Evan Hultman—U.S. attorney and member of the prosecution team at the Peltier trial.

Ann M. Johnson—FBI stenographer who took notes of radio communications from various FBI agents on the day of the firefight.

Wallace Little, Jr.—lived at the Jumping Bulls and left the crime scene with his father and Gerald Mousseau after the shooting of the agents.

Winthrop Lodge—FBI fingerprint specialist who allegedly made notes while examining Coler's car (where the .223 casing was found) but neglected to note down the contents of other cars at the crime scene.

John Lowe—attorney and member of the defense team, Peltier trial.

Dr. Thomas Noguchi—pathologist who testified for the government and possibly perjured himself.

George O'Clock—FBI Special Agent who "assisted" stenographer Ann Johnson transcribe radio transmissions.

Myrtle Poor Bear—testified she signed three false affidavits under FBI coercion, two of which indicated she observed Peltier kill the agents. Also testified she did not know Leonard Peltier and was not at the Jumping Bulls area on the day in question.

David Price—FBI Special Agent and member of a SWAT team who helped Myrtle Poor Bear prepare her affidavits. May have been involved in the cover-up of Annie Mae Aquash's death/murder.

Bob Robideau—indicted for murdering agents Coler and Williams on 25 November 1975. Acquitted summer 1976 in Cedar Rapids, IA.

Robert L. Sikma—Assistant U.S. Attorney and member of prosecution team, Peltier trial.

Edward Skelly—FBI Special Agent and member of SWAT team who testified to hearing Williams say over the radio that someone should get to the top of the ridge and cover agents Coler and Williams.

Madonna Slow Bear—testified she had never been questioned by the FBI regarding her alleged presence at the Jumping Bull area and did not know Myrtle Poor Bear.

Marvin Stolt—BIA police officer and SWAT team member who testified to observing Eagle and Peltier through binoculars.

Joe Stuntz—Native American killed at Pine Ridge on 26 June 1975.

Elliott Taikeff—attorney and member of defense team, Peltier trial.

Dallas Thundershield—assisted Peltier escape from Lompoc Federal Prison. Shot in the back during the escape.

Gerard P. Waring—FBI Special Agent and SWAT team member who testified to hearing Williams' radio transmission that firing was coming from the ridge above him and that he was hit. Waring possibly changed his 302 (FBI report) to fit the government scenario.

William Webster—current FBI director. Sat on the panel that heard Peltier's appeal, but resigned when he was appointed director.

Ron Williams—FBI Special Agent who was killed at Pine Ridge on 26 June 1976.

Dick Wilson—tribal chairperson of the Pine Ridge Reservation 1972-1976.

Norman Zigrossi—Assistant Special Agent in charge, Rapid City, SD.

Jimmy Zimmerman—Eleven-year-old Native American who lived in tent city.

CHRONOLOGY OF EVENTS

December 1890—Wounded Knee I—Massacre of 300 women, children and men near Wounded Knee by the U.S. Cavalry.

February 1973—Wounded Knee II—Approximately 300 traditionals and AIM supporters occupy the village of Wounded Knee to protest tactics of Wilson and the goon squad.

March 1975—Members of AIM arrive at the Jumping Bull Ranch and set up a spiritual camp. A grassroots movement of AIM and traditional people continues to grow, challenging Wilson's abuse of power and corporate exploitation on Indian land.

Between 1 March 1973 and 1 March 1976—Extensive clashes between Wilson's goon squad and supporters or members of AIM, resulting in 66 documented violent deaths and 200 murders overall.

24 April 1975—FBI does a study of its "paramilitary operations" preparedness on Indian land.

Between 27 May 1975 and 6 June 1975—FBI inspects reservation and concludes that "bunkers" exist which would take a paramilitary assault to overcome resistance against the FBI by AIM members and supporters. The FBI notes pockets of AIM members on the reservation.

Late May 1975—Build-up of FBI personel in and around reservation (mostly SWAT trained agents). The FBI begins training a ten-man BIA SWAT team.

16 June 1975—FBI again supplements its manpower by ordering special agents into South Dakota for a temporary 60 day period.

26 June 1975—FBI agents Ron Williams and Jack Coler enter the Jumping Bull Ranch and a firefight ensues. Both FBI agents and Native American Joe Stuntz are killed. The firefight lasts all day, and the grassroots movement is disrupted with the ensuing military-type occupation of the Reservation by FBI and other law enforcement agencies.

27 June 1975—Church Committee cancels plans to hear testimony concerning relationship between FBI and AIM.

5 September 1975—FBI invades Rosebud Reservation in search of Peltier and others.

10 September 1975—Automobile carrying Michael Anderson, Bob Robideau, Norman Charles and others explodes on a turnpike near Wichita, KS. The government obtains a damaged AR-15 from this automobile and claims it is the murder weapon.

25 November 1975—Leonard Peltier, Jimmy Eagle, Bob Robideau and Dino Butler are indicted for the murder of agents Williams and Coler.

2 January 1976—Six months after the firefight, Dick Wilson officially signs over to the Department of the Interior jurisdiction for one-eighth of Pine Ridge Reservation land, which contains uranium, gas, oil and gravel.

6 February 1976—Peltier arrested in Canada and held for extradition hearings.

26 February 1976—Annie Mae Aquash's body found on reservation. Government autopsy states she died of exposure; independent pathologist determines she was shot in the head.

February and March 1976—Myrtle Poor Bear signs three false affidavits under coercion by the FBI which directly implicate Leonard Peltier. These affidavits are used in extradition proceedings of Peltier.

Summer 1976—Butler and Robideau acquitted of charges in Cedar Rapids, IA.

8 September 1976—Charges against Jimmy Eagle dropped.

18 December 1976—Peltier extradited to the U.S.

March and April 1977—Peltier stands trial for the murder of SA Williams and Coler in Fargo, ND.

18 April 1977—Peltier found guilty of two counts of murder in the first degree.

1 June 1977—Peltier sentenced by Judge Paul Benson to two consecutive life sentences.

December 1977—Oral argument on Peltier's appeal first held in St. Louis. Judge William Webster is one of panel of three judges hearing appeal.

January 1978—Webster named Director of FBI. Tells American people they must help combat domestic terrorism.

February 1978—Peltier acquitted of attempted murder of Milwaukee Police Officer Ronald Hlaviaka.

14 September 1978—Peltier's appeal before the Eight Circuit Court denied.

10 March 1979—Supreme Court refuses to review Peltier's case.

May to June 1979—Government plot to kill Peltier in prison unfolds before his eyes.

20 July 1979—Leonard Peltier, with the assistance of Bobby Garcia, Dallas Thundershield and Roque Dueñas, flees from Lompoc Federal Prison, in fear for his life.

26 July 1979—Leonard Peltier recaptured.

14 November 1979—Escape trial begins, Judge Lawrence Lydick denies "duress and coercion" defense, prohibits Peltier from presenting evidence concerning his reasons for fleeing prison.

22 January 1980—Peltier convicted and given maximum sentence, seven years, on charges of prison escape and illegal possession of a weapon. Bobby Garcia sentenced to five years for the escape conviction.

13 December 1980—Bobby Garcia found dead in his cell.

20 **March 1981**—Peltier's escape conviction appealed to U.S. 9th Circuit Court. The three-judge panel reverses escape conviction, ruling that the trial judge erred in denying Peltier the opportunity to ask a government witness questions pertaining to his personal bias against Peltier. The court also "suggested" that the lower court permit the assassination plot evidence at a new trial ordered to take place.

2 **October 1981**—Roque Dueñas' fishing boat found upside down. Kevin Henry, Dueñas' nephew, found dead due to drowning and being hit by a blunt object. Dueñas remains missing.

11 **April 1982**—Writ of habeas corpus filed in U.S. District Court, Fargo, ND. Writ indicates substantial suppression of exonerating evidence by the government during the Peltier trial as well as knowing use of false evidence to obtain a conviction.

30 **December 1982**—Judge Paul Benson refuses to remove himself from the case as well as order the release of 6,000 FBI documents on Peltier.

31 **December 1982**—Judge Paul Benson denies Leonard Peltier a new trial.

ACKNOWLEDGEMENTS

Many people devoted much time and energy to help make this book possible.

I am particularly indebted to Bruce Ellison, who read the manuscript several times, providing valuable insight and detailed comments at each stage of the process. He also supplied me with valuable prison and FBI documents and happily tolerated long telephone calls as well as an abundance of correspondence.

I owe considerable thanks to members of the South End Press collective whose strong commitment to an anti-racist posture puts them far above any other "left" publishing house today. Special thanks go to Michael Albert who supported and believed in this book from the beginning, and to Mary Lea, whose brilliant copy editing and dedicated hard work and long hours made the organization and clarity of the book much better.

Maluca van den Bergh and Elizabeth and Joe Merz furnished me with an unpublished manuscript they had prepared, which helped guide my initial voyage through the 5,300 pages of trial transcripts. John Snider and John Sherman both read early drafts of the manuscript, contributing important comments and editorial assistance. Lilias Jones read the final chapter and helped clarify what I wanted to say. Ward Churchill read the final draft of the manuscript and rendered important information that helped me avoid historical errors. Lynn Wilson and Nancy Gililand read the initial draft of the trial chapter and contributed important suggestions.

Many thanks also go to Michael Garitty who provided me with the government documents discussed in the last chapter; to John Privitera for sending the trial transcripts and the writ of habeas corpus; to Ed Asner for financial assistance; to Linda Kalland for typing the first draft of the manuscript; and to Mark Fredrickson, Kathy Sullivan, and Ulla Eurenius-Messerschmidt for continued emotional support throughout the last two and one half years.

Finally, I would like to thank Ward Churchill, John Johnson, Ulla Eurenius-Messerschmidt, and Lea Storch for their work on the front cover.

TABLE OF CONTENTS

One

INTRODUCTION

Leonard Peltier is a political prisoner. At this time he is serving two consecutive life terms at the maximum security federal prison in Marion, Illinois. He was convicted by an all white jury for a crime he did not commit, the murder of two FBI agents. But as we will see, Peltier was tried and convicted because he was an American Indian leader, struggling to defend the rights and land of his people.

On the morning of 26 June 1975, at a ranch occupied by members of the Jumping Bull Family (within the boundaries of the Pine Ridge Indian Reservation, South Dakota), a firefight occurred between traditional Native Americans aligned with members of the American Indian Movement (AIM) and the Federal Bureau of Investigation (FBI). When the shooting had ceased, Lakota Joseph Stuntz and FBI agents Ron Williams and Jack Coler were dead. Four Native Americans were subsequently charged with the murder of the two agents, yet only one, Leonard Peltier, was convicted. The reasons for Peltier's trial and subsequent conviction are the subject of this book.

Leonard Peltier, a Chippewa-Lakota activist and an important leader of the American Indian Movement, has been described by fellow AIM activist John Trudell as "this generation's Geronimo, this generation's Crazy Horse." Peltier, like the great Indian leaders Trudell mentions, has opposed government control and takeover of Indian land,

1

while the FBI, not the Seventh Cavalry, persecutes Peltier and other Indian leaders like him.

The trial of Leonard Peltier was, in fact, the result of his political history. Peltier, in the late '60s, was committed to a national movement of Indians striving to restore their traditional culture and reclaim the rights guaranteed them by treaties made over a period of one hundred years. Peltier was then living in Seattle where he assisted a group of Indians in the occupation of Fort Lawton, which had been declared surplus by the United States Army. Since federal regulations grant Indians first rights to all land declared "surplus," the occupation was proclaimed "lawful" by the federal government. As a result, the United Indians of All Tribes have built and continue to maintain on this land the Daybreak Star Cultural Center.

During this time in Seattle, Peltier owned a large body and fender shop. He provided voluntary services to the Indian community and was highly respected by his friends.

In the 1970s, Peltier moved to the midwest where he met Dennis Banks, Russell Means and some other individuals who had organized the American Indian Movement in Minneapolis in 1968. AIM was founded for the purpose of protecting the lives and treaty rights of American Indians across the country. Peltier joined AIM and became active in struggles revolving around treaty rights.

In 1972 Peltier was living in Milwaukee, Wisconsin, where he joined the "Trail of Broken Treaties," a demonstration requesting that the U.S. Government investigate treaty violations over the last one hundred years. Over 200 people arrived in Washington, D.C. on 30 October 1972, and when the Bureau of Indian Affairs officials told the caravan to go home, they occupied the BIA offices. The offices were held for one week, forcing the White House to promise a hearing on the grievances set down by AIM.

However, the FBI also became aware of the leaders of this occupation. According to Rex Wyler, in a memo from then Attorney General William Saxbe, the FBI was told to "put AIM leaders under close scrutiny and arrest them on every possible charge until they can no longer make bail." Dennis Banks, Russell Means and Leonard Peltier were three of the AIM leaders specifically targeted by the FBI.[1]

It was during this time that the power of Pine Ridge Reservation (South Dakota) Tribal Chairman Dick Wilson was being challenged by traditional Indians on the reservation. Wilson was elected tribal chairman in 1972 and has since ignored traditional Indian demands. For instance, shortly after his election, the traditional people organized the Oglala Sioux Constitutional Rights Organization to obtain such things as higher rents for land Indians leased to ranchers. Yet Wilson, representing big business, refused to allow this issue to go before the Bureau of Indian Affairs for consideration.[2] Instead, Wilson misused federal money to employ, train and arm a despotic personal police force, known to the residents of the Pine Ridge Reservation as the "goon squad."*

In February 1973, Banks, Means and approximately three hundred traditionals and supporters or members of AIM occupied the village of Wounded Knee, South Dakota to protest the tactics employed by Wilson and his goons. For 71 days, Native Americans outlasted a siege by the FBI, U.S. Marshalls and the Bureau of Indian Affairs Police. Wounded Knee "precipitated the most recent series of governmental prosecutorial and armed ferocity [savageries] against the Indian Nations and flowed directly from the land thefts, under guise of treaty, conducted by the U.S. government and its Bureau of Indian Affairs."[3]** On 6 May 1973 the occupation came to a close as representatives of the U.S. Government agreed to carry out congressional investigations of and meetings on the conditions at Pine Ridge and the violations of the 1868 treaty. These investigations never occurred.

In the year following Wounded Knee (1974), Russell Means ran for the office of tribal chairman of the Pine Ridge Indian Reservation and, "in one of the most outrageous miscarriages of Justice, Richard Wilson (the right-wing incumbent) stole the election."[5] The U.S. Commission on Civil Rights later documented how this election was fraudulently won.

In the primary, Means was the victor by approximately 150 votes.[6] Yet when the final election came around on 7 February 1974, Wilson won by a vote of 1,714 to 1,514.[7] The Commission found through their investigation that,

- Many individuals voted who were ineligible to vote because they were not enrolled members of the tribe. An examination of 743 names on the official voting records identified 154 such non-enrolled voters.

*Members of the goon squad, which numbered approximately 100 individuals, called themselves "goons," meaning "Guardians of the Oglala Nation."
**The Sioux signed the Fort Laramie Treaty in 1868, which recognized the Sioux Nation as a sovereign nation. This treaty originally guaranteed the Sioux approximately 50 million acres of traditional homeland in Nebraska, North and South Dakota, Montana and Wyoming. However, when gold, oil, coal, uranium and other natural resources were found on this land, "the government and private corporations took back the land in violation of this treaty."[4]

- Many people voted in the election who were not on the official voting list without complying with the election ordinance requiring a proper affidavit of eligibility.
- No method was set up to disqualify ballots cast by voters who were ineligible.
- Many people voted who were not residents of the reservation or who did not meet the one year residency requirement.
- No method was used to check the identity of individuals presenting themselves at the polls.
- The voter lists distributed to the precincts were out of date and extremely inaccurate.
- No poll-watchers or observers were present at any time during the official count of the votes.
- No record was kept as to the distribution of official ballots or the exact number of official ballots printed.
- Many ballots were taken out of the polling places, marked, placed in the ballot boxes and counted without following the procedures set down for absentee voting.
- When the election was contested by Russell Means, Wilson, the only person with the legal authority to call the Tribal Council into session, refused to do so.
- The Bureau of Indian Affairs refused to oversee the election and refused to investigate charges of irregularities and fraud.
- The election was held in a climate of fear and tension.[8]

Wilson's manipulation of the election was only one aspect of his administration. During his tenure in office he sacrificed his people to larger economic interests. For instance, he attempted to convince the tribal council to sell the Black Hills, but was unsuccessful.[9] On 2 January 1976 he signed away one-eighth of the Pine Ridge Reservation to the Badlands National Monument.[10] Moreover, according to Johansen and Maestas, he has continually facilitated the transfer of Lakota land from traditional Indians to either non-Indian or minimally-Indian (less than full-blood) ranchers and farmers. In short, Wilson's administration has furthered the process of removing land from Lakota people such that by the mid-1970s approximately thirty percent of the grazing land and eighty-seven percent of the cultivated land on the Oglala Lakota Nation was in the hands of non-Indians.[11] Of the seventy percent grazing land in Indian hands, approximately ninety percent is owned and used by individuals who are less than half Indian blood.[12] Sixty-three percent of all Indian-owned agricultural land is being cultivated by non-Indians today.[13] This "giving away" of Indian lands to non-Indians is nothing new to traditional Indians. It has been happening for the last five hundred years as people like Wilson cater to the needs and enticements of big business. The energy companies in this country are now working on the final land thefts.[14]

The depleted Indian land base destroys Native Americans' ability to sustain and reproduce life. Hundreds of thousands have left the reservations for the cities in search of work. Of approximately 1,500,000 American Indians in the United States today, only about one third, or 500,000, live on or near reservations.[15] As early as 1969, few reservations had as many as 3,000 people, and the average population density was only one person per 4.2 square miles. The result of these trends has been devastating poverty for American Indians.[16]

Not only is the means of sustaining life for American Indians being stolen, but also, the means of reproducing life. Many traditional American Indian men and women have been forced to submit to sterilization. Lee Brightman, President of the United Native Americans, estimates that of the overall Native population "as many as 42% of the women of childbearing age and 10% of the men have already been sterilized."[17] All information, from Dr. Connie Uri's inquiry in 1976 for then U.S. Senator Abourezk (D.-South Dakota) to more recent studies, indicates that "sterilization of Native people is on the increase" and there is much evidence "that full-blood Indian women are being singled out."[18] The blatant racism of such efforts at birth control can only be seen as significantly contributing to the genocide of full blood Indians.

Pine Ridge Reservation is one of the parcels of land allocated to the Sioux after the 1934 Indian Reorganization Act, and the social and economic conditions of the marginalization process are clear:

> The reservation exceeds 4,500 square miles without any public transportation. Its one library and bank are located in the white settlement areas. Less than one percent of the land is cultivated by Native Americans, while more than half the acreage is used by whites for grazing . . . By 1973 about 70 percent of those at Pine Ridge were unemployed . . . the life expectancy was 44 years, 30 years less than that of white persons . . . While the BIA and other federal agencies billed American tax payers over $8,000 a year per Oglala Sioux family at the Pine Ridge, the medium income there remained at less than $2,000.[19]

Wilson's abuse of power, because it supported the incessant alienation of traditional Indian land and resources, as well as the destruction of the traditional way of life, motivated the traditional community to challenge his practices even more. The Oglala Sioux Constitutional Rights Organization attempted to impeach Wilson, but the tribal chairman "sat . . . at his own impeachment hearing and of course denied the traditional's challenge." The Constitutional Rights Organization then turned to the Bureau of Indian Affairs for help, only to be ignored.[20] One result of this conflict between the traditionals and Wilson was the seventy-one day occupation of Wounded Knee. Wilson responded with his goon squad.

Between 1 March 1973 and 1 March 1976 sixty-three documented violent deaths occurred on the Oglala Nation.[21] The majority of these deaths were those of supporters or members of the American Indian Movement, who were killed primarily by the goon squad.[22]

The Treaty Council believes that overall "more than 300 people have been murdered on the Pine Ridge Reservation since 1973."[24] As a result, the yearly murder rate between 1973 and 1976 has been estimated to be 170 per 100,000, making it the highest in the country. This was more than eight times the 1974 murder rate in Detroit, the nation's urban leader.[25] Furthermore, when the police and goons were not killing people, they were engaging in attempted murder, beatings and the destruction of property. All of which have become a fact of life for traditional people on the reservation.[26]

Many witnesses at the trial of Leonard Peltier testified to these oppressive conditions existing on the reservation. Della Starr's testimony summarized the plight of the traditional people:

> . . . the goons and the BIA police would start coming around you know, start shooting around. And they'd start, you know, start some kind of trouble and then we'd have to break up, you know—we try to avoid trouble, and they were even shooting at our houses. And we have, you know, there's alot of kids in some of these houses. And what the goons done (is) alot of harassing. But there was nothing that could be done. We couldn't go to the BIA police because they were right with them. So finally, the traditional, the elderly people got together and asked, you know, that we'd have our own security around the Oglala area so we can have at least a little protection.[27]

Although the FBI is charged with investigating major crimes in Indian country under the Major Crimes Act (23 Stat. 385), it continually avoided this legal responsibility on the Pine Ridge Reservation. In fact, according to Bruce Johansen and Roberto Maestas, the FBI purposely evaded the issue, stating it "lacked manpower," even though all evidence indicates this was not so.

> . . . before Wounded Knee the full-time staff of the Rapid City office had been three agents; after Wounded Knee eleven were assigned there. On the reservation, agents conspicuously walked the streets of Pine Ridge Village, looking appropriately colonial with their short haircuts and shiny black, round-toed shoes. Paramilitary gear, such as tanks and armored personnel carriers, reminders of Wounded Knee, sometimes stood on street corners.[28]

With the Wilson regime, BIA police and FBI against them, the traditional people again turned to the American Indian Movement for assistance.

Francis He Crow, co-coordinator and researcher for the Traditional Council of Chiefs of the Oglala Sioux Tribe, brought to the trial a document drawn up in early 1975 and signed by every member of the Council of Chiefs. This document specifically requested the American Indian Movement to come to the Reservation "and protect Indians and property and the fish and wildlife." AIM was needed, according to He Crow, because "there is no law on the reservation."[29]

According to the prosecution, seven members of AIM arrived at Pine Ridge Reservation in March of 1975: Dino and Nilak Butler, Leonard Peltier, Jean Day, Anna Mae Aquash, Melvin Lee and Michael Anderson. They first lived outside the Oglala village. In May, Joe Stuntz and Norman Charles came to the Reservation and the entire group moved to the Jumping Bull area. The Jumping Bull land (owned by Harry and Cecilia Jumping Bull) lies within the White Clay district of the Pine Ridge Reservation. This district "is like a stronghold of the traditional peoples traditionalism on the Reservation." At White Clay, "the traditional philosophy is more prevalent."[30] After a trip to an AIM sponsored spiritual conference in Arizona, Norman Brown, Wilford Draper, Bob Robideau and Jimmy Zimmerman joined the group at Jumping Bulls.

Jimmy Durham, Executive Director of the International Indian Treaty Council and their United Nations representative stated at the Peltier trial that the traditional Council of Chiefs is the *legal* government on the Reservation, not the U.S.-imposed government instituted by the Indian Reorganization Act of 1934. This legality, according to Durham, was

> . . . recognized by the U.S. through the 1868 Fort Laramie Treaty. Different congressional Acts have tried to pretend this treaty is not valid to the extent that those congressional acts say it is not valid. That is not constitutional in our vision and so there is a constant conflict of what amounts to a colonial government, the United States taking over our land, giving us the form of government on every reservation that is not our form of government, setting up different economic factors that pit Indians against other Indians. The government uses every way that it can, the only way I can frankly say it, to harass us and divide us.[31]

The tribal government is recognized and supported by the U.S. government and was not consulted with or approved by the Council of Chiefs. As a result, the Bureau of Indian Affairs, a subdivision of the Department of the Interior, controls Native Americans, Native American land and other natural resources, and Native American capital.

Jimmy Durham summarized the underlying causes of the conflict between traditional and non-traditional Native Americans:

> The traditional vision of American Indians with the pipe centers around a harmony of a circle, harmony of every part of life with our animal brothers and sisters and with our human brothers and sisters and a reverence for the sacredness of life. And this seems to come in direct conflict with white people's mentality. The only way I can see it, and the situation on Pine Ridge is that the non-traditionals, the mixed-bloods, have accepted the white man's money, the white man's way of life and that is the difference.[32]

In contrast to non-traditionals, members of AIM were described by witnesses at the Peltier trial as being the same as traditional Native Americans "because the thoughts are the same," in the sense that both are committed to constructing a socio-economic system based on and able to preserve traditional Indian cultures. The American Indian Movement was "organized to help the people, the Native American people throughout the United States to get to know their traditions and to live the traditional way, and teach it to our young . . . and also if there was anything that we might be able to help them with in their community, to come in and help them. More or less a supportive group than anything else." In short, "The American Indian Movement is a group of people organized to struggle for their freedom, against hatred, oppression and against people in power."[33]

The traditional people on the Pine Ridge Reservation were increasingly concerned with the continued alienation of their land and resources, and their resulting impoverishment. As a result, a grassroots movement which included Peltier emerged to challenge the illegal conveyance of Indian property to non-Indians. The movement was countered by Richard Wilson's repressive police force, which indicated through its actions a dedication to the destruction of full-blood Indians. In addition the Federal Bureau of Investigation did *not* move to help prevent the criminality of the goon squad, nor did it even attempt to investigate the crimes that had been committed. Instead, the FBI, in an indirect way, aligned with Wilson in repressing the traditional people and American Indian Movement, who were resisting Wilson's actions, which seemed to support big business.

The government's stake in the status quo and the reasons for Peltier's trial and subsequent conviction are the subject of this book. We will investigate in the pages to come the government's role in repressing dissent; the subsequent use of the legal system to secure control over the movement; and the causes of the repression and its effect on American Indian land, resources and way of life.

Chapters two and three concentrate on the FBI and judicial apparatus and show their involvement with events at Pine Ridge. Chapter two provides a brief historical overview of the FBI, its main concerns throughout its years of operation and its more recent relation to American Indians. Chapter three describes, through an analysis of the trial of Leonard Peltier, how the legal system legitimates its repressive tactics by appealing to legal codes and procedures, and how the state effectively secures control while at the same time masking its own criminal behavior.[34] In Chapter four we look at what has more recently happened to Leonard Peltier. And finally, in the last chapter, we consider the political-economic motivations for the legal repression and the subsequent effect of this repression on American Indian land, resources and way of life.

Two

THE FBI

Historically, individuals and groups in the U.S. who oppose capitalism and advocate social change have been defined as subversive and threatening to free enterprise, democracy, and thus the security of the nation-state. As a result, under the guise of defending the "free enterprise system" and "national security," the FBI has, from its inception, denied, through direct criminal actions, anti-capitalist activists their first amendment rights. We, therefore, begin by looking historically at the emergence of the Bureau of Investigation and its early role in American society in the 20th century. Then we turn to the later years of the Bureau and analyze its change of emphasis in the 1960s and 1970s. Finally, we close out this chapter with a look at the relationship between American Indians and the FBI, with particular emphasis upon its role at Pine Ridge. This survey allows us to understand the trial of Leonard Peltier in the broader social and historical context which contours its real lessons and meaning.

Early Years

The forerunner of the modern FBI was the Justice Department's Bureau of Investigation. The Bureau was established in 1908 under Theodore Roosevelt's administration, but did not turn its attention toward dissent until the years surrounding World War I. During that

11

time, 1917-1918, agents from the Bureau of Investigation investigated the activities of thousands of draft resisters, while enforcing the Espionage and Sedition Acts, which were enacted for the purpose of criminalizing pronouncements and publications critical of U.S. governmental policies. In combination with vigilante groups and state officials, the Justice Department repressed dissident individuals and organizations. Supporting the capitalist class, agents raided offices of radical groups, such as the Socialist Party; in 1918 alone, they secured the conviction of 166 leaders of the Industrial Workers of the World.[1]

During this time, socialists, anarchists and unionists opposed the militarism generated by WWI. The IWW was a leading element in the resistance movement. Thus, in early September 1917, Bureau agents raided forty-eight IWW meeting halls throughout the country, seizing evidence for prosecution. Eventually 101 of the 166 went to trial for conspiring to hinder the draft, encouraging desertion and intimidating others in connection with labor disputes. The jury found them all guilty, many receiving lengthy sentences of 20 years. They were fined a total of $2,500,000.[2]

In 1917, the revolution in Russia surprised the world. As a result of the victory of the Soviet Bolsheviks, Bolshevism in the United States became a major focus of attention for the Justice Department. Rather than directing their activities toward "common criminals," agents for the Bureau mounted a massive intelligence gathering operation against all left-wing groups and dissidents in the country.[3]

Then Attorney General A. Mitchell Palmer, received $500,000 from Congress to apprehend radicals. On 1 August 1919 he established within the Bureau of Investigation a department called the General Intelligence Division (GID). As head he appointed J. Edgar Hoover, "charging him with the responsibility of gathering and coordinating all information concerning domestic radical activities."[4] One of Hoover's first maneuvers in October of that year was a campaign to frame black radical Marcus Garvey on fraud charges. This operation culminated in Garvey's deportation.[5] Under Hoover's leadership, the GID set up a file of over 200,000 radical leaders, publications, organizations, and activities in various localities.[6] The result of this information gathering was the roundup and eventual deportation of 10,000 individuals in the infamous Palmer Raids on January 2 and 6, 1920. Those arrested came mainly from the Communist and Communist Labor Party organizations.[7] Moreover, as blacks became members of the Communist Party, the Bureau attempted to destroy interracial unity. Special strategies were specifically directed at black leaders such as Paul Robeson and Richard Wright; the Bureau may even have been involved in Wright's later death in Paris.[8] In short, although agents of the Bureau of Investigation were charged with enforcing the criminal law, they spent a major part of their time making illegal arrests of thousands of alien communists and undertaking counterintelligence activities that would undermine radical organizations.

One of those "rounded up" was an anarchist by the name of Andrea Salsedo. After his arrest he was held for eight weeks in a New York Bureau office, not allowed to have contact with family, friends or a lawyer. Shortly thereafter his crushed body was found on the pavement below the building. Bureau agents stated he committed suicide by jumping from the fourteenth floor window.[9]

Shortly after Salsedo's death, two of his friends were arrested by Bureau agents on trumped up charges. These individuals were Nicola Sacco and Bartolomeo Vanzetti, both charged with robbery and eventual murder at a shoe factory. Being arrested for crimes they did not in all probability commit, Sacco and Vanzetti

> . . . went on trial, were found guilty, and spent seven years in jail while appeals went on, and while all over the country and the world, people became involved in their case. The trial record and the surrounding circumstances suggested that Sacco and Vanzetti were sentenced to death because they were anarchists and foreigners. In August 1927, as police broke up marches and picket lines with arrests and beatings, and troops surrounded the prison, they were electrocuted.[10]

American radicalism was practically destroyed by the Palmer Raids and the resulting deportations, trials, and counterintelligence activities. Bolshevism was no longer a threat to American capitalism. Nevertheless, the Bureau of Investigation did not stop. It began to increase in strength considerably. By 1923 the Bureau received an annual budget of two and a quarter, million dollars, grew to 697 employees, and became the largest bureau in the entire Justice Department. With this amount of money, the Bureau was able to employ an efficient network of paid informants to infiltrate unions and radical organizations.[11]

Such Bureau activities were "extralegal." There was no federal law that could be used to prosecute radicals and communists. Consequently, no federal statutes justified their continued infiltration and investigation of radical leaders and groups. As a result, "the Bureau turned to the states, many of which had enacted vague laws proscribing such offenses as criminal anarchy, criminal syndicalism, and sedition."[12] In other words, *federal* agents began investigating radicals for prosecution of crimes that fell under *local* statutes. However, this was clearly not under their authority to perform. Yet, as Michael Belnap has shown, in 1922 alone, the Bureau

> . . .obtained state convictions against 115 such individuals, despite the fact that nothing in the bureau operation gave it any authority to assist local prosecutors in building cases against Communists who had violated no federal law.[13]

This was not the only thing Bureau agents did illegally. Agents perjured themselves and covered up wrongdoings to obtain the convictions of communists and other "radical elements."[14]

After 1924, the year J. Edgar Hoover was made head of the Bureau, the postwar boom began to take effect, ushering in a new era of prosperity for U.S. capitalism. This lasted throughout the twenties and up to the stock market crash of 1929. Although labor strife was still prevalent, it declined considerably when compared to the 1917-1923 period.[15] In this economic context "the deportation of alien radicals virtually ceased. Presidents Harding and Coolidge freed most federal political prisoners, and a number of governors released radicals from state confinement."[16]

However, this liberalism was not to last long. With the onset of the Great Depression in the thirties, communists, socialists and anarchists became active again in organizing workers' alliances.[17] As a result, the newly elected President, Franklin D. Roosevelt, asked J. Edgar Hoover to collect intelligence on political organizations he deemed "subversive." The following is an excerpt from a "strictly confidential" Hoover memorandum, dictated on 10 September 1936.

> In talking with the Attorney General today concerning the radical situation, I informed him of the conference which I had with the President on September 1, 1936, at which time the Secretary of State was present and at which time the Secretary of State, at the President's suggestion, requested of me, the representative of the Department of Justice, to have investigation made of the subversive activities in this country.[18]

Not long after, Bureau agents once again became profoundly committed to the suppression of radicalism in the United States. The

Federal Bureau of Investigation, as it was renamed in 1938, directed the majority of its activities toward radicalism. Consequently, the Bureau performed law enforcement duties unrelated to the enforcement of Federal Criminal laws. The Church Committee Report investigating FBI intelligence activities since its beginning came to this very conclusion:

> Thus it appears that one of the first purposes of FBI domestic intelligence was to perform the "pure intelligence" function of supplying executive officials with information believed of value for making policy decisions. This aspect of the assignment to investigate "subversion" was entirely unrelated to enforcement of federal criminal laws.[19]

The FBI's work began to entail "pure intelligence," or in other words, the amassing of information to implement political repression. By 1938, according to a Hoover memorandum to then Attorney General Cummings and President Roosevelt, the FBI had *illegally* investigated subversion in (1) the maritime, steel, coal, clothing, garment, fur, automobile, and newspaper industries, (2) educational institutions, (3) organized labor, (4) youth groups, (5) black groups, (6) government affairs, and (7) the armed forces.[20]

The intelligence gathered in these investigations was accomplished through forms of misconduct by the agents themselves. Through wiretapping (in violation of the Federal Communications Act of 1934 which prohibited wiretapping), bugging, mail opening and breaking-and-entering, the FBI gathered information on radical individuals and groups and conveyed it directly to the White House.[21]

During the Cold War, the breadth of FBI investigations led to massive amounts of information on law abiding citizens. The most important program during this time was COMINFIL, meaning communist infiltration. Through this program, the FBI collected intelligence about alleged communist activity in the government, educational system, industry, and groups associated with blacks, youths, women, farmers and veterans. In short, the FBI infiltrated the "entire spectrum of the social and labor movement in the country."[22]

The FBI gathered intelligence on so-called communist infiltration, even though the FBI knew the Communist Party was steadily declining in the fifties and early sixties. The FBI, however, fabricated memos to the White House which were, according to the Church Committee Report, "deliberately used to exaggerate the threat of Communist influence."[23] Furthermore, went on the Church Committee, this "distorted picture of communist 'infiltration' later served to justify "the FBI's intensive investigations of the groups involved in protests against the Vietnam War and the Civil Rights Movement."[24] In the late 1950s and early 1960s the Civil Rights movement had emerged in the south. During this time, more than one-fourth of all members of the Ku Klux Klan in the south were known to be either FBI agents or informants, who initiated much of the violence directed toward blacks.[25] Also, as early as 1960 the FBI had begun a campaign to "disrupt" and "neutralize" both the Nation of Islam and the Puerto Rican Independence Movement.[26] Regarding the Nation of Islam, the FBI's primary purpose was to "exacerbate the tensions between Malcolm X and Elijah Muhammed, and these activities either directly or indirectly led to the assassination of Malcolm X in 1965."[27]

By 1963, the FBI had opened approximately 441,000 files on individuals and groups deemed "subversive." It gathered its intelligence illegally through the use of "microphone surveillance" and "surrepetitious entries to install microphones." Yet extensive bugging and breaking and entering were not the only methods. The FBI once again opened mail and wire-tapped to thwart a contrived communist threat and destroy other radical movements. The FBI even admits that "legal considerations were simply not raised at the time."[28]

Later Years

The major thrust of the FBI since at least 1941 was its counter-intelligence program, more commonly known as COINTELPRO. This program went beyond intelligence gathering to include strategies and tactics for the purpose of "disrupting" and "neutralizing" organizations threatening to U.S. capitalism. William C. Sullivan, former head of the FBI Intelligence Division has stated:

> We were engaged in COINTELPRO tactics, to divide, confuse, weaken, in diverse ways, an organization. We were engaged in that when I entered the Bureau in 1941.[29]

From the 1940s to the early 1960s, COINTELPRO was primarily directed at two organizations: the Communist Party and the Socialist Workers Party.[30] However, in the sixties and early seventies it encompassed the addition of new groups on its roster, implementing seven "counterintelligence" programs as a whole and some 2,370 separate COINTELPRO actions.[31]

Two examples were the "Black Nationalists" and "New Left"

COINTELPRO operations. In 1967, the "Black Nationalist" COIN-TELPRO was initiated "to expose, disrupt, misdirect, discredit, or otherwise neutralize," black groups struggling against their oppression. Specifically targeted was the "leadership, spokesmen, members and supporters," with larger objectives being to "frustrate" their efforts to "consolidate their forces."[32]

The Black Panther Party was of special interest, FBI Field Offices being directed by headquarters in 1968 to develop "imaginative and hard hitting counter-intelligence measures aimed at crippling the BPP."[33] Moreover, other groups and individuals on the FBI's "hit list" were the Student Non-Violent Coordinating Committee, the Southern Christian Leadership Conference, the Revolutionary Action Movement, the Nation of Islam, the Deacons of Defense, as well as Stokely Carmichael, H. Rap Brown, Elijah Muhammed, Dr. Martin Luther King Jr., Maxwell Stanford, and many more.[34]

Under COINTELPRO, "New Left," agents were directed to disrupt and neutralize such groups as Students for a Democratic Society. FBI headquarters directed field offices in July 1968 to:

(1) prepare leaflets using "the most obnoxious pictures" of New Left leaders at various universities;

(2) instigate "personal conflicts and animosities" between New Left leaders;

(3) create the impression that leaders are "informants for the Bureau or other law enforcement agencies" (the "snitch jacket" technique);

(4) send articles from student or "underground" newspapers which show "depravity" (use of narcotics and free sex) of New Left leaders to university officials, donors, legislators, and parents;

(5) have members arrested on marijuana charges;

(6) send anonymous letters about a student's activities to parents, neighbors, and the parents' employers;

(7) send anonymous letters about New Left faculty members (signed "A concerned Alumni" or "A concerned Taxpayer") to university officials, legislators, Board of Regents, and the press;

(8) use "cooperative press contacts";

(9) exploit the "hostility" between New Left and Old Left groups;

(10) disrupt New Left coffee houses near military bases

which are attempting to "influence members of the armed forces";
(11) use cartoons, photographs, and anonymous letters to "ridicule" the New Left;
(12) use "misinformation" to "confuse and disrupt" New Left activities, such as by notifying members that events have been cancelled.[35]

All of the methods used by the FBI under COINTELPRO were, according to the Church Committee, "secret programs . . . which used unlawful or improper acts" to carry out their desired goals. In short, from 1942 to 1968, the FBI conducted hundreds of illegal burglaries against "threatening" individuals and organizations, stealing private files and documents.[36] Moreover, the FBI clearly knew this was criminal behavior as the following quote from an FBI memorandum reveals:

> Such techniques involve trespassing and are clearly illegal;
> therefore, it would be impossible to obtain any legal sanction
> for it. Break-ins . . . have been used because they represent
> an invaluable technique in combating subversive activities
> of a clandestine nature aimed directly at undermining and
> destroying our nation.[37]

These "unlawful" and "improper" acts however did not end with COINTELPRO, which allegedly was abolished in 1971. Indeed, on 18 November 1974, then FBI Director Clarence Kelly specifically drove the point home that COINTELPRO had "helped bring about a favorable change" in U.S. society and was a major part of the FBI's duty.[38] A month later, Kelly stated that the FBI may need to engage in such disruptive actions again, especially "under emergency situations."[39] The Director could not have been closer to the truth, since criminal behavior by the FBI continues unabated, of which a small portion is revealed below. The FBI continues to invade the privacy of Americans. A Senate Subcommittee found that federal intelligence agencies maintain at least 858 data banks, containing 1.246 *billion* files on individuals.[40] Agents of the FBI are permitted to open mail without a warrant from a federal judge and have, as a result, continually engaged in warrantless secret mail cover operations.[41] The FBI has to date infiltrated labor unions.[42] Moreover, in late June 1978 when a Teamsters strike broke out in San Francisco, the FBI used more than a dozen of its agents (who had posed as workers) in an attempt to break it up.[43]

The FBI has also planted agent provocateurs in labor unions. One individual received from the FBI over $5,000 and a new job at a non-union shipyard in New Orleans for information on union organizing and advocating aggressive, violent behavior.[44] The FBI also maintains, unconstitutionally, a "security index" listing 15,000 dissidents who will be "targeted for detention" in a declared national emergency.[45] The FBI has infiltrated and attempted to disrupt the Women's Liberation Movement, gathering at least 1,377 pages of "intelligence."[46]

In 1974, the FBI admitted keeping a "subversive" file on a 16-year-old high school woman who wrote a letter to the Socialist Workers Party (SWP) as part of a school project. She requested information about the SWP as part of a social studies project entitled, "From Left to Right"; she received a copy of the party newspaper and some other printed material from an affiliated youth group, the Young Socialist Alliance. Her letter was intercepted as part of the FBI's ongoing mail cover of the SWP. This is a form of surveillance where all data on the outside of first-class letters are copied, and the contents of second, third and fourth class mail are examined before being sent to the target of the surveillance. The FBI subsequently investigated the woman's family's credit, her father's employment, police records on the family, as well as her own background and interests.[47]

From 1960 to 1976, the FBI used 316 informers against the Socialist Workers Party and the Young Socialist Alliance. As of June 1976, the FBI was still using more than 60 informers against the party. Overall, at least 42 of the informers held offices within the organization. Subsequently, the SWP filed a $40 million civil lawsuit against the FBI, charging them with illegally manipulating the party's political activities, sowing discord within the organization, stealing documents, and affecting the membership's rights to free association, speech and lawful political activity.[48]

During the trial, which began 2 April 1981 in New York, the FBI continued their political harassment of SWP members. On April 13 an FBI agent visited the Vermont Secretary of State's office, inquiring about the political past of Bernard Sanders, the newly elected mayor of Burlington, Vermont. Sander's name had come up in trial testimony on April 12 as a member of the SWP. Similarly, the FBI investigated the voting records of Mel Mason, a city councilman in Seaside, California and SWP member. Mason was also named in courtroom testimony the day before as being a party member. The FBI does not deny the charges made by SWP, but claims the actions were justified because of the "subversive nature" of the SWP.[49]

Even though Director Kelly stated in 1976 he was "truly sorry" for all these wrongs and that these times were over, the FBI persists in its war against lawful dissent by members of the left.[50] In that same year (1976) the FBI was budgeted over $7 million for its domestic security informant program, which, according to the Church Committee, was "more than twice the amount it spends on informants against organized crime."[51]

And in December of 1980, the FBI announced its "new" guidelines on the use of informants. These guidelines bar an informant from breaking the law "without authorization or approval of an appropriate government official." The FBI maintains the right to determine if the criminal behavior is necessary "to obtain information or evidence for paramount prosecutive purposes." William Webster, who succeeded Kelly as Director of the FBI, has also interpreted these guidelines as giving the Bureau freedom to withhold information regarding criminal behavior by one of its informants from local officials. For example, if an informant murdered someone, as happened in Birmingham or Chicago, "the FBI would not be bound under the guidelines to report the slaying to local officials if the informant's role outweighed the individual killing."[52] Yet as we will see below, these guidelines only make "legal" what informants have been doing illegally for years.

Contrary to its relationship with leftist groups, the FBI has not only allowed, but assisted, activities carried out by many right-wing organizations. The FBI created and financed a "crypto-fascist" group in San Diego called the Secret Army Organization (SAO), whose members carried with them automatic weapons and explosives. All the activities performed by the SAO, which included burglary, mail thefts, bombings, kidnapping, assasination plots, and attempted murder, were supervised by the FBI.[53] Howard Berry Godfrey, an informant for the San Diego FBI office has stated that even though some assasination plots were reported to the local police and FBI many times, nothing was done about it.[54] Agents of the FBI have also infiltrated the Ku Klux Klan, not for the purpose of disrupting it or neutralizing its leadership, but rather, to participate in its racist terrorist actions. Even though the Bureau had been warned in advance many times, its "agents rarely acted to head off Klan attacks against blacks and civil right workers."[55] One informant has stated that he warned "the FBI three weeks in advance about plans by the Klan to attack freedom riders in Birmingham, Alabama," yet the racist onslaught took place as planned; the FBI and the local police simply allowed the terrorism to happen. According to the informant,

. . . the Klan moved in with baseball bats, clubs, chains, and pistols after having been promised free rein for 15 minutes by members of the Birmingham police force.[56]

This same informant, as a member of the FBI, participated in such criminal actions as the murder of civil rights worker Viola Liuzzo, the bombing of a church in the south which killed four black children and the killing of a black man during a racial disturbance in 1963.[57] These tactics continue to date by the FBI. On 3 November 1979, five members of the Communist Workers Party (CWP) were murdered by members of the Ku Klux Klan and American Nazi Party in Greensboro, North Carolina. Even though the local police and FBI knew the KKK and Nazi Party were armed and planning to disrupt the CWP demonstration against racism, they did nothing to prevent the assault and were many blocks away when the murders took place. The members of the Klan and American Nazi Party were acquitted despite overwhelming evidence of their guilt.[58]

And finally, the FBI has worked with, in the past, the Shah of Iran's secret police (SAVAK), by helping them coordinate violent attacks on the Iranian Student Association in this country.[59]

The FBI argues that the treatened use of violence forces them to infiltrate leftist organizations. However, as Michael Parenti has shown, the FBI is hardly concerned about violence. The following three examples indicate how the FBI feels about violence toward Chicano and Cuban people.

- In 1973, the Center for Cuban Studies was bombed and even though right-wing Cuban exile groups had repeatedly threatened to blow the center up, the FBI made no arrests;
- In 1974, two Chicano socialists were killed by bombs planted in their cars, yet the FBI made no arrests;
- A Cuban-American leading an organization seeking normalized relations between the U.S. and Cuba was murdered in San Juan, Puerto Rico; the FBI took no action even though right-wing organizations frequently threatened his life.[60]

On the other hand, the FBI is "right there" with these right wing groups, harassing and attempting to disrupt the Chicano and Puerto Rican movements for liberation.[61]

Unfortunately, the same is true for the American Indian Movement. The following section demonstrates how the FBI has used practically every method thinkable to undermine American Indians on the Pine Ridge Reservation.

At the Pine Ridge Reservation

The FBI began to enter and become established obtrusively on the Pine Ridge Reservation in 1973. Their undertaking was spurred by the challenge of the traditional people during this time and specifically by the events revolving around the tribal elections between Russell Means and Dick Wilson. As a result of these events, Tribal Chairman Wilson asked for help from the FBI, whose agents filtered onto the reservation, joining ranks with the goon squad to harass AIM members and other traditional Lakota. The following two testimonies given before the Minnesota Citizens Review Commission on the FBI reveal this harassment:

> Under the direction of FBI agent Skelly . . . they surrounded a private land . . . where there was a memorial feast, a quiet one. The FBI surrounded the whole geographical area, set up machine guns in three separate positions . . . they used infantry tactics with M-16s, running toward the house and laying down, crawling . . . And in that house that they surrounded that they invaded in battle dress, was my wife and five children. They held an M-16 on the three girls . . .

> Recently, and specifically, on November 18, 1977, upon this quiet hillside village (Porcupine) came four FBI cars to a house across the street. There were two FBI men in each car. And like "storm troopers" of Germany, they pushed their way into the home of Oscar Bear Runner. The leading FBI man carried an M-16 or riot gun, pushed the door in, bumping Mrs. Grace Bear Runner and her daughter Valding. Valding (age 30) was bumped on the side of her face by the door. Mrs. Bear Runner and her daughter are severe diabetics (sworn affidavit has been executed). The FBI showed no ID, no warrants, no search warrants. They violated the 4th Amendment.[62]

As such, it was the traditional people who aligned with AIM in struggle against Wilson's administration, against the goon squad, the BIA and its police, as well as the FBI.

The FBI did not waste any time engaging in their "disruptive" and "neutralizing" programs. Within three years of the occupation of Wounded Knee, federal officials made 562 arrests which resulted in only 15 convictions, 5 of which were for "interfering with federal officers" as individuals attempted to pass through an FBI road block to bring food to those inside the occupation.[63] Trumped-up charges against massive numbers of dissidents, like charges made during the anti-war and civil rights movements, is a method the state effectively employs to thwart the efforts of a movement.[64] Activists, and especially leaders, are tied up in the court system through fabricated charges. Such events frustrate their organizing effort and divert time and money away from the movement. Instead, it becomes necessary to organize for their defense in the courts.

The following are some examples of the methods the state has employed against various leaders of the American Indian Movement. In 1974, Dennis Banks and Russell Means, both active in AIM, were on trial in federal court for a variety of crimes allegedly committed during the occupation of Wounded Knee. If convicted of those crimes, both could have been sentenced to 85 years in prison. However, after both the government and defense rested, and the jury was about to deliberate an acquittal, the government came up with a surprise rebuttal witness. His name was Louis Moves Camp. After FBI Special Agent in charge of Minnesota, North Dakota and South Dakota, Joseph Trimbach, refused to give Moves Camp a lie detector test, Moves Camp took the stand. He testified to being at Wounded Knee from the beginning of the occupation to the end, and he allegedly witnessed all of the events there. Under cross examination, however, Moves Camp was thoroughly discredited. During the occupation, he was actually in the state of California. The defense presented testimony as well as documentary evidence to dispute Moves Camp's earlier attestations under direct examination.[65]

What is more important, however, is the further evidence which came out during cross examination. Prior to Moves Camp's testimony, he was involved in a rape incident in River Falls, Wisconsin *while* under the "protection" of the FBI. Moves Camp was released and never charged with the rape after two FBI agents (which according to Rex Wyler were Special Agent David Price, whom we will hear more about, and Special Agent Ron Williams, one of the agents killed at the Pine Ridge firefight) had informed the Wisconsin prosecutor and police officers that Moves Camp was to be a witness in the Wounded Knee Trial. Moves Camp agreed to give testimony favorable to the government, and the Wisconsin prosecutor dropped the rape charges.[66]

The defense moved for a dismissal based on prosecution and FBI misconduct which consisted of the following:

1) Conspiracy to [commit] perjury and to cover up said subornation in the case of Louis Moves Camp, a prosecution witness;

2) suppression of an FBI statement exposing the perjury of Alexander David Richards, a prosecution witness;

3) illegal and unconstitutional use of military personnel and material at Wounded Knee and the government's effort to cover up said use;

4) violation of applicable professional, ethical and moral standards; and

5) various other incidents of government misconduct.[67]

Judge Fred Nichol dismissed the charges, stating, "the waters of justice have been polluted." And it was his belief that the misconduct by the government and FBI "in this case is so aggravated that a dismissal must be entered in the interests of justice."[68] Members of the jury finding the tactics employed by the FBI and government attorneys repulsive, agreed strongly with the judge. Consequently, ten jurors sent a letter to then Attorney General William B. Saxbe asking that the Justice Department not appeal the dismissal and that the government dismiss charges against ninety other persons awaiting trial because of their part in the occupation.[69] Moreover, it was found after the dismissal that the FBI and government prosecutors had placed an informer inside the defense camp, even though "in a sworn affidavit at the trial" the prosecution contended that they "had no informer in the defense ranks."* The informer was none other than Douglas Dur-

---

*FBI Special Agent in Charge of Minnesota, North Dakota and South Dakota, Joseph Trimbach (who refused to give Moves Camp the lie detector test) testified that the FBI had used informants against AIM, but had *not* infiltrated them into the defense camp. His testimony was as follows:

Q. To your knowledge, and I am asking for your knowledge based upon reports made to you orally or in writing. . . have any of these informants attended the meetings at which there were present defendants in matters arising out of any of the incidents of Wounded Knee and the lawyers?

A. The answer is no.

Q. You are sure of that?

A. Yes.

Q. Have any of the informants about whom you have given testimony. . .talked to any of the members of the Wounded Knee Legal Defense/Offense Committee?

A. Not to my knowledge.

ham who had become security chief for AIM and was chief aid and confidant of Dennis Banks during the trial. Durham recounted later for a Senate Subcommittee his duties at the trial:

> . . .I was the person who issued the passes for the defense attorneys to get to their rooms. I was the person who cleared the defense attorneys, to see if they were cleared to go into their room. I issued passes for the others to go into the room and controlled the security around them.. . .I was charged with, for a short period of time, maintaining the trial records.[71]

Durham was involved extensively with AIM as an FBI informer. An FBI memorandum of 1975 states that "the key to the successful investigation of AIM is substantial, live, quality informant coverage of its leaders and activities. In the past, this technique proved to be highly effective." Moreover, the memo went on to say that "when necessary, coverage is supplanted by certain techniques which would be sanctioned in preliminary and limited investigations."[72] The memo obliquely refers to other ways the FBI could effectively disrupt the group.

The following is an example of one of the FBI's techniques. Two AIM activists, Paul Skyhorse and Richard Mohawk, were charged in January 1975 with the murder of a taxi cab driver in Ventura County, California on 10 October 1974. Durham, as well as another informant, Virginia DeLuce, also known as Blue Dove, worked together to implicate the two activists.[73] Initially, three individuals (two Indians and one white, none of whom were members of AIM) Marvin Redshirt, Marcella McNoise and Holly Brussard, were charged with murder, kidnapping, robbery and conspiracy. The evidence made the charge seem plausible as Redshirt's bloody fingerprints were found on the cab's hood, and his clothes as well as Broussard's and McNoise's were covered with blood. Yet, several days following the killing, Skyhorse and Mohawk were arrested in Phoenix, Arizona while attending an Indian Educational Conference. They waived extradition as they thought they were being detained as material witnesses. In January

> Q. And what is your knowledge based on?
> A. The fact that I have no such affirmative information plus the fact that the FBI as a matter of policy is not going to try to infiltrate the defense circles or defense strategy plus the assurance that I have. . . that this was a situation wherein there were no such efforts on our part.[70]

1975, however, the events turned a clear 180 degrees. The charges against the original suspects were dropped, and Skyhorse and Mohawk were immediately indicted for murder and robbery. McNoise and Broussard were granted immunity in exchange for their testimony implicating the AIM activists, while Redshirt pleaded guilty to assault with a deadly weapon and received five years probation. They were all, furthermore, given jobs and other forms of financial support. Doug Durham then engaged in the following in an attempt to hinder AIM support for the two.

- He wrote a phony letter and pinned it to a post at the L.A. AIM encampment with a bundle of hair, supposedly the "scalp" of the cab driver;
- He leaked a story to the local media that the murder of the cab driver was the start of an anti-white campaign by AIM during the bicentennial year;
- He posed as an Indian psychiatrist, testifying at a sanity hearing for Skyhorse and stating that he was irrational and dangerous.[74]

The trial lasted approximately three years, producing seventeen thousand pages of transcripts. On 24 May 1978, despite Durham's dirty tricks, the two were found not guilty.[75] Although the two were freed, this event demonstrates the method by which the FBI tied up two AIM activists in the court system. Consequently, the growth of an AIM chapter in Los Angeles, the city with the largest urban-Indian population in the United States, was effectively impeded.[76]

When the FBI has been unable to tie leaders up in the courts, it uses other methods to attempt to impede their political activity. One prime example is the relationship between the Bureau and ex-National Chairman of AIM, John Trudell. In 1975, the FBI was clearly aware of Trudell's political activities. An FBI memorandum, dated 1975, states in part the following:

JOHN TRUDELL has been involved in the area of Indian conflicts/demonstrations longer than any other AIM member. He is intelligent and extremely eloquent when he speaks. TRUDELL has the ability to meet with a group of "pacifists" and in a short time have them yelling and screaming "right on." In short, he is an extremely effective agitator. . .TRUDELL favors the forming of coalitions among minority activist groups for increased "political clout."[77]

John and his wife Tina worked together in many activities. For instance, they lead the struggle to retain water rights for American

Indians on the Duck Valley Reservation in Nevada. They also worked together organizing the Minnesota Review Commission on the FBI.[78]

In December 1977, while serving 60 days for a contempt citation, Trudell apparently received word from FBI agents that unless he halted his political activities or left the country, the FBI would get either him, his family, or both. On 11 February 1979 Trudell was the featured speaker at a rally in front of the FBI building in Washington, D.C. Trudell spoke about the repressive nature of the FBI and their actions against movements for social change. At approximately 2:00 p.m. Trudell burned the American flag in contempt for the continued genocidal policies of the United States government. At around 2:00 a.m. the next morning (12 hours later), Trudell's home on the Duck Valley Reservation, with his wife Tina, their four children and Tina's mother inside, was burned to the ground by an arsonist.[79] They all died in the blaze. To date, there is no evidence of any inquiry by the FBI, which is charged with investigating such crimes under the Major Crimes Act.

These events, (the trials of Means/Banks and Skyhorse/Mohawk, the deaths of the Trudell family and lack of investigation) clearly revealed the feelings of the FBI for AIM activists. Such feelings were also prevalent at Pine Ridge. During February of 1977, the Minnesota Citizens Review Commission on the FBI (with a Hearing Board composed of 25 persons representing different religions, labor, minority, educational and political communities) held hearings to investigate reports of harassment and extralegal activity by the FBI. The FBI, which was invited to testify, refused. Much of the testimony concerned the role of the FBI at Pine Ridge, and after 18 hours of testimony the Hearing Board concluded that "the FBI has engaged in systematic and extensive efforts to harass, intimidate, and otherwise 'neutralize' AIM," and further, "the FBI is conducting a full-scale military operation on the reservation."[80] Donald Holman, in a letter of resignation (to South Dakota Governor Richard Kniep) from the South Dakota Criminal Justice Commission, echoed the Hearing Board:

> I have become increasingly aware of the fact that Native Americans who hold traditional views and are political activists are singled out for special attention by the criminal justice system in South Dakota. Members of the American Indian Movement, in particular, are singled out for harassment. Every law enforcement agency in the state, including the S.D. Highway Patrol, B.I.A. police, F.B.I., D.C.I. and seemingly all local police authorities apparently agree on one thing, that the American Indian Movement is in-

nately evil and that they should do everything in their power
to suppress the Native people who adhere to goals of that
organization. They have formed units which go by names
"Tac Team," Initial Response Team, Special Operations
Group, etc. All these organizations have two things in common. The first is that they all practice military tactics,
something more properly left to the Army and National
Guard. The second is that they were all formed for the same
purpose, namely the suppression of Indian uprisings.[81]

By the end of May and in early June 1975 Holman's words were a
reality as there were at least 18 and possibly as many as 60 FBI agents
on or near the Pine Ridge Reservation, and a SWAT (Special Weapons
and Tactics) unit which spent a considerable amount of its time "prac-
ticing assaults on houses" scattered throughout the Pine Ridge Village.[82]

In addition to the law enforcement people on or near the reservation, there were, of course, members of AIM who were living at a
spiritual encampment (called "tent city" by the government attorneys)
approximately one third of a mile from the Jumping Bull houses (see
Figure 1 on page 36). The group engaged in spiritual and social
gatherings, discussed treaty rights and the oppressive environment
Indians were forced to live under. The traditional people from the
surrounding communities joined in, speaking about their treaty and
civil rights and what was happening to their land. The changes resulting from the presence of AIM at the White Clay district is expressed
by Indian Reorganization Act Tribal President Al Trimble:

It's my personal belief that the traditional and full-blooded
people are much more cognizant of their own, personal,
individual rights and seem more willing to try to exercise
them now.[83]

A grassroots movement had emerged. Dick Wilson and his goon
squad were also cognizant of this increasing political consciousness of
the traditional people of White Clay. Late in the morning of June 26
as AIM members were in camp preparing the breakfast meal, shots
were heard from the direction of the Jumping Bull house. Fearing that
the goon squad was attacking the house, the men at the encampment
grabbed rifles and ran in the direction of the shooting. They spotted
two men (wearing street clothes and later identified as FBI agents Jack
Coler and Ron Williams) behind their unmarked cars shooting at the

Jumping Bull house. They returned fire in order to help those staying at the home escape the attack. The government and FBI allege these two agents were pursuing a "red and white van," possibly carrying Jimmy Eagle, who had an outstanding warrant pending against him.[84] A gun battle broke out. A large number of FBI, BIA and South Dakota State police officers converged upon the Jumping Bull area. The gun battle turned into a firefight and continued until late in the afternoon when all Native Americans escaped the area.* However, as the dust settled and the smoke cleared, two important events had occurred. First, Joe Stuntz, an Indian man was found shot to death, as were the two FBI agents, Ron Williams and Jack Coler. And second, on the same day as this firefight, Dick Wilson, in Washington, D.C., was discussing the possibility of signing away one eighth of the reservation, the Sheep Mountain Gunnery Range, to the Department of the Interior. A U.S. Geological Survey had found that this area contained varying amounts of uranium ore, gas, oil and gravel. At the same time in western South Dakota, twenty-five major corporations were quietly leasing over one million acres for projects such as uranium mining, coal strip-mining and coal gasification.

It should be pointed out that the Senate Select Committee on Intelligence (Church Committee) had decided on 23 June 1975 to investigate the relationship between the FBI and the American Indian Movement. However, as the citation below (from an FBI memorandum, dated 6-27-75) indicates, immediately following the firefight at the Jumping Bull's, the decision was *gently* hushed up.

> Attached is a letter from the Senate Select Committee (SSC) dated 6-23-75, addressed to the Honorable Edward H. Levi. This letter announces the SSC's intent to conduct interviews

---

*I refer throughout the book to the battle between AIM and FBI as a "firefight" for the following reasons. A number of SWAT (Special Weapons and Tactics) teams attacked the houses at the end of the day, firing automatic and semi-automatic weapons. They also shot tear gas with the use of grenade launchers and called for high explosives. Fixed-wing aircraft flew overhead. All of the surrounding homes, outhouses, garbage cans, etc. had a large number of bullet holes in them, the "white house" having at least 100 such holes. After the area was secured, some agents entered the Jumping Bull house and in a deranged manner devastated the insides, concentrating on personal items. Pictures of Cecilia and Harry Jumping Bull's nephew and grandson (one who was killed in Vietnam, the other in Korea) were demolished with bullets, as were a wash basin, the inside walls, and even a doll, which was shot between the eyes.

relating to Douglas Durham, a former Bureau informant. The request obviously relates to our investigation at "Wounded Knee" and our investigation of the American Indian Movement. This request was received 6-27-75, by Legal Division.

On 6-27-75, Patrick Shea, staff member of the SSC requested we hold in abeyance any action on the request in view of the killing of the Agents at Pine Ridge Reservation, South Dakota.[85]

Within thirty-six hours of the firefight, 175 FBI agents had swarmed the reservation, seeking suspects, not for the murder of Stuntz, but of the two agents. Assault teams, equipped with M-16's, helicopters, and tracking dogs carried out a series of raids on the reservation "in the largest display of force ever mustered by the Bureau." Agents "broke into homes without warrants, violated Sacred Sun Dance grounds and used their weaponry to intimidate dozens of innocent bystanders."[86] Unable to find anyone connected with the shootings, the FBI moved its invasion to the Rosebud Reservation on 5 September 1975. During the early morning at Leonard Crow Dog's they harassed the traditional people in a fashion similiar to that at Pine Ridge. Yet once again no suspects were found.*

Although there were estimates of between 20 and 30 armed people at the Jumping Bulls on the morning of June 26, the identity of some of these people seems beyond dispute. There was the Long Visitor Family: Angie, Ivis and their children. There were the AIM people, who were mostly residing in what the government called "tent city." On June 26 this group consisted of women, including Nilak Butler, Jeanne Bordeaux and Lynn (not further identified), at least four adult men, Dino Butler, Bob Robideau, Leonard Peltier and Joe Stuntz, at least four teenagers, Wilford Draper, Michael Anderson, Norman Brown and Norman Charles, and twelve year old Jimmy Zimmerman.

Unable to net any arrests during the FBI's hunt across two reservations, the Justice Department settled for the indictment of four active AIM members for the murders of the two agents. Joseph Stuntz's death was never investigated; the government maintained he was killed by law enforcement officers while lawfully performing their official duties. Two of the four indicted, Dino Butler and Bob Robideau, were

*Dino Butler and Anna Mae Aquash were arrested at this time; however, it was for other charges than the murder of the two agents.

acquitted in Cedar Rapids, Iowa in the summer of 1976. The reason for the acquittal was partly due to FBI misconduct during the trial.[87] Charges against the third individual indicted, Jimmy Eagle, were dropped September 1976. At the time of the firefight the government concluded that Eagle was 15 miles away at his grandmother's house. Leonard Peltier was the last remaining individual of the four originally indicted on the charge. Peltier had fled to Canada, where he was arrested on 6 February 1976 as a fugitive from justice. He was in Canada seeking political asylum, since there was reason to believe that the Justice Department and the FBI were committed to an organized, well-orchestrated plan to disrupt and demolish the American Indian Movement and put its members behind bars, or have them killed.

Peltier had reason to feel the way he did. In 1972 he was allegedly involved in a fight with two off-duty police officers in Milwaukee, Wisconsin. The officers claimed Peltier had made an attempt on the life of one of them, and he was subsequently charged with attempted murder. However, as it turned out, this was a fabricated charge.* On 30 July 1974 Peltier failed to appear for trial. This charge was outstanding on 26 June 1975.

At least by February of 1975 the FBI had targeted Leonard Peltier. An FBI report sent to field offices on 25 February 1975 (four months before the firefight at Pine Ridge) indicates there was a *national* search by the FBI for Peltier in connection with this fabricated charge. In this report, Peltier was identified as a leader in AIM, who was "armed and extremely dangerous." The trumped-up attempted murder charge served the function of neutralizing a leader of the American Indian Movement, and of possibly discrediting or disrupting further the organization.

The pending murder charge was also brought up at the Fargo trial, the government arguing that this charge might have been one of his motives for killing the agents. The defense argued that this disclosure (to the jury) was in clear violation of the Federal Rules of Evidence, which are rules to protect the defendant from evidence that is irrelevant, immaterial, and incompetent. However, these rules are

---

*Nine months after the Fargo trial, in January 1978, Peltier was acquitted by a jury in Milwaukee of this charge. At this trial, defense witnesses testified Peltier had been severely beaten by the off-duty police officers. One of the officers affirmed that for three days following the incident his hands had been too swollen for him to work. Interestingly, this particular trial is the only one where Peltier's defense team was not restricted and, consequently, was the only case where he was acquitted.

subject to the discretion of the judge, who, in this case, allowed the disclosure (Judge Paul Benson).

Regarding the FBI raid on the Rosebud Reservation discussed above, it seems the purpose of the raid was to arrest Peltier. An FBI document dated 2 August 1975 reveals that an informant gave information to the FBI that Peltier was staying in early August of 1975 at the residence of Leonard Crow Dogs' mother on the Rosebud Reservation.* However, the FBI decided this would not be a good time to arrest Peltier, since "there's a good chance a gun fight could break out." Thus, the raid was delayed one month.

What is important is that the evidence points to the fact that at least by February of 1975 (if not earlier) the FBI had targeted Leonard Peltier. The trumped up Milwaukee charge served the FBI purpose well. Moreover, the FBI continued to target Peltier after the firefight at the Jumping Bulls.

Like Peltier, but several months before the firefight at Jumping Bull ranch, Russell Means and Richard Marshall were charged with the murder of a Martin Montileaux, who was shot and killed in a bar in Scenic, South Dakota. Approximately a year after the shooting in Scenic and nine months after the events at Jumping Bulls, Special Agents of the FBI discovered a Lakota woman, Myrtle Poor Bear, who signed two affidavits (19 and 23 February 1976) that implicated Leonard Peltier in the June 26 murders. She also made two other statements associating Marshall with the murder of Montileaux.

At the same time that these two "eyewitness" accounts were obtained from Myrtle Poor Bear, the body of Anna Mae Aquash, an AIM member and strong activist, was found by the roadside on the Pine Ridge Reservation. The story of Anna Mae is highly important to the issues at hand. Anna Mae was arrested during the FBI raid of Crow Dog's Paradise (Rosebud Reservation) on 5 September 1975, allegedly for possession of weapons. According to one source, Special Agent David Price told her then that he would "see her dead within a year."[88] After her arrest on the Rosebud Reservation, she was taken to Pierre, South Dakota for interrogation. Anna Mae was accused of

---

*According to Bruce Ellison, Attorney John Privatera uncovered through the Freedom of Information Act approximately 12,000 pages—of 18,000 total—which the FBI has accumulated on Peltier and related events. This document, as well as all others which are not footnoted throughout the book are drawn from those recovered documents. The FBI will not give up the remaining 6,000 pages.

involvement in the killings of Ron Williams and Jack Coler (the two agents killed at Pine Ridge), and Agent Price and others wanted to know who else was involved. Aquash insisted she knew nothing and asked the agents to leave her alone. They refused and continued to badger her, demanding she provide them with information. An FBI report of the interrogation then revealed what occurred next:

> She advised at this point that, "You can either shoot me or throw me in jail, as those are the two choices that I am taking." She was asked specifically what she meant by this, to which she replied, "That's what you're going to do to me anyway."[89]

She was released on bond a few days later. On 14 November 1975 she was arrested in Oregon and returned to South Dakota to face trial on the weapons charge. On November 24 she appeared before Judge Robert Merhige, who released her on personal recognizance pending her trial the following day. She failed to appear for that trial.

In February 1976 Anna Mae's body was discovered. FBI agents, including Special Agent Price, had gone to the scene and taken pictures but did not identify her. An autopsy was performed by a Bureau of Indian Affairs coroner, Dr. W.O. Brown, who attributed her death to exposure. Her *hands* were *cut off* and sent to Washington, D.C. for fingerprint identification, though apparently the FBI knew who she was. (This behavior is only one small instance of the FBI's attitude toward Native Americans.) According to pathologist Gary Peterson, Chief Coroner for Hennepin County at the time, Anna Mae's fingerprints could have easily been taken without cutting off her hands. Seven days after her body was found Anna Mae was buried without a burial certificate in an unmarked grave. Fingerprint examination confirmed her identity. When her family was notified of her death and burial, they demanded another autopsy. This was carried out by a different pathologist, who found a bullet in her forehead and a bullet hole and powder burns on the back of her neck, indicating an execution type murder.[90]

When Myrtle Poor Bear became uncooperative in the latter part of March 1976, Special Agent David Price threatened Myrtle Poor Bear with the story of Anna Mae. In Poor Bear's words, "The agents are always talking about Anna Mae . . . they would just talk about that time she died." If she failed to cooperate with the FBI, she would end up like Anna Mae did. As a result, Poor Bear signed affidavits stating she was Peltier's girlfriend and had seen Peltier kill the two agents. These affidavits were completely false, as we will see in the following chapter. Nevertheless, they "proved" to Canadian authorities that evidence existed for extradition, and thus Peltier was returned to the United States on 18 December 1976. Peltier's response to this decision was in part the following:

> This type of selective political persecution against AIM lead-
> ers is no different from the abuses of the FBI against the
> Black Panther Party and the Socialist Workers Party. The
> FBI has abused the court system by harassing and jailing
> people who resist . . . an attempt to push us off our reser-
> vations because . . . what was once called worthless land
> contains valuable mineral and oil resources.[91]

A few days before Myrtle Poor Bear signed the third affidavit implicating Leonard Peltier she was under "protection" by Special Agents Price and William Wood; interestingly, she signed two statements alleging that she was Richard Marshall's girlfriend and that he confessed the murder of Montileaux on two occasions to her. Later, at Richard Marshall's trial, she stated this evidence was false and "contrived by FBI agents." Myrtle Poor Bear went on to say that the agents forced her to testify against Marshall by threatening to take her and her daughters' lives.[92] No one knew, except the agents (and possibly the government attorneys) that Myrtle Poor Bear was simultaneously signing affidavits all falsely stating she was an eyewitness to two murders.

Myrtle Poor Bear's fabricated and coerced affidavits were the only testimonial evidence which directly linked Peltier to the killings. She was the only alleged eyewitness. However, three young Native American boys testified they had seen Peltier at the scene of the crime. Yet their attestation revealed that the FBI had also coerced each of them in presenting this testimony: As we will see, Michael Anderson was threatened with a beating, Wilford Draper was tied to a chair for three hours and forced to say what agents wanted, and Norman Brown was threatened with his life if he failed to cooperate with the FBI.

Two law enforcement officers, one of them an FBI agent, testified to sighting Peltier and Jimmy Eagle in the vicinity of the Jumping Bull Ranch. The testimony regarding Eagle was highly inconsistent and contradictory. As for Peltier, Special Agent Fred Coward testified he had recognized Peltier from one half mile away through a 2x7 power rifle scope. The defense duplicated this sighting, and found it impossible to identify an individual at such a distance through this power of a scope. However, the judge would not allow the jury to make the test.

Other testimony throughout this trial was in a similiar vein. It did *not* connect Peltier with the murder of the agents. Rather, it characterised a consistent pattern of misconduct on the part of the FBI and possibly the government attorneys in their preparation for the trial. In short, the FBI and Justice Department did everything they could (legal, illegal and extralegal) to convict Leonard Peltier, regardless of his presumed guilt or innocence of the specific crime charged.

As Norman Zigrossi, Special Agent in charge of the South Dakota FBI office put it, the American Indians are a "conquered nation . . . and when you're conquered, the people you're conquered by dictate your future." Consequently, the FBI must function as a "colonial police force."[93]

Figure 1: JUMPING BULL RANCH
Pine Ridge Indian Reservation, South Dakota

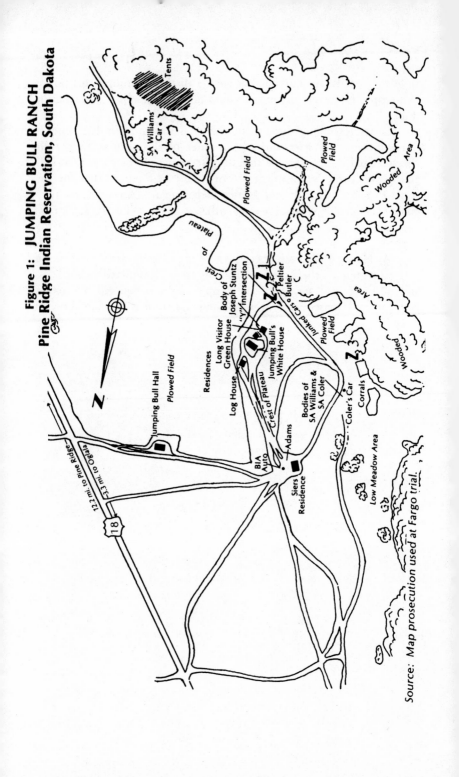

Source: Map prosecution used at Fargo trial.

Three

THE TRIAL

In this chapter we will investigate the most important evidence and testimony presented at the trial of Leonard Peltier and their relation to the role of the FBI and court system in the United States.[1] We will also examine the way procedural rules of evidence were used to manipulate the outcome of the trial and mask the criminal acts of the state.

Judge Paul Benson presided over the trial. He is a former law partner of the law firm, Shaft, Benson, Shaft and McConn of Grand Forks, North Dakota. He was also previously an Assistant City Attorney of Grand Forks and Attorney General for the state of North Dakota. Benson was appointed to the federal bench in 1971 by the Nixon administration.

The government was represented by Evan Hultman, United States Attorney from Waterloo, Iowa, Lynn E. Crooks, Assistant United States Attorney from Fargo, North Dakota, Robert L. Sikma, Assistant United States Attorney from Sioux City, Iowa, Bruce Boyd, Assistant United States Attorney from Rapid City, South Dakota, and Richard Vosepka, Assistant United States Attorney from Minneapolis, Minnesota.

Leonard Peltier was represented by attorneys Elliott A. Taikeff from New York City, New York, John Lowe from Charlottesville,

37

Virginia, Bruce Ellison from Rapid City, South Dakota, Stanley Englestein from New York City, New York and Terry Gilberg from Cleveland, Ohio.

Jury selection resulted in an all white jury of ten women and four men, two of whom were alternates. They were sequestered for the duration of the trial. The government presented fifteen days of evidence to the jury after which the defense presented six days of evidence, although the Judge allowed only two and a half days of the defense case to be heard by the jury. On April 15 the government and defense made their closing arguments. On Saturday April 16 Judge Paul Benson instructed the jury on the law regarding the case. After eleven hours of deliberation, the jury reached a verdict around 3:30 p.m. on the following Monday, 18 April 1977.

Leonard Peltier was the only remaining individual to be charged for the murder of the two agents. The charges against Jimmy Eagle had been dropped; the government stipulated that he was not on the reservation the day of the firefight. Dino Butler and Bob Robideau were acquitted in Cedar Rapids, Iowa, in July 1976.

The trial of Butler and Robideau had uncovered much FBI misconduct, such as tampering with witnesses and evidence, perjury, COINTELPRO-type activities used against AIM, substantial evidence indicating there was a full scale paramilitary assault on Pine Ridge by the FBI and other law enforcement officials on the day in question. The jury as a result concluded that Butler and Robideau were acting in self-defense.[2]

Peltier's defense team had this same evidence, and, in fact, more which strongly indicated FBI misconduct in their preparation for the trial of Leonard Peltier. Yet they would never be able to present a major portion of it to the jury. The following Table briefly points out the major differences between the two trials. Also included in the chart are direct quotations from an FBI investigation of the Butler-Robideau trial (dated 20 July 1976), specifically analyzing the "reasons why [the] jury found the defendants Robideau and Butler not guilty on July 16, 1976." It is important that the reader compare this FBI study to the subsequent rulings in the Fargo trial.

We begin by looking at the government's story about what happened on the day in question and the testimony of FBI agents and Bureau of Indian Affairs' police officers. Then we turn to the testimonies of two pathologists about how the two agents died. Following this we scrutinize important testimony of the three teenagers, Anderson,

Draper and Brown, as well as that of Myrtle Poor Bear. Next we investigate the physical evidence of the case and the circumstantial evidence against Peltier. Finally, we provide a theoretical analysis of the trial.

The chapter is based on the original Trial Transcript (approximately 5300 pages) and FBI documents. Throughout the chapter I refer to FBI documents which have recently been disclosed to Leonard Peltier's attorneys through a Freedom of Information Act (FOIA) Suit. These documents help shed additional light on the many behind-the-scenes happenings of "our" criminal justice system. References to the transcript are found in parentheses at the end of each paragraph in the text.

Cops, Sightings and the Red Pickup (Van)

In this section we will explore the testimony of the law enforcement officers directly involved in the events leading up to, during and after the killing of the agents. At the trial, one Assistant Special Agent of the FBI, five Special Agents of the FBI and two Bureau of Indian Affairs police officers attempted to present a uniform account of the events. In other words, all these law enforcement officials attempted to report the same version of the events. We will first provide a narrative of the evidence these officers supplied at the trial. Following this, we will point out several important contradictions in the officers' testimony. And finally, we will look at some new evidence uncovered through the Freedom of Information Act.

On the evening of 25 June 1975, Bureau of Indian Affairs (BIA) policeman Robert Ecoffey testified he went looking for Jimmy Eagle. He was accompanied by Special Agents Ron Williams and Jack Coler and another BIA officer, Glenn Littlebird. Eagle was wanted on a robbery charge, and there was an outstanding warrant against him. In the course of their search, Ecoffey, Williams, Coler and Littlebird first went to the home of Wanda Siers in the Jumping Bull area (See Figure 1). There, they were told by several individuals that Jimmy Eagle had not been at this particular home in the last few days. Following this interview, the four law enforcement officers allegedly continued their search at LaVete Little's residence in Oglala. Jimmy Eagle was not there either. Some residents reported, however, that Jimmy Eagle was "staying down at the Wallace Little's residence." When they arrived at Wallace Little's outside of Oglala, a young

A COMPARISON OF THE TWO TRIALS

Butler-Robideau Trial Cedar Rapids, Iowa	FBI analysis of Cedar Rapids Trial: Reasons for Not Guilty verdict*	Peltier Trial Fargo, ND
—Only a few autopsy photos of dead agents were allowed for fear of prejudicing the jury.		—All autopsy photos were entered into evidence, plus FBI Academy graduation photos of the two agents.
—FBI Special Agent Gary Adams testified to the presence and departure of a red pickup truck at 12:18 p.m., moments after the agents were shot.		—FBI Special Agent Gary Adams denied existence of 12:18 pm red pickup truck.
—Extensive FBI 302's entered into evidence.	"The Court rulings. . . forced the government to furnish the defense with all 302's prepared by Special Agents who testified for the government."	—No 302's entered as evidence if agent who wrote it testified.
—Witnesses told of FBI coercion in obtaining their testimony.	"The defense was allowed freedom of questioning of witnesses. . ."	—FBI coercion of important defense witnesses not allowed to be presented to jury.
—Defense allowed to present testimony concerning the number of unsolved murders that occurred on Pine Ridge Reservation as well as climate of fear on the reservation.	"The Court continually overruled government objections . . ." and "As a result, the defense inferred the FBI created a climate of fear on the reservation which precipitated the murders".	—Defense allowed to talk of unsolved murders occurring on Pine Ridge only in a general sense, and were not allowed to exhibit evidence of FBI creation of climate of fear.

—History of FBI misconduct allowed as testimony.	—No evidence regarding past history of FBI allowed to be introduced.
	—"The Court allowed testimony concerning past activities of the FBI relating to COINTEL PRO and subsequently allowed the Church Report into evidence"
—Defense lawyers and members of Butler-Robideau Support Group held frequent meetings and rallies in an effort to educate the public about June 26th and events leading up to it. National press blackout existed, but local press carried daily related articles.	—"The defense was uncontrolled in its dealings with the news media. . ."
	—Judge ordered the only news carried about Peltier could come from the courtroom. Defense lawyers and potential witnesses were not allowed to speak publicly about the trial.
—The jury was not sequestered.	—"The jury was not sequestered."
	—Jury sequestered under complete control of U.S. Marshall Service

*Three additional reasons the FBI gave for the not guilty verdict at the Cedar Rapids trial were: 1) the government was prohibited from entering into evidence certain collateral exhibits; 2) there was a lengthy recess after completion of the government case; 3) the jury had a difficult time putting things together because it was a complicated case.

woman told the officers and agents that Jimmy Eagle had just left in a *red pickup* (656,654,662,663,665).*

Ecoffey's testimony further revealed that while the four were in Oglala, they observed three young male Indians walking down the road toward the highway. Special Agent Williams, suspecting one of them was Jimmy Eagle, asked the three boys who they were and where they lived. Although none of the boys could be identified as Eagle, Williams searched a rolled up towel one of the boys was holding. He discovered in the towel a "clip full of rifle ammo." Consequently, the three youths were taken to the Pine Ridge jail for identification. At the jail, none of the boys could be identified as Jimmy Eagle, so they were all released and given transportation, at their request, to the Jumping Bull area. Later testimony established that these three youths were Norman Charles, Michael Anderson and Wilford Draper (666,-667,669).

This event, according to the government, provoked great anger among the AIM members after the three boys were released and returned to the Jumping Bull area. The boys told the leaders of the encampment, especially Peltier, what happened. According to the government, this resulted in a furious decision by AIM members to kill the agents if they ever came around. There is no evidence, however, to back up such an argument; there is no testimony at the trial to indicate a premeditated ambush on the part of AIM.

Let's now direct our attention to the morning of 26 June 1975, the day of the firefight. The following narrative of the law enforcement officers' testimony exhibits several important contradictions.

Around mid morning of that day, SAs Williams and Coler continued their search for Jimmy Eagle in the Oglala area. Shortly before noon, Special Agent Ron Williams purportedly made some radio transmissions. A stenographer at the FBI office in Rapid City, South Dakota, as well as four Special Agents out in the field, testified to overhearing these communications. Stenographer Ann M. Johnson heard Ron Williams transmit, "There is something wrong here, we are being fired on." Special Agent George O'Klock came to "assist" her in interpreting successive communications; he dictated what was said, and she wrote it down. O'Klock continued this "assistance" for approximately one half hour (1653, 1655, 1656, 1833).

---

*The significance of the "red pickup" will become clear later. For now, however, the reader should keep in mind the number of references during testimony to such a vehicle.

On 28 June 1975 Special Agent Leon Canton interviewed Ann M. Johnson. During this interview she did not mention that she received help from anyone between 11:15 a.m. and 12:36 p.m. on June 26 (1663,1678). This omission in her report is important because it points out the kinds of problems the FBI testimony presented throughout the trial. As we will see, Ann Johnson's recordings of radio transmissions provide very valuable evidence which contradicts, in particular, Special Agent Gary Adams' testimony concerning a crucial suspect's vehicle (a red and white pickup that left at 12:18 p.m.). Therefore, it was imperative that the government present to the jury that because agent O'Klock "assists" Johnson in *interpreting* the radio communications, Johnson's recordings are not accurate. Yet only two days after the event there was no mention of anyone assisting her.

Four agents of the FBI (Adams, Hughes, Waring and Skelly) also heard some transmissions by Ron Williams that morning. Special Agent Gary Adams testified that on 26 June 1975 he was in his car at 11:45 or 11:50 a.m. driving to White Clay, Nebraska, to eat lunch. He was approximately two miles from Rapid City when he heard over his radio the following communications by Special Agent Ron Williams: "Looks like there's some guys around that house. It looks like they're going to get into that *pickup*. Looks like they're going to take off" (emphasis added). After a few minutes, according to Adams, Williams continued, "I hope you've got a lot of guys . . .looks like they're going to shoot at us . . .We've been hit (sound of gunfire)" (72-73).

After asking about Williams' location, Adams was told " . . .that he was at some houses behind Jumping Bull Hall" and Adams should "get on a high hill and give us some fire cover. We'll be killed." Williams related further to Adams that help should "come to a house" that was some distance, a house that has an outhouse some distance from it, but he did not give any specific location yet (74-75).

At approximately the same time, Special Agent Dean Hughes was transporting a prisoner to Rapid City, South Dakota, for arraignment when he heard Special Agent Williams' voice over the car radio. Hughes testified Williams made the following communications: "We are being fired on, we are in a little valley in Oglala, South Dakota, pinned down in a cross fire between two houses." Williams then allegedly directed Adams to his rescue: "Get to the high ground... Hurry up and get here, or we are going to be dead men." The last statement Hughes heard Williams speak was "I am hit" (2870-71).

Special Agent Gerard P. Waring testified that on the morning of 26 June 1975 he awakened at 7:30 a.m. and finished his "administrative work," then had coffee with both Ron Williams and Jack Coler in their motel coffee shop. Williams and Coler left together, in search of Jimmy Eagle. Waring remained behind until approximately 11:00 or 11:15 a.m. He, along with Special Agent Vince Breci, then went to Pine Ridge (1831, 1833, 1835).

About "halfway" to the Pine Ridge Indian Reservation, Waring heard Agent Williams come on the car radio. The first transmission he heard from Williams was "that there was a *red and white vehicle* traveling near him and there appeared to be a number of Indians in the vehicle" (emphasis added). Shortly thereafter, "his next transmission was that the individuals appeared to have rifles" and then immediately following, "that he was being fired on by these individuals" (1836-37).

Waring also heard Adams come on the radio and ask Williams his location. Williams replied that he was in the Oglala, South Dakota area near the Little residence and then again asked for help to get there as quickly as possible. Williams maintained "the firing was coming to him from the ridge above him and they needed help quick . . . and that if we didn't arrive quickly to help him that they were dead men." A short time later Waring heard Williams say, "I have been hit" (1837-38).

Special Agent Edward Skelly only heard one transmission to the effect that, "If someone could get to the top of the ridge and give us some cover, we might be able to get out of here" (4379).

The government presented the testimony of the law enforcement officers' recollection of radio transmissions to help bolster its scenario of the events prior to the firefight. What the government argues is that Special Agents Williams and Coler were proceeding southeast in two different cars on highway 18 (see Figure 1) when they came upon a "vehicle" which was carrying several Indians. They chased this "vehicle" into the Jumping Bull area because they assumed Jimmy Eagle was inside the car. The agents stopped at the spot marked "Coler's car" on the map. The "vehicle" carrying the Indians, according to the government, stopped at the Y intersection to the south of the residences. A firefight ensued.

As one can see from looking at Figure 1, the Jumping Bull Compound consists of principally three major houses which sit on a plateau just above the flood plain of the White Clay Creek. The ground level drops sharply into a small valley on the western side of the residences. The spot marked "Colers' Car" is in this valley. The AIM encampment was located approximately a quarter of a mile southeast of the residences.

Adams was the first to arrive at the Jumping Bull Compound after Williams and Coler. He came to the area around noon and was followed by a BIA automobile. The tires of both their cars were shot flat; they consequently retreated off the road for cover (see Figure 1). Meanwhile, Ann M. Johnson took down the following radio transmissions dictated to her by Agent O'Klock.

> 12:06—Adams was receiving fire
> 12:10—An ambulance was called
> 12:18—Adams stated that he saw a *red pickup* leaving the Jumping Bull Hall area, and the Pine Ridge Police were instructed to stop this *pickup*.
> 12:21—Both Adams and the BIA unit have flat tires, and they didn't know where the shooting was coming from.
> 12:23—Adams was receiving fire from several directions.
> 12:24—Special Agent Hughes arrived on the scene.
> 12:27—They were receiving fire from Jumping Bull Hall (1658-59) (emphasis added)

Special Agent Gerard Waring arrived at the Jumping Bull Compound near Gary Adams around 12:30 p.m. He received fire upon arrival and Agents Breci, Adams, another individual and himself were, according to Waring, the only law enforcement officers in the vicinity at that time (1848).

Between 12:30 and 1:00 p.m. Waring testified that other agents and BIA police officers kept arriving, although Marvin Stoldt testified that he had come to the Jumping Bull Hall soon after noon but was turned back by gunfire (1849, 3658).

Meanwhile Special Agent Hughes had gone to Hot Springs, dropped "his prisoner" off there, and then driven rapidly back to Oglala. He arrived in Oglala around 1:00 p.m. (see the listing of radio transmission by Ann Johnson above) and organized a search team for Agents Williams and Coler. The search party, which included Gerard Waring and several BIA officers went west and followed the creek south. They worked their way around the northwest section of the creek bed, emerging from the woods just southeast of the green house (see Z-1 on Figure 1). Upon appearing beyond the treeline, they received fire and retreated back into the woods for cover (2871, 2874, 2875, 1853, 1854, 1855, 2876).

Between noon and 1:00 p.m. law enforcement officers began to enter the Jumping Bull area. A number of these officers were organized into a search party to locate Agents Williams and Coler.

Gary Adams remained with his car throughout the day. At approximately 12:30 p.m. Adams saw a woman enter the area to negotiate. Failing to accomplish what she expected, she left around 1:30 p.m. and refused to discuss anything with the officers. At this time Adams also observed a man in a red pickup enter the area. It stopped close to the log house for a few minutes and then left with at least two additional passengers. Ann M. Johnson, the FBI stenographer, had recorded this event in the following manner: "1:26 p.m. Adams to Coward, *pickup* came in here, and he just left, can't get any BIA people on it" (90-94, 4230) (emphasis added). We will look more closely at this piece of evidence toward the end of this section.

Another Special Agent, Fred Coward, testified he left his office around 12:20 p.m. and arrived at the Jumping Bull area around 1:30 p.m. At approximately 2:00 p.m. he, Marvin Stoldt (BIA officer), and six others occupied the Pumpkin Seed family residence which sits on highway 35 (1160, 1165) (located to the south, not shown on the map). Between 2:00 and 4:30 p.m. Stoldt was called to assist in a gun battle in the wooded area near the creek. At this time according to Marvin Stoldt, there was shooting coming from both the Jumping Bull residence and the Wanda Siers home (3662, 3663).

It is important to keep in mind the areas where shooting was coming from. Stolt testified there was shooting coming from *both* the area of residences and the Siers house. As we will see, the prosecution throughout the trial emphasized the shooting from the area of the residences and completely ignored that from the Wanda Siers house. This method of manipulating the evidence effectively deceived the jury.

Special Agents Hughes and Waring and their group were still under cover just inside the treeline to the east and south of the green house. At around 2:15 p.m., after Hughes had yelled to those in the green house to surrender because they were surrounded by the FBI and BIA, according to the government, two individuals emerged from the area on Figure 1 labelled residences, and started shooting. Subsequently, members of the search group began to return fire, and one individual stated, "I think I have hit one." Another yelled, "The guy in the white shirt is hit also." After this, firing ceased (1856, 1857, 2877, 2878).

Shortly thereafter, Waring climbed a tree (Z-2), and with his rifle scope identified Special Agent Coler's car about 200 to 250 yards away. He could not, however, spot anyone near the automobile (1857, 1860).

Hughes and several BIA officers then split off from the group to get a better view of the area where the Coler car was. Waring remained at the original location with a few BIA officers to keep "visual contact" with the green house. They remained there for approximately forty-five minutes but did not hear any further gunshots. At approximately 3:00 p.m. Waring's group then joined Hughes and the rest of the search team where they had emerged from the woods, just behind the corrals (Z–3) (1864, 2879, 2880, 2881).

However, at roughly the same time Special Agent Gary Adams observed Edgar Bear Runner enter the area of the three houses (labelled residences on Figure 1). Somewhat earlier, Adams received a radio transmission from the state police "that there was a young individual walking on the crest of the plateau with his hands up." The young boy, Jimmy Zimmerman, and Mr. Bear Runner walked over to Adams, who attempted to interrogate them, but they told him only that there were thirty armed individuals in the trees. (Jimmy was the twelve year old Native American youth mentioned earlier who was living in "tent city.") Both Zimmerman and Edgar Bear Runner left the area around 3:30 or 3:45 p.m. Adams, who remained in the Jumping Bull area until approximately 4:00 p.m., heard gunfire from the Siers house, the Jumping Bull houses, from near Coler's car as well as from the "Y" intersection. He also testifed that at least one individual or possibly more was shooting an automatic weapon from the Siers house (96-97).

At 3:09 p.m. and 3:14 p.m. Special Agent Edward Skelly made radio transmissions. The first asserted that three or four individuals were running between the swamp area and the plowed fields toward highway 18. The second transmission declared, "some people were chased back into the red house and they fired at our guys." Skelly identified this "red house" as being the Siers house (4354, 4355, 4374, 4375, 4377).

Marvin Stoldt, while inside the Pumpkin Seed house, saw five people running up a hill. Using binoculars, Stoldt allegedly identified two people out of this group, Jimmy Eagle and Leonard Peltier (3669, 3670).

Fred Coward was also in the Pumpkin Seed residence at this time. At around 3:45 p.m. he allegedly observed through a 2x7 power riflescope several people at a distance of approximately one half mile running from the Jumping Bulls home into the woods. Through this scope, Coward claimed he could identify one of the persons running from the Jumping Bulls in a southerly direction; this person was Leonard Peltier (1169, 1168).

Special Agent Dean Hughes and Special Agent Gerard Waring remained in the area of the corrals until approximately 4:20 p.m. when they observed Edgar Bear Runner coming toward them with his hands up. Bear Runner told the agents that as he passed Agent Coler's car "he saw two individuals lying on the driver's side of the vehicle, lying in the grass." Bear Runner was sent back to the houses to negotiate peace. Proceeding past Coler's car, he stopped near the three houses for a few moments, then disappeared. A few minutes later he reappeared, coming from the vicinity of the junked cars (see Figure 1) with a second individual identified as "the commissioner." They went directly to Coler's car. Agent Hughes and an unidentified BIA officer likewise walked to the FBI vehicle and found that both agents "had been shot a number of times and both were dead." Hughes and the BIA officer walked back to the corral area; the commissioner and Bear Runner disappeared behind the residences (1869, 1872, 1873, 2883, 2884, 2885).

Reinforcements (several SWAT teams) had arrived when Hughes returned. At 5:50 p.m. Hughes, Waring, BIA officers and the reinforcements attempted to "secure" the residences. They divided into three groups and attacked the houses from all possible sides. They shot tear gas into the houses, and many of the officers were carrying M-16's, the automatic rifle designed for use in Vietnam. On their way up to the houses they came under heavy fire from, as Hughes testified, unidentifiable locations. Once they had secured the houses, they found them empty. However, Waring found the body of Joe Stuntz, allegedly wearing "a dark fatigue jacket with the letters FBI stamped over the pocket." Underneath the jacket was a light color shirt (1875, 1879, 2889, 2890).

Between 5:30 and 6:00 p.m. Skelly warned over the radio that "Some or all of the escaping individuals might possibly be in a position to outflank us." These individuals were in the hills, about ¼ mile west of highway 35 (4360, 4362).

The government argued that the AIM group, which was allegedly firing from the residences, met back at tent city before the police secured the area and then escaped to the south, on foot.

From 6:00 to 7:00 p.m. Ecoffey, Coward and Adams all observed individuals fleeing the area. Adams heard firing until seven, but was unable to pinpoint the source (4460).

After the residential area was assaulted, all law enforcement personnel thoroughly searched it and meticulously gathered evidence, although leaving untouched expended law enforcement shells and casings. None of these casings were sent to FBI labs for analysis, as far the FOIA documents indicate.

This concludes a summarization of the government's (and police officers') scenario as to the law enforcement activities on 26 June 1975 in the Jumping Bull area.

Pickup or Van?

Throughout the trial, the government maintained that Special Agents Coler and Williams were following a "red and white van" into the Jumping Bull area that contained Indians, one of whom was allegedly Leonard Peltier. He supposedly owned a red and white Chevrolet suburban van. Government attorneys Robert Sikma and Evan Hultman continuously referred to either a "vehicle" or "van" and avoided ever using the word "pickup." However, almost all witnesses on the stand talked about a "pickup" rather than a van. Let's look closely at some interesting testimony.

According to testimony we have presented, Gary Adams heard Williams refer to the vehicle in the following manner: "It looks like they're going to get into that *pickup*" (emphasis added). Gerard Waring heard Agent Williams report that "there was a *red and white vehicle* . . ." (emphasis added). Robert Ecoffey heard on the evening of June 25 that Jimmy Eagle had just left in a *red pickup*, and the next day that Williams had chased a "red *vehicle*, van or *pickup*" (emphasis added).

Ann M. Johnson testified Special Agent Gary Adams radioed at 12:18 that he saw a *red pickup* leaving Jumping Bull Hall. At the trial in Cedar Rapids, Iowa, in the summer of 1976 where Dino Butler and Robert Robideau were tried and acquitted on the same charge as those lodged against Peltier, he testified he made that transmission.

Q: And did you not give instructions at 12:18 that there was a red pickup leaving Jumping Bull Hall area going north, and you instructed people to stop this pickup?

A: Yes (350).

At the trial in Fargo, however, he denied making such a transmission.

Q: But you are sure you didn't make that transmission at 12:18 p.m.?

A: Yes (347).

Also, at 1:26 p.m. Ann Johnson recorded a transmission made by Adams to Coward that a red pickup with only a driver stopped at the log house, but that it left with three people in it! (There was never any evidence presented at the trial to indicate Peltier was ever around this house.) (263)*

Michael Anderson, a government witness who testified to the events leading up to the killing of the agents, stated that he saw the agents chasing a vehicle into the Jumping Bull area, which the government, of course, wanted the jury to believe was Peltier's alleged red and white van. Consider then the following exchange:

Q: (Evan Hultman) And what if anything then happened?
A: (Michael Anderson) Well, I guess they seen the *orange pickup* going down that way and they followed it.
Q: Now, when you say "orange pickup" is that the red and white van to which—
(Objection by the defense, sustained by Judge Benson)
Q: Mr. Anderson, tell us what the car was—
A: The orange and white and red and white van that was going down the hill (774-775) (emphasis added).

In Gerard Waring's 302 reporting the events of the 26th, he asserted hearing Williams radio, "red and white vehicle."[3] Waring was the only agent or officer to specify the description in such a way; all others used the word "pickup."

Waring's insistence on the vaguer term, "vehicle," was important in the government case. The more specific references to a "red pickup" coming into and going out of the Jumping Bull area, especially as it turned up in the radio transmissions of Special Agent Williams, did not fit conveniently into the case against Peltier. We will discuss why the government played down this evidence of a red pickup at greater length toward the end of this section. Let's now look at another important inconsistency in the law enforcement officer's testimonies, the alleged sightings of Jimmy Eagle and Leonard Peltier.

The Sightings of Peltier and Jimmy Eagle

Special Agent Fred Coward testified he saw Leonard Peltier on 26 June 1975. This alleged sighting, which he said took place around 3:45 p.m., was made through a 2x7 power rifle scope at a distance

---

*The individual driving the pickup was later identified as Wallace Little Sr., who entered the area to negotiate. The two passengers were later identified as Wallace Little, Jr., and Jerry Mousseau, both considered suspects by the ¯BI (discussed later).

of one half mile as he was looking east. He supposedly identified Peltier running south. Therefore, Peltier would have been seen in profile. It was a hot, sunny June day, and the day before had been rainy so the mirage factor was high (1305).

The defense requested Judge Benson to look through Fred Coward's rifle scope and attempt to recognize an acquaintance at that distance. The judge both refused to do this himself and would not allow jury members to try it. The defense then brought in James R. Hall, retail store manager of a sporting goods shop specializing in the sales of firearms, scopes, and reloading devices. He testified that in the presence of a defense attorney and FBI agent, he looked through a rifle scope equal in power to that of Coward's at an acquaintance facing him one half mile away on a sunny, cold (38 degrees) and bright day. Mr. Hall could not determine any facial features and could not recognize his friend (1797, 3786, 3790).

Fred Coward testified that from June 26-30 there were all-agent conferences each morning and evening. Agents spoke freely concerning the development of the investigation and, according to Coward, they worked out a theory of what happened (1227, 1228).

Coward met with Special Agents Skelly and Waring specifically during these conferences where he stated that he had sighted Leonard Peltier. However, on the stand later neither Skelly nor Waring recalled any mention of Leonard Peltier during those conferences (1306, 1307, 2052, 4364).

Assistant Special Agent in Charge Norman Zigrossi arrived in Rapid City on the evening of the 27th. Even though thoroughly briefed on the investigation up to that time, Zigrossi told defense attorney Taikeff the afternoon before he testified that he did not recall any mention of Leonard Peltier during the period June 27-30—in contradiction to Coward's testimony that a sighting was discussed. However, when he was on the stand he changed his story and stated that Leonard Peltier's name was mentioned during this time period (4450, 4451).

There were inconsistencies in Coward and Stoldt's testimonies as well. At the time Fred Coward made his alleged sighting, BIA officer Marvin Stoldt, who was with him at the Pumpkin Seed house, also looked at two fleeing figures through a pair of 15-power binoculars. At the time of the sightings, however, Stoldt failed to mention whom he saw to anyone, including Coward. Stoldt testified that when he looked through the scope of a rifle, which he thought was "possibly" Special Agent Coward's, he could not identify either of these individuals. Stoldt further stated he could not recollect telling Coward about

the sighting later in the day. He didn't see Coward after June 26 until
4 September 1975 (3671, 3673, 3685, 3686).

Coward testified he had conversations with Stoldt during the
whole day on June 26. Coward claimed that during these conversations
Stoldt told him he had spotted Jimmy Eagle in the same group in
which Coward had spotted Peltier. Although Coward testified that this
was a highly important fact, it was not recorded in his 302 report of
the activities of 26 June 1975. The defense attempted to offer this 302
into evidence, but the government objected, and Judge Benson sustained the objection. Consequently, the jury never saw this important
piece of evidence.

Coward stated on the stand that the *first* time Stoldt mentioned
the sighting of Jimmy Eagle was on the 26th, during a car ride. This
alleged identification was never recorded in his 302 (1308, 1310, 1320,
1321). This testimony is additionally interesting once we uncover
Stoldt's recollection of the events.

Q: (Elliott Taikeff) Well, how about the possibility that instead
   of making a formal statement, in a car ride later that day or
   perhaps on your way home with Agent Coward you may have
   just casually mentioned to him the sighting of a person who
   appeared to you to be Jimmy Eagle?

A: (Marvin Stoldt) I think that's highly improbable also because
   I and Coward did split up, you know... and he was quite a
   ways from me (3750-3751).

There were other problems. Stoldt was interrogated by Coward
on 4 September 1975. Coward testified that this date was the first time
he had interviewed Stoldt about the alleged sighting of Jimmy Eagle.
Defense attorney Elliott Taikeff then handed Coward a report and asked
him:

Q. What is it?

A: It's a 302.

Q: Of what?

A: Marvin Stoldt.

Q: Do you mean an interview of Marvin Stoldt?

A: Yes, Sir.

Q: By whom?

A: By myself and Vincent Louis Breci.

Q: And according to that 302 what was the date of the interview?

A: June 28, 1975.

Q: And what was the subject matter of the interview?

A: Well, basically it was a sighting by him at approximately

3:45 p.m.

Q: Of?

A: Of Jimmy Eagle (1345).

This 302 was offered into evidence by the defense but was disallowed by Judge Benson. Therefore, the jury never saw this evidence either (1351).

Coward stated in response that the date on the 302 was wrong, due to a typographical error, and Stoldt actually told him about his sighting of Jimmy Eagle on the 26th, rather than the 28th. Stoldt's testimony reveals once again the ludicrous nature of the FBI story.

Q: (Elliott Taikeff) Now, might it be possible that you made that statement to him [Coward] on June 26th and that there's a typographical error there when it says that you were interviewed June 28th?

A. (Marvin Stoldt) No, I don't, I think that's highly impossible because of the fact that we were involved in so much. It wasn't time for anybody to sit down and give statements, you know...There was no time for anybody, you know, to make any kind of statements or anything (3750).

Defense attorney Elliot Taikeff read the following from Coward's September 4 interview of Marvin Stoldt.

Stoldt stated that during the first statement he had given to the FBI *a few days after the shooting of the agents*, he told the agents then, one of the agents being Coward, that he saw Jimmy Eagle in the group that he had just identified but was not absolutely positive during the interview (emphasis added).

Coward's reply was he was misled by the wrong date on the previous 302. Elliot Taikeff then asked Coward the following question:

". . . explain why you did not recognize the error of June 28th, only two months later, considering the fact that in this courtroom you instantly recognized that fact and said 'Oh, that date is wrong, that couldn't be the 28th.' "

A: (Fred Coward) ". . . because of the fact that some things, some impulsive thing that you asked me a few weeks ago about this, you know, it triggered my memory, it refreshed it" (4240, 4241).

Marvin Stoldt also gave testimony regarding this interview on 4 September 1975. Defense attorney Taikeff asked Stoldt if he in fact did tell Coward then he was positive he sighted Jimmy Eagle on June 26.

A. (Marvin Stoldt) Can you give me a little time to think about it?

Q. Absolutely.

A. All right.

Q. You can have all the time you want.

THE COURT: The witness may be advised that you do not have to answer the question yes or no. You can also answer it whether or not you remember.

A. Then in that case I'll take the alternative, I'll say I don't recall.

Q. I see (3758).

Was this confused testimony the result of an attempted cover-up, since Jimmy Eagle *was* in fact on the reservation? Why such a problem with Jimmy Eagle? As we have stated earlier, the government stipulated that Jimmy Eagle was *not* on the reservation June 26. Why did they stipulate that?*

The Vehicle Question Revisited

New evidence, obtained under the Freedom of Information Act by Peltier's attorneys exposes the problems with the government story. Regarding the "red and white van," previously undisclosed evidence indicates that the government was in possession of and possibly suppressed reports demonstrating the involvement of other vehicles. And it is these vehicles which likely contained the individuals who

---

*The prosecution presented evidence at the trial that Coler and Williams were looking for Eagle and had information that he was traveling in a red pickup. However, in the writ of habeas corpus filed by Peltier's attorneys, the defense argues with much documentation that the prosecution was in possession, yet it suppressed, "evidence that the agents believed Eagle was at the Jumping Bulls, that Williams observed him in such a vehicle, chased Eagle in the vehicle, and were subsequently fired upon by *that* vehicle's occupants." This evidence against Eagle was inconsistent with the prosecution of Peltier; consequently, Eagle was dismissed, and evidence concerning his presence on the reservation was kept away from the jury.

At a meeting between the prosecutors of the reservation murders (the FBI code named it RESMURS) and top FBI and Department of Justice officials on 10 August 1976, Evan Hultman made the statement that "the Resmurs case on *James Eagle was weak* and he felt there was not sufficient evidence to get it to the jury" (emphasis added). The FBI memorandum revealed that the prosecutors' reason for wanting to dismiss the charges against Eagle was "so that the *full prosecutive weight of the Federal Government could be directed against Leonard Peltier*" (emphasis added).

actually killed Agents Coler and Williams.

At no time prior to the trial did any document exist which showed involvement of a 1966 red and white Chevrolet van.* The documents that do exist show that Peltier was *not* even the owner of such a van. The government in fact knew as early as 9 July 1975 that the red and white Chevrolet van belonged to Donald Matthew Loud Hawk, who was being considered as a suspect. According to an FBI report from the special Agent in Charge at Pine Ridge to the Director on 15 August 1975,

> Loud Hawk is considered a suspect inasmuch as one witness states he is quite sure he saw Loud Hawk running from the crime scene on June 26, 1975. He is also the registered owner of a 1966 Chevrolet van which was found in "tent city." He is an associate of suspect James Theodore Eagle and was recently involved in a shooting with him.

The FBI was also aware on 14 July 1975 that Loud Hawk had either sold or given the van to Joseph Stuntz, who was considered a suspect. Interestingly, the government made no attempt to challenge the testimony of Angie Long Visitor that this van belonged to Leonard Peltier (2672).

The Pickup. As shown above, there was only limited reference in testimony to the agents chasing a pickup into the Jumping Bull area and one leaving immediately after the killings. Why was this testimony kept low-keyed? FBI documents reveal that the Bureau was concerned and very interested in a red pickup almost immediately. The day following the firefight (6-27-75) an internal FBI memorandum stated,

> At approximately 6:25 a.m., Minneappolis office telephonically advised that an explosion had occurred at the Visitor's Center, Mt. Rushmore, S.D. ... There were earlier reports that a *red pickup* truck had been spotted in the vicinity of the Visitor's Center shortly before the explosion and this *may have a significant connection to captioned matter since a red pickup truck was also reported in the vicinity of the shooting on 6-26-75* (emphasis added).

---

*This is not totally true. Angie Long Visitor made a statement to the FBI on 28 June 1975 that she saw a van in the vicinity of the crime scene.

On 1 July 1975, a few days after the above memorandum, Clarence Kelly, Director of the FBI, held a news conference in Los Angeles concerning the killing of the two agents. Kelly discussed SA Williams' radio transmissions overheard by other agents.

> The first of these was apparently to the effect that there's some people by the house and it looks like they are leaving. We found later that probably they were speaking of the fact that some subjects or possible subjects were leaving the area in a *red pickup and this red pickup had become the subject of some concern in this investigation* (emphasis added).

The red pickup became an object of deep concern to the FBI. For example, a member of the Fall River County Sheriff's Office, Hot Springs, South Dakota, was interviewed by two SA's of the FBI on 9 July 1975. This Sheriff was present at the Jumping Bulls on 26 June 1975 and remembers seeing:

> a *red 1965 Ford pickup* driving in the vicinity of where the Agents took fire on several occasions and he stated that he did not think that it was a law enforcement vehicle. The individual driving the *red pickup* was identified as an Indian male wearing a light western straw hat (emphasis added).

On 11 July 1975, the FBI interviewed an individual who stated that Jimmy Eagle rode around "in an orange and white pickup."* On 9 July 1975, Wallace Little, Sr., was seen driving a "red Ford pickup." On 22 August 1975 witnesses told the FBI that on 26 June 1975, they observed Wallace Little enter the crime scene area in a red Ford pickup truck and leave with two individuals, Wallace Little, Jr., and Jerry Mousseau. Both Little, Jr., and Mousseau were considered suspects by the FBI. Moreover, an FBI document reveals that when the red pickup left the Jumping Bull area, a BIA officer observed that it was followed out by suspect Richard Little.

The International Scout. FBI documents also reveal another type of automobile referred to in their investigation. David Price, a former partner of Ron Williams, reported on 26 June 1975 that he

---

*Robert Ecoffey testified at the trial, as we discussed above, that he assisted Coler and Williams' search for Jimmy Eagle on 25 June 1975. Ecoffey observed a *red pickup* at the Wallace Little residence. When they went to the residence, the vehicle was gone and they were informed that Eagle had "just left in the red pickup."

heard Williams state the following over the radio:

> He's supposed to be in a *red Scout*....That looks like the *red Scout* over there....There's alot of people around....They're getting in the *red Scout* with rifles. They're shooting at us (emphasis added).

As they had done with the "red pickup," the FBI began to search for clues and evidence concerning who might have been in the "red Scout." For example, on 27 June 1975 the FBI interviewed Rayford Featherman, who later became a suspect. He claimed he had no knowledge of the events at the Jumping Bulls. However, he did exclaim that "the story in Oglala about the events of June 26, 1975, are that the men in the *red Scout are body guards for Dennis Banks*" (emphasis added).

On 4 July 1975, two BIA police officers told the FBI that they had spotted a red Scout in March of 1975 parked in the area where the agents had been shot. One BIA officer "stated that their two BIA police cars *chased* this red *International Scout* to the residence of Richard Little" (emphasis added). The other BIA officer provided the interviewing agent with a Federal Criminal Violation Report, dated 25 March 1975. According to this document, Trudy Pumpkin Seed reported to the BIA "that she went out to dump garbage when she heard some gun shots" and that "she observed a red International Scout" after hearing the shots fired. Her residence is across the river from where the two agents were shot (where Coward and Stoldt made their alleged sightings). When the officers chased the Scout to the Little residence, they observed three individuals running into the house.

The government, in its closing argument, emphasized the testimony of Angie Long Visitor that the red Scout was a junked car, which had been sitting for weeks. Yet the Scout was one of only three seized at the scene, along with the 1967 Ford and the 1966 Chevrolet Suburban van. Special attention was given to photographing the Scout, examining its contents, conducting a fingerprint analysis of items inside, and finding its owner.

The Red Jeep. FBI documents uncovered through the Freedom of Information Act also indicate their concern about a *red jeep* possibly being involved in the events of 26 June 1975. For example, on that day a Special Agent working at his desk in the Rapid City resident agency heard Williams' voice over the radio: "I paid little attention to the transmission at that moment, but did hear him mention the name Jimmy Eagle and something about *chasing a red jeep*" (emphasis added). Moreover, while SA Dean Howard Hughes was transporting a prisoner, FBI documents indicate that he heard a similar transmission as the one above:

> SA Hughes heard over the Bureau radio the voice of SA Williams, and SA Williams was talking to another unnamed agent that he thought he saw Jimmy Eagle in a *red jeep* (emphasis added). *

And a teletype from Minneapolis to the Director et al. on 3 July 1975 pointed out the following:

> ...Jimmy Eagle, has been sighted in a red jeep at the Jumping Bull area. Radio transmissions seconds later from SA Williams determined that SA Williams was under fire from unknown individuals from the jeep at that location.

Once again, as with the previous "red pickup" and "red Scout," the FBI began to investigate this "red jeep." For example, while attempting to serve a grand jury subpoena on Wanda Siers, two FBI agents wrote in their report that she was "located exiting from the Richard Little residence driving a *red jeep* pickup truck" (emphasis added). While several agents attempted to interview Martha Tranquilli of Oglala, they observed an Indian male "in an area adjacent to the Weasel Bear residence and near a *red jeep* pickup truck" (emphasis added).

Peltier Van Theory. What the above evidence indicates is that the government had grave problems with their Peltier van theory. Not *one* FOIA document indicates a concern about a "van." As such, the prosecution possibly withheld the confused vehicles evidence from the defense, as well as the judge and jury, making the Peltier van theory much easier to argue.

The "Peltier van theory" apparently came to fruition in late September 1975. The FBI at Rapid City teletyped the Director, summarizing an interview by SA J. Gary Adams and Q. Victor Harvey, 9-22-75, with future prosecution witness Norman Brown. The summary stated erroneously that the interview had produced a statement that "a white over red 1966 suburban van recovered at Tent City on

---

*This document contradicts Hughes' testimony at trial where he stated that the first transmission he heard was, "We are being fired on; we are in a little valley in Oglala, South Dakota, pinned down in a cross fire between two houses" (2870). He did *not* testify to overhearing something about a vehicle.

June 27, 1975, was identical with one that agents were pursuing prior to confrontation." According to Adams and Harveys' 302 of that interview, what Brown *really* said was the following:

> Regarding the red and white Chevrolet Suburban, Brown referred to this as a *bus* belonging to Peltier. He stated he observed this *bus* on numerous occasions, always being driven by Peltier (emphasis added).

Moreover, the above inaccurate summary is unsupported by any other statement made by Brown, including his trial testimony. However, the "summary" does paraphrase the trial testimony of Michael Anderson, the prosecution's most important witness. We will point out some important problems in a later section with Anderson's testimony, as well as some new evidence uncovered through the Freedom of Information Act, which sheds some light on the government's "one vehicle" theory. Let's now turn to the pathologists' reports.

The Pathologists' Reports

The government presented the testimony of two pathologists to the jury, Dr. Robert Bloemendaal and Dr. Thomas Noguchi. Both had concluded Special Agents Ron Williams and Jack Coler were each hit with three bullets. Williams was shot once through the outer portion of the left arm by a bullet that proceeded through the arm and penetrated the body just above the belt line. The wound was judged "potentially fatal" and was discharged from a .44 magnum at a distance greater than ten feet. Williams received a second gunshot wound to the left instep, which broke the main bone to the big toe. This wound, also caused by a distant shot, would have been "very painful" and disabling, but not fatal. The third gunshot wound which Agent Williams received was through his right hand as he held it in front of his face. According to the pathologists, the gun, a high velocity weapon, was in contact with Agent Williams' hand; the bullet went through it, struck his face, and continued out the back of his head. This third and final gunshot wound was established by the pathologists to have been immediately fatal (587, 588, 623, 624, 593, 589).

Special Agent Coler also received three gunshot wounds. The first, to the left arm, incapacitated it by destroying the muscles at the elbow joint. Without immediate treatment this injury would have been potentially fatal "in a matter of minutes" because of major bleeding. Coler was allegedly found with Williams' shirt in use as a tourniquet around his arm. This particular bullet had come from a distance;

it first pierced the open trunk lid of his car and then struck his arm. Coler's second gunshot wound, to the top of the head, entered the right side and exited on the left. This wound, judged "potentially and immediately fatal," came from a high velocity weapon at close range. Coler's third wound was to the chin and the right side of the jaw. According to the pathologists, this too would have been immediately fatal and was also from a high velocity weapon shot at close range (592, 591, 626, 633, 635, 593).

In summary, one or more individuals standing within ten feet of the agents, fired three shots which took the lives of the two agents. One of the shots went through the right hand of Agent Williams, struck him in the face and killed him instantly. Two shots fired from ten feet at most struck Agent Coler in the head and at least one was immediately fatal (643).

Both pathologists were aware of the death of Joe Stuntz, the Native American who was shot and killed the same day as the two agents. The pathologists, however, were not asked to do a postmortem examination of Joe Stuntz in conjunction with the other examinations. There was no reason why this examination could not have taken place (588-589).*

Photographs taken at the crime scene and during the autopsy were introduced into evidence by the government during the pathologists' testimony. These pictures were extremely gory, and the defense accordingly strongly objected to their admission into evidence. The issue was not how the agents died—the point the government was emphasizing—but rather, whether or not the defendant participated in the killing of the agents. Defense attorney Elliot Taikeff further argued that the doctors were able and willing to describe adequately the murders of Special Agents Williams and Coler. Therefore, introducing these pictures into evidence—and allowing the jury to see them would only serve to arouse the passions of the jury and, in turn, would likely lead to a prejudiced decision based on outrage rather than a rational one supported through fact. Judge Benson, however, ruled that the relevance and probative value of the photographs outweighed the possible prejudicial effect on the defendant. Consequently, the government used these pictures extensively throughout the trial, displaying them to the jury many times (544-546). The government had two points to make in relation to the actual shooting of the agents:

*Interestingly, it was W. O. Brown who performed the examination of Joe Stuntz, the same pathologist who cut off the hands of Anna Mae Aquash.

(1) that it was "the last gunshot wound" that Williams received which "would have been immediately fatal" (Dr. Bloemendaal's testimony at the trial), and (2) that the projectile which killed both agents "was a high velocity missile" (589, 593).

FBI documents indicate that Bloemendaal's initial conclusion of Williams' autopsy was quite different from his testimony. A 27 June 1975 teletype from the Minneapolis Division of the FBI to Headquarters reported that Bloemendaal's autopsy conclusion was "that the bullet which entered Williams' head was *first* in sequence and *caused death instantaneously*" (emphasis added). However, FBI headquarters questioned the autopsy findings. Special Agent in Charge Richard Held was "instructed," according to a Special Agent 30 June 1975 internal FBI memorandum, to clear up the matter prior to (SA) J. Gary Adams' flight to Los Angeles to brief the Director for a news conference.

According to FBI headquarters,

> One of the chief concerns by the way of inconsistencies that should be resolved today, is the autopsy report saying that SA Williams was instantly killed by the first bullet at close range . . .

What the FBI was concerned about was the inconsistency with their theory of events at trial: simply that Williams transmitted prior to his death the message over his car radio, "I'm hit." As the FBI memo went on to say, "The Director has stated that it is obvious that this transmission would be impossible if the autopsy report was accurate and he desires this clarified before any statement to the press is made." However, for the time being the FBI decided to adhere to the initial conclusion by Bloemendaal. Clarence Kelly reported to the media on 1 July 1975 the following: "We know that the first wound suffered by Agent Williams was in his head and killed him instantly."

The FBI did not drop the issue but became very concerned about the discrepancy. They therefore hired pathologist Thomas Noguchi, who, they felt, was more qualified, to "corroborate the testimony of eyewitnesses." Since Noguchi was hired at such a late date, he would obviously be unable to examine the bodies of the deceased agents prior to his testimony. Consequently, Assistant United States Attorney Robert Sikma participated in a conference with a Special Agent and an Inspector, who together proposed that the FBI "provide Dr. Noguchi with the necessary support for his testing involving use of animal parts." Animal parts were to be used since "Noguchi must conduct some testing to provide him with data upon which to have his opinions." In a teletype from the Director to both the Assistant Special Agent in charge at Rapid City and the Special Agent in charge at Los Angeles 24 March 1976 the following was pointed out:

> Through conversations with Special Prosecutor Sikma it is the understanding of the laboratory that the main purpose of any testing to be conducted by Dr. Noguchi is to establish 1) That the the wound to SA Coler's Jaw was caused by bullet entry near the right side of the mouth with bullet exit under the jaw; 2) That the wound to SA Williams' left foot was caused before death; 3) A distance estimate for the wound in Williams' right hand.

The memo continued to make clear:

> The first two points are in opposition to Dr. Bloemendaal's autopsy reports and *Bloemendaal will not be used for medical opinion testimony* (emphasis added).

What these documents expose is that the FBI realized that Dr. Bloemendaal's findings (and possible future testimony) were not consistent with their theory of what happened on 26 June 1975.* Consequently, rather than question their theory, the government questioned Bloemendaal's findings and found an individual more "qualified" for their purposes. Although Noguchi demanded the opportunity to perform certain tests, the FBI lab felt they would be "highly speculative and not worth the cost." Yet the tests were authorized, since it was "in the Bureau's best interest not to alienate him [Noguchi] at this time."

The tests took place on 14 and 15 April 1976. They involved an AR-15, .308 caliber rifle, .30-30 rifle, M-1 carbine, .45 caliber rifle, .222 caliber rifle, .44 magnum rifle, hogs legs and ribs, and various car parts. An FBI teletype from the Los Angeles office to the Director and Rapid City on 15 April 1976 noted that "photos and 16 MM motion pictures were taken" during the testing, and a SA from Rapid City planned "to hand carry reports of Dr. Noguchi to special prosecutor Sikma regarding Noguchi's findings obtained after analysis of photos and x-rays at time of autopsies of SAS Williams and Coler."

---

*As stated already, how could Williams have made such a statement, "I'm hit," if he was killed instantly by the first bullet, as Bloemendaal's initial conclusion indicates. Did Bloemendaal and/or the agents commit perjury?

Yet, according to Peltier's lawyers, no photographs, motion pictures, X-rays or reports were ever provided to them. Nor did the FBI ever inform the defense about these tests.*

It was the government's contention that a single individual (Peltier) using a high velocity weapon (AR-15) fired a small caliber projectile (.223) which killed agents Coler and Williams.** Yet documents reveal that this conclusion could only be argued by ignoring important evidence. On 27 June 1975 the Minneapolis Division of the FBI teletyped to the Director that "the first bullet to strike SA Williams was," according to Bloemendaal, *"possibly* from a high velocity shoulder weapon..." (emphasis added). And in February 1976 Bloemendaal confirmed that only *one* of the agents had been killed by a high velocity bullet, attributing this to an AR-15. The government further argued that this AR-15 was Peltier's. These documents thus challenge the testimony that both agents were killed by a high velocity weapon.

Consequently, there seems to be a substantial amount of evidence either "hushed up" or simply suppressed that clearly questions the government's theory about the killing of the agents.*** The patholo-

---

*At the trial, Noguchi made no references to what these tests involved, but only referred to his "findings." Such vagueness about what these tests entailed casts more doubt on their value. Had the jury been able to hear about this situation, what would they have thought?

**It should also be made *very* clear that the AR-15 and FBI-issued M-16 deliver the *same* .223 caliber round.

***When I state "suppressed evidence" or "withheld evidence" a few things need to be understood. Peltier's attorneys state in their writ of habaes corpus that the government suppressed the majority of FBI documents discussed in this book (see, *Motion to Vacate Judgment and for a New Trial*, U.S. v. Leonard Peltier, #C77-3003). However, as this book goes to print, the government filed an opposition to that writ, stating the following:

> The only documents which the Court can be reasonably assured were not given to the defense were the FBI's progress reports to headquarters, communications sending out leads and summarizing the status of the investigation, case summaries and witness summaries which were prepared for the prosecutors and other internal administrative documents of like nature.

The government went on to state, however, that these types of documents are "rarely provided" to the defense in criminal cases. They pointed out that all fingerprint reports, all firearms reports, and a "high percentage" of the FBI interview memoranda (302's) were provided to the defense at trial (see U.S. v. Leonard Peltier, *Brief Resisting Motion for New Trial*: 1).

It is clear that the government has admitted withholding a number of documents and that, therefore, the "suppression of evidence" did take place. It is in this light that I argue that the government attorneys suppressed evidence.

(cont., p. 64)

gists' reports and evidence add up to the following conclusion: Either both pathologists were utterly incompetent (because they couldn't differentiate between wounds inflicted by large and small bore weapons) or the evidence was deliberately fudged to conform to the prosecution's Peltier/AR-15 theory. In either event, the range of ballistics "options" entered into evidence at one point or another is simply too vast to be credible, since it should have been obvious by the kind of wound inflicted what type of weapon was used. Either the pathologists never knew enough to impart anything of value to the case (and were used only to add to the confusion), or they knew *too* much to submit honest and accurate testimony, in which case they were asked to suppress evidence in order to assist the government's case.

Anderson, Draper and Brown

The government's most important witnesses were Michael Anderson, Wilford Draper and Norman Brown. In front of the jury the government called these three young Native Americans "eyewitnesses," in the sense that they testified to having seen Peltier at the murder scene. None of them, however, would testify he actually saw Peltier shoot the agents. Further, their often contradictory, inconsistent attestations showed without a doubt that the FBI had tampered with and manipulated their stories. We will first look specifically at their individual testimonies given under direct examination. Then, as in the preceding section, we will look at some important contradictions in their testimonies and at the role the FBI played in helping these individuals prepare their statements.

Michael Anderson testified that on the evening of 25 June 1975, Norman Charles, Wilford Draper and he were stopped and questioned by two FBI agents. Subsequently, they were taken to the Pine Ridge jail since the agents suspected one of them was possibly Jimmy Eagle. Since none could be identified as Jimmy Eagle, all three were returned to the Jumping Bull area later that same day (750-768).

The government asked Anderson whom the three of them saw when they returned to the tent area. As the following exchange shows, Anderson met both Peltier and Dino Butler, but oddly only remembered what Peltier had to say.

Even with this said, it is clear that far more crucial questions remain: Does the "rarely provided" evidence call into question the government's scenario? Does it in fact help to exonerate Peltier? Is it valid policy on the part of the government to "rarely provide" certain evidence to the defense? Does such a policy assist or impede justice?

Q: (By Mr. Hultman) And what if anything took place when you saw Peltier?

A: Well, we just told him we got stopped by the FBI.

Q: And what if anything did he do or say?

A: We just got yelled at.

Q: And what did he indicate to you when he yelled at you?

A: We were dumb to get in the car.

Q: Did you talk to anybody other than you remember that night?

A: To Dino.

Q: All right. And do you remember what you talked to him about at all?

A: No (770).

Regarding the events leading up to the shootings, Anderson testified during direct examination that he went to Wanda Siers' residence on the morning of June 26 in order to eat breakfast there. After breakfast, Anderson climbed up on the roof of the Siers house and observed a "red and white van" arriving. He "knew" this van belonged to Leonard Peltier, since there were only two cars in the tent area which people used from time to time. However, surprisingly, he supposedly did not know who owned or even drove the other vehicle (773, 771, 772).

When the van arrived at the Siers house, Anderson was on the roof and he could allegedly see Leonard Peltier, Joe Stuntz and Norman Charles exit the vehicle and begin to visit with one another. Immediately following this, two FBI agents cars approached the Siers residence. At this time, Peltier, Stuntz and Charles also observed the agents and got back into the van and drove down the hill (see Figure 1). The agents stopped at Wanda Siers' residence to look for Jimmy Eagle. However they spotted the van going down the hill and followed it. The van went a little further, parked beside a fence, and the three occupants jumped out. The last matter Anderson recalls was the agents' following the van and then the sound of gunfire (773, 776).

Following this, Anderson evidently ran back to the tent area, picked up a rifle and ran back to the Jumping Bull residence where he found Norman Charles, Norman Brown and Joe Stuntz. Anderson promptly commenced firing at the agents as well as at another automobile coming in from the highway (777, 778, 779, 781).

During the ensuing firefight, Anderson testified to looking down at the agents' cars four times and observing the activity of Agents Williams and Coler. The *first* observation by Anderson revealed, "one guy was behind the trunk shooting a rifle, and the other one had a pistol." The *second* time Anderson looked down upon the agents and their cars he allegedly noticed the following.

A: (Michael Anderson) One of them was hit.

Q: Do you remember anything about the looks of the two?

A: One had no shirt on.

Q: One of them had no shirt on. You said one of them was hit. How do you know one of them was hit?

A: I don't know. I guess the guy with the shirt off was trying to help him, bandage him up or something (784).

Regarding the whereabouts of Leonard Peltier, Anderson testified he observed Peltier at the treeline, close to where the van had allegedly stopped (see Figure 1). Anderson, however, consistently contradicted himself concerning the sightings of Peltier. He first testified he did *not* see Peltier anywhere else except at the treeline. Later he would testify he observed Peltier down at the agents' cars, even though just prior to that he affirmed seeing "nobody" at the automobiles. This self-impeaching testimony came out during the government's questioning of Anderson's recollection of the *third* time he looked down at the agents' cars. He allegedly made this third observation immediately following his sighting of Leonard Peltier at the treeline.

Q: (Evan Hultman) What did you see at the next time you looked down to the agents' cars?

A: (Michael Anderson) Nobody.

Q: Was anything going on at that time?

A: No.

Q: Did you see any individuals down at the agents' cars at any time?

A: Yes.

Q: And tell us who it was you saw at the agents' cars.

A: Butler, Robideau and Peltier.

Q: And did they have weapons with them?

A: Yes.

Anderson added that Peltier had an AR-15, Butler an M-1 and Robideau some kind of "weapon" (778-791).

Anderson was questioned about a *fourth* time he looked down at the two agents and cars. At this time he allegedly was unable to see anything, including the agents. Following this sighting attempt, "we ran back down to camp," where they all met with the women, Jimmy Zimmerman and Leonard Peltier. Peltier asked Anderson to help "load the van" and suggested they all make a run for it. The group agreed with his suggestion of using the van and decided instead to go on foot. During the escape, Anderson testified he carried out a .44 Ranger, Peltier carried an AR-15 and Robideau carried a shotgun and pumpgun (791, 792, 793, 801, 804, 805).

Wilford Draper testified that on 25 June 1975 Mike Anderson, Norman Charles and he went into Oglala to take showers. On their way back they were stopped by Special Agents Jack Coler and Ron Williams as well as some BIA police officers. All three were taken to Pine Ridge jail since the agents thought one of them was Jimmy Eagle. They were identified by the booking officer at the jail, released and given a ride back to the Jumping Bull area. There they met Leonard Peltier who said to them, " 'I heard you guys went to Pine Ridge with some agents, and did they do anything to you guys, or anything like that, did they harm you?' We told him no, because we went along with them. Told him they were looking for Eagle. He said, 'It's okay' " (1016, 1024).

On the morning of June 26, Draper testified that he awakened in his tent (which was set up behind Jumping Bull's house) around 8 or 8:30 a.m., then hauled water down to the tent area, his usual chore. He arrived at the tent area around 9 or 9:30 and saw Jimmy Zimmerman, Norman Charles, Dino Butler, Leonard Peltier and Nee-lock. During direct examination by the prosecution, Draper testified, "later that morning" he heard some shooting, and, when the gunfire sounded, he was the only one in the tent area. After a while Jimmy Zimmerman appeared, then he saw Joe Stuntz and Norman Charles, a little later, Dino Butler and Norman Brown. All of these individuals ran up to the Jumping Bull area, except Draper, who went off and hid in a ravine. When he came back to the tent area, which was after "quite awhile," he saw Leonard Peltier, Dino Butler and Bob Robideau. Butler, Robideau and Peltier, according to Draper, were loading up the red and white van when he arrived. After a while Norman Charles came into the tent area, and still later, he saw Norman Brown and Mike Anderson. The whole group left the area together by foot. He carried out two brown bags of dynamite fuse, Peltier had an AR-15 rifle, Robideau had a rifle and shotgun, the latter having a sticker that said "Denver FBI." Dino Butler, Norman Charles, Norman Brown and Mike Anderson were all carrying rifles with them (1026, 1028, 1029, 1020, 1022, 1041).

Norman Brown was the third major witness for the prosecution. Prior to giving testimony, Norman Brown was granted by Judge Benson (at the request of the government) immunity from prosecution for any testimony he gave on the witness stand or any proceedings connected with the trial. Brown's private attorney was given a reserved, front row seat in the courtroom so that anytime Brown became confused on the witness stand, Judge Benson could grant a short recess, enabling Brown and his attorney time to confer (1382).

Brown swore on the sacred pipe that his testimony would be truthful.[4] On the evening of 25 June 1975, Brown "pulled security," that is, he "just walked around camp and looked to see how everything was because, reasons why we had security was because we were afraid of the goons" (1392, 1420).

On the following morning, June 26, Brown was in tent city talking with Joe Stuntz when he heard some shots. Brown and Stuntz ran to a "little hill" and found that the shooting was coming from the direction of the houses. They went back to camp for their guns and informed Dino Butler and Bob Robideau of what they had seen. The four left the camp together but split up approximately half way to the houses. Dino and Bob went southwesterly while Norman and Joe went northwesterly. Brown and Stuntz arrived at the residences, finding there Michael Anderson and Norman Charles (1425, 1426, 1444, 1441).

Brown allegedly observed Peltier at the treeline shooting a gun, which he thought resembled a M-16, and he also saw the agents. One was standing behind his raised trunk lid shooting a pump gun, the other was on the side of the second car with a hand gun. Both agents were shooting at Brown and at the people with him (1446, 1472, 1481, 1484).

After a while, Brown observed two cars coming into the area from Highway 18. He and Norman Charles began to shoot at these cars. The automobiles backed up, and some individuals got out and started shooting at Brown and the others (1492).

Once again Brown looked down at the agents' cars and saw both agents: One was crawling "through the front of the car and he crawled out. He was there for a while, and then he crawled back out and got in the same place where he was at"; the second agent was shooting a handgun. Brown also saw the agents a third time; however, they had merely "moved around the two cars, you know, and shooting back of it" (1494, 1495, 1504).

Following this, Joe Stuntz came to Norman Brown and stated, "There is women and children in the camp, you know. Our sisters are down there . . . why don't you go down there? The agents are coming in this way, so this is the time to be a man. This is the time to be a warrior . . . why don't you go over there and take somebody with you. They might be coming in from this side." So Norman Brown and Michael Anderson left the houses and ran over to an area close to tent city as guards (1493, 1497).

Brown and Anderson were in this area for approximately two hours, watching the camp to see if anyone entered. According to Brown not a *single* car or person went into or left the camp during their watch. Norman Charles and Wilford Draper then came to them and said that Joe Stuntz had been killed. The four then entered tent city where they found Peltier, Butler and Robideau loading the red and white van (1512, 1511, 1513, 1514).

Peltier allegedly told everyone, "we'll make a run for it" in the red and white van. That did not seem feasible to the group, so all decided to go out on foot, "southeast to the woods." All of the males— Brown, Peltier, Robideau, Butler, Draper, Charles and Anderson— went out along the creek. After some distance they met the women, who were coming back in the opposite direction. The women stated that all the roads were blocked and there was no way out; ". . . we didn't know what to do" stated Brown. He then continued, "that would be the end of us, but we got together and told Jimmy to give himself up because they might hurt him or might shoot him." So they sent Jimmy Zimmerman back toward the houses while the others escaped to the south (1526, 1538, 1539, 1540).

This ended the testimony of Anderson, Draper and Brown as government witnesses. We will now, through the remainder of this section, analyze the contradictory character of the above testimonies to uncover how unreliable, untrustworthy and unbelievable it all is. Further, we will see how members of the FBI coerced and eventually forced these individuals to give as their testimony a story which would delineate Leonard Peltier as the killer.

Michael Anderson's Testimony Examined

Contrary to his testimony during direct examination, Michael Anderson testified during cross examination that when the FBI cars approached the Siers house, he jumped off the roof and "went inside the house and hid in there." Further, he remained hiding in the house until after the agents conversed with June Little to determine whether Jimmy Eagle was around. After the agents had driven past, Anderson ran back to tent city. At camp he picked up a .22 caliber rifle and ran back to the houses (875, 876, 877, 878, 885).

Under cross examination Anderson made some interesting "changes" in his testimony regarding the sightings of agents Williams and Coler. After running back up to the houses, Anderson *first* observed the agents from the Jumping Bull house. One agent was kneeling and shooting a handgun while the other was standing, shooting a rifle from behind the open trunk of his car. He maneuvered over to the log house, shot for awhile at incoming police cars and then returned back to the Jumping Bull house (877). He then made his *second* sighting of the agents.

> Q: (John Lowe) And as I made my notes, you said the second time you saw the cars one of the special agents, one of the people down there that you saw, had no shirt on; is that correct?
>
> A: Yes.
>
> Q: And he was tying a bandage on the other person; is that true?
>
> A: Yeah, I think so.
>
> Q: What made you think he was tying a bandage on?
>
> A: I don't know. The other guy got hit. I didn't see him sitting up or anything.
>
> Q: Was he tying it on his leg, arm or head?
>
> A: I don't know.
>
> Q: Why would you say he was tying a bandage on if you can't even tell what part of the body he was looking at?
>
> A: I don't know. I didn't know what he was trying to do.
>
> Q: Well, did you see him take his shirt off?
>
> A: No.
>
> Q: Did you see him holding his shirt in his hand?
>
> A: No.
>
> Q: Did you see the other agent with the shirt on him somewhere?
>
> A: No. I didn't see the other agent (900).

Michael Anderson denied that the government had given him this information (901).

Anderson stated during cross examination, in contrast to his testimony under direct examination, that after he saw the agent standing without a shirt, he ran back down to the camp. John Lowe then corrected him and Anderson agreed, declaring he actually ran to the log cabin rather than tent city. He remained there for approximately twenty minutes shooting at the Jumping Bull Hall, even though there was no evidence that anyone was there. Further, during cross examination, Anderson testified that when he looked down at the agents' cars for the *third* time he saw no one. Contrary to what Anderson said during direct examination, he testified that after this sighting, he *ran back to tent city*. The following exchange then took place.

> Q: (John Lowe) And you then described in your direct testimony a fourth time that you looked at the FBI cars; and did you

run back up from the tent area, or walk back up from the tent area again to the white house for that fourth look?

A: No.

Q: How did you get back up there?

A: I don't remember that.

Q: You don't remember that?

A: No.

The Court: Court is in recess until 3:25.

Mr. Lowe: All right, sir. (Recess taken) (903-904)

After the recess, Anderson changed his testimony again regarding the *third* time he looked down at the agents; Anderson claimed he saw no activity at the cars, nor did he see anybody present. However, he did then allegedly observe Leonard Peltier in the treeline. Anderson then moved to the white house (Jumping Bull's), looked a fourth time down toward the cars, and saw Butler, Robideau, and Peltier. Defense attorney John Lowe then went through a lengthy summation of the four times Anderson allegedly looked down at the agents (918).

Q: (John Lowe) . . . Did I correctly summarize those four times?

A: I can't remember that now. I think it was the third time I saw the three standing down there by the car.

Q: Was that before or after you saw Mr. Peltier in the wood line?

A: Before.

Q: It was before you saw him in the wood line?

A: Yes.

Q: Did you go directly from the white house to the tent area at that time when you saw them down by the cars?

A: Yes.

Q: Mr. Anderson, if you left the white house while you saw them down at the cars and went directly to the tent area, will you tell the jury how you could thereafter see Mr. Peltier in the tree line?

A: I think that was there the second time.

Q: . . . When you arrived in the tent area, I thought you told us that Mr. Peltier was there and he told you to load the red and white van.

A: Yes, he was.

Q: Now will you tell the jury if you were at the white house and saw the three men at the two cars down there and you went directly to the tent area, will you tell the jury how Mr. Peltier could be at the tent area when you got there if you had left him at the three cars?

A: I don't know.

And finally, during cross examination, John Lowe questioned Michael Anderson on the religion of the pipe. Anderson regarded himself a firm believer in the religion of the pipe.

Specifically, the sacred pipe to a believer in the ancient Lakota religion is much like the Bible to a Christian or Jew who, when testifying in court, swears on the Bible to "tell the whole truth and nothing but the truth." Anderson, despite or because of being a firm believer in traditional Indian ways and religions, refused to take the oath of the pipe before he testified in court.

Q: (John Lowe) I believe you told me that you believe the religion of the pipe, is that correct?
A: Yes
Q: . . . do you believe in the ancient Indian ways and religions?
A: Yes
Q: I call your attention to this object which is on the defense table, and ask you if you know what it is?
A: Yes.
Q: What is it?
A: Pipe.
Q: Is that the sacred pipe?
A: Yes
Q: . . . When I told you this morning we were going to be talking with you and you were asked whether you would take your oath on the pipe, weren't you?
A: Yes.
Q: You didn't do that, did you?
A: No.

Mr. Lowe: I believe that's all I have, Your Honor (857).

Under direct and cross examination Anderson talked about the events leading up to his testimony. He established that on 10 September 1975, he, Bob Robideau, Norman Charles and some other people were in a car which exploded on a turnpike near Wichita, Kansas. Anderson was arrested on nine charges, among them transporting firearms and explosives across a state line. Each of these charges carried a maximum penalty of ten years in a federal penitentiary. In addition, there was also, at this time, a burglary charge pending against Anderson in Arizona (837, 838, 845).

On 11 September 1975 Special Agents Gary Adams and O. Victor Harvey came to Wichita to interview Anderson. He asked for an attorney to be present, but none was called. Anderson testified in Fargo that for the first hour of this interview he had refused to talk to the agents. Then Gary Adams made the following statement, "If you don't talk, I will beat you up in the cell." Anderson then feared that the agents would beat him up if he failed to provide them with the answers *they* wanted.

> Q: (John Lowe) And did you then give him the answers that you understood he wanted?
>
> A: Yes.
>
> Q: Did you believe that Special Agent Gary Adams was capable of hurting you if you didn't do what he wanted?
>
> A: Yes (841-842).

Adams asked questions generally in the style of "Isn't it true that a certain fact is true," and then asked Anderson to respond whether or not it was true. Anderson understood the substance of the question was in fact the answer wanted by Adams (843).

Special Agent O. Victor Harvey testified Anderson was initially "somewhat reluctant," but they talked with him awhile and "he became less reluctant and furnished information." Harvey affirmed they had persuaded Anderson that he had nothing to worry about and that it would be in his best interest if he told them all he knew on the subject. Anderson testified the FBI promised to help him on the burglary charge in Arizona if he cooperated (4263, 845).

Adams and Harvey's 302 report of this interview indicates that, contrary to his testimony in Fargo, Anderson on 26 June 1975 was in tent city at 11:30 a.m., preparing to eat the noon meal. Further, Anderson informed Adams and Harvey that the *first* time he "looked down" at the agents' cars the agents were lying prone and he was certain they were already dead since they failed to move or in any other manner indicate they were alive. Anderson was also shown thirty-six photographs, and he identified almost all of them. Subsequent investigation revealed that these individuals were around the Jumping Bull area on June 26 (4264, 4284).

On 1 February 1977 Special Agents James Doyle and Gary Adams arrested Anderson in Albuquerque, New Mexico, for probation violation. At approximately 10:50 a.m. of that day these agents attempted to interview Anderson, and his reply was he did not desire to be interviewed about his activities of 26 June 1975. The agents brought him to the marshall's office to await his hearing on the probation violation. At 1:40 p.m. Anderson signed a waiver of his constitutional rights and made a statement that in effect said after he returned to the top of the hill, he did in fact see Peltier, Robideau and Butler down by the agents' cars (4298, 4203, 4305).

Interestingly, at the time of the trial, Michael Anderson had not been prosecuted for that burglary charge in Arizona. Moreover, all charges pending against him in Wichita had been dropped (845). All of Anderson's pre-trial statements placed him in tent city at the start of the shooting and not, as he testified at the trial, on top of Wanda Siers' house where he allegedly saw the red and white van chased by agents. Recent FBI documents, uncovered through the Freedom of Information Act, indicate that the FBI was highly concerned about the vehicle theory. The FBI, on 11 June 1976 did an analysis of the first days of the Butler-Robideau trial. They specifically concentrated on the defense's cross-examination of witnesses. One of their most important points was stated as follows: "There was an effort to confuse the jury as to pertinent vehicles and their locations on the day of the murder, June 26, 1975." Did Michael Anderson change his story, the credibility of which was made possible only by suppressing FBI documents revealing concern about *three* vehicles, in order to make the job easier for the prosecution? The ultimate result of changing the testimony and possibly suppressing FBI reports was to prevent the jury from gaining clarity about what type of vehicle was actually chased into the Jumping Bull area.

Moreover, FBI documents have revealed that the prosecution possibly suppressed information of a grand jury subpoena issued for Mike Anderson on 7 July 1975. The subpoena was served on July 9 to Mike's brother Larry who "stated he would deliver subpoena to Michael." And a teletype from Rapid City to the Director, dated 27 July 1975, states that "Michael Anderson appeared as scheduled before federal grand jury." The fact that neither the grand jury appearance nor a transcript of testimony was revealed by the prosecution at or before the trial indicates that its contents may be in conformance with Anderson's pre-trial statements and in serious conflict with his trial testimony.

Wilford Draper's Testimony Examined

Under cross examination in Fargo Wilford Draper testified that approximately one hour before he heard shooting, Leonard Peltier was not in "tent city." At the Cedar Rapids trial, Draper had testified that Peltier was in the tent area 30-45 minutes before the shooting took place. Additionally, and contrary to Michael Anderson's testimony that he was at Wanda Siers' when the shooting began, Draper testified both Norman Charles and Michael Anderson were in the tent area when he first heard the shots (1125, 776, 1127).

On 9 January 1976, Wilford Draper was arrested by Special Agent Charles Stapleton on an alcohol charge and strong-armed robbery in Arizona. He was handcuffed and tied to a chair while being interviewed for three hours by Stapleton and a BIA police officer, Frank Gadake. According to Draper's testimony, on the following day he was taken to "Gallup, New Mexico, and there I met some more agents." At Gallup he was interviewed by Special Agents Doyle and Stapleton. Draper was told then that if he refused to cooperate with the FBI, he would be indicted for the murders of Agents Williams and Coler. The FBI agents also told him what was in the offing if he did cooperate: Draper would receive (1) a new identity, (2) protection, (3) a job elsewhere, (4) education and training, and (5) financial security, all if he cooperated with the FBI. Draper additionally "felt" that all of the charges pending against him would be "taken care of." Subsequently, Draper signed a statement that was satisfactory to the agents, and, as a result, all charges against him were dropped (1083, 1085, 1086, 1087, 1088, 1115).

After a few days, Draper was taken to Pine Ridge, South Dakota. He was escorted about the reservation by Special Agent Doyle. He was also interviewed extensively: by Doyle for approximately nine hours, by Special Agent Gary Adams for approximately five hours, and by United States Attorney Robert Sikma for approximately eight hours. The next day he went to Sioux Falls for the Grand Jury proceedings (1087, 1097, 1098).

Q: (John Lowe) On January 13, 1976 at Sioux Falls, South Dakota, did you appear before the Grand Jury?

A: (Wilford Draper) Yes.

Q: Did you testify under oath?

A: Yes.

Q: Would I be correct in saying that some of the testimony you gave was false?

A: Yes.

At the Fargo trial, Draper was asked if parts of his testimony referred "to something that some agent may have told you happened rather than what you actually saw or heard yourself, is that possible?" Draper's reply, "Yes, that's possible" (1116).

Norman Brown's Testimony Examined

Norman was interviewed on various dates, and the content of these sessions showed contradictions in his testimony. For example, he testified that on 10 October 1975, at twelve midnight, he was interviewed by three FBI agents. James Doyle's 302 that reported this interview stated (contrary to Brown's direct testimony at the Fargo trial) that while Brown went to "tent city" for a meal prior to the shooting, Joe Stuntz, Jimmy Zimmerman *and* Michael Anderson were there. However, this 302 contained the word "lunch" crossed out, and in its place was written the word "breakfast." When Brown was asked on the stand in Fargo if the first meal they ate was the noon meal, he replied "Yeah, right" (1561, 1564, 1566, 1568).

On 5 September 1975, at around 5:30 a.m. Norman Brown and his wife were awakened at Crow Dogs Paradise by 80-100 FBI agents. These, "officers of the law" were "dressed like Vietnam, army fatigues and those greens . . . carrying M-16's . . . sawed off shotguns and bullet proof vests." There were also helicopters flying around (4805).

Brown and his wife were told to come out of the house with their hands up and lie on the ground. They were then searched. Brown testified that this terrifying experience with the FBI had influenced the testimony he gave to the Grand Jury (4806, 4807).

On 22 September 1975, Brown was interviewed in Chinle, Arizona by Special Agents Gary Adams and O. Victor Harvey. Norman and his mother were at his sister's house when a BIA officer came and ushered Norman and his mother to a trailer where some other BIA officers were waiting. Once inside the trailer he was not allowed to leave. After awhile Adams and Harvey arrived, read him his rights and began questioning him about 26 June 1975. Brown asked for an attorney, but was not allowed one. The agents first were friendly, but when he steadfastly refused to talk with them, the agents became angry and stated "If you don't answer our questions we can indict you; we can charge you with those two murders of those two agents." Brown's mother did not know what had taken place on the 26th and was very upset. The agents explained to her that Norman was involved in the shootout, and as his mother cried the agents pressed on, "You won't see your son again for a long time . . . you won't see your family again." And to Norman, "If you don't talk to us, you might never walk the earth again." Brown's mother begged him to cooperate as she did not want to see Norman in jail or hurt. She told Norman to think of her, his brothers and sisters, and the whole family. Brown then began answering the agents' questions (4799, 4801, 4803, 4804).

Agents Adams and Harvey asked Brown "we know you saw this and that" kind of questions, and they told him "people" stated to them that Brown was a witness to the shootings. Norman Brown became exceptionally scared, was worried about his mother and, therefore, told the agents he saw Butler, Robideau and Peltier in the vicinity of Williams' and Coler's cars (4804, 4805, 4810).

On 13 January 1976, Norman Brown testified in front of the Grand Jury in Sioux Falls, South Dakota. There he implicated Peltier, Robideau and Butler as being at the agents' cars. Later at the Fargo trial, Brown repudiated the Sioux Falls testimony.

Q: (Elliott Taikeff) When you testified before the Grand Jury that you saw Leonard and Bob and Dino down by the agents' cars, where did you get that information?

A: (Norman Brown) FBI.

Q: Did you ever see that on June 26, 1975?

A: No (4812).

In addition, Brown explained to Evan Hultman during recross examination that he lied to the agents during the above discussed interview and told them what he "thought they wanted to hear" (4827).

At the completion of Brown's testimony in Fargo, the following interesting exchange took place:

Q: (Elliott Taikeff) Were you afraid of the FBI when you were before the Grand Jury?

A: Yeah.

Q: When you got finished testifying in the Grand Jury and you came out, did you see any of the lawyers sitting at the government table?

A: Yeah. It was that guy (indicating).

Q: Mr. Sikma?

A: Yeah.

Q: Did he say anything to you?

A: Yeah.

Objection by the government. Judge Benson asks Counsel to approach the Bench. The following discussion being had at the bench.

The Court: What do you expect the answer to be?

Mr. Taikeff: I expect the answer will be Mr. Sikma said, quote, "You did good. We could have put you away for a long time."

Mr. Hultman: I object to that.

Mr. Sikma: That's a lie. That's an absolute lie.

The Court: In view of the denial, the question will not be allowed (4842, 4843).

Taikeff's final question to Brown was, "When you testified before the Grand Jury, did you swear on the sacred pipe?" Brown's response, "No" (4843).

And finally, on 23 March 1977, while shopping in Mission, South Dakota, Norman Brown was served with a subpoena to appear at the trial in Fargo. The FBI took him at this time by car to Pierre, South Dakota, and from there they flew in a private plane to Fargo. He asked for an attorney but none was provided. The agents locked him in a hotel room, and the next morning he was taken to the Federal Court-house where he testified for the government (4793, 4796, 4797).

Myrtle Poor Bear

In February and March of 1976, Myrtle Poor Bear signed three affidavits, two of which alleged she had observed Leonard Peltier and others murder the two FBI agents. These affidavits were the prime evidence submitted by the United States government in its successful attempt to extradite Leonard Peltier from Canada.

There were discrepencies in the three affidavits as well as evidence to indicate that Poor Bear was nowhere in the vicinity of Pine Ridge at the time of the shooting. We will look at these affidavits, Poor Bear's subsequent testimony attesting to their falseness, and examine how and why the FBI utilized these stories.

It is important to note that the jury at Peltier's trial never heard the above testimony. What they heard was scanty indeed. For instance, Michael Anderson testified he did not know if he saw Myrtle Poor Bear either at the Jumping Bull's or in "tent city." He knew everyone residing in "tent city," yet testified to not knowing if one of these individuals was Myrtle Poor Bear. Norman Brown testified he had never seen Myrtle Poor Bear in the Jumping Bull area or on the Pine Ridge Reservation. Angie Long Visitor, granddaughter to the Jumping Bull's, testified she had never seen Myrtle Poor Bear in the Jumping Bull area during the seven years she had lived there. (Angie Long Visitor lived in the green house, next to the Jumping Bull's residence.) She further stated on the stand in Fargo that Jean Day, and not Myrtle Poor Bear, was Leonard Peltier's girlfriend. Finally, Jean Day tes-tified that she had lived with Leonard Peltier in the Jumping Bull area from the end of May 1975 until 22 June 1975 when she left the Reservation. She had seen Leonard Peltier every day during this time, and Myrtle Poor Bear did *not* live with him. Myrtle Poor Bear, in fact, lived with her father and sisters in the village of Allen on the Pine Ridge Reservation. This was all the testimony concerning Myrtle Poor Bear the jury would hear (849, 850, 1597, 1598, 2701, 2703, 3520).

In the trial of Dino Butler and Bob Robideau at Cedar Rapids,

Iowa (June 1976) for the murder of the two agents, Myrtle Poor Bear was on the government's lists of potential witnesses. Yet she was never called to testify. At the trial in Fargo, she was likewise on the government's list of potential witnesses and, for this purpose, she came to Fargo in March 1977. However, the government felt that the trial was "going all right" and therefore would not need to use her. The defense, consequently, subpoenaed her as a defense witness. The Prosecution objected, and Judge Benson sided with the prosecution on a critical issue, stating her testimony was irrelevant. The defense argued that the jury should hear her testimony since the government had used her affidavits in the extradition proceedings and since she was on the government's list of potential witnesses for both the Cedar Rapids and Fargo trials. Moreover, the contents of the affidavits, statements which (we will see below) she was forced to make by the FBI, were very revealing and hence significant. The conduct of the FBI in connection with the inducement of Myrtle Poor Bear directly reflected on all of the evidence presented by the government at the trial. Simply, it exhibited vividly what the FBI was willing to do in order to connect Leonard Peltier with the shootings and convict him of murder (4619, 4401, 4403). Judge Benson ruled that the testimony relative to Myrtle Poor Bear and her affidavits would be presented to the Court initially (once again) in an offer of proof. Following this, the Judge would make a determination whether or not the jury could hear it (4406, 4407).

The following evidence given by three Special Agents of the FBI, one Native American woman and Myrtle Poor Bear, also a Native American, was presented *outside* the presence of the jury.

The final texts of the three affidavits signed by Myrtle Poor Bear were put together, according to Special Agent David Price, in the U.S. Attorney's office in Rapid City. These affidavits were composed there by William Halperin of the Canadian Justice Department and U.S. Attorney Bruce Boyd. They were based, however, on Special Agents William Wood's and David Price's "rough notes" of interviews with Myrtle Poor Bear (4540, 4532, 4533).

Testimony exhibited that Special Agents Wood and Price had been meeting Myrtle Poor Bear frequently on another matter, which David Price stated was very serious. Myrtle Poor Bear was allegedly furnishing information to the FBI and consequently had been beaten and was in a great deal of danger. Therefore, she was placed in motels by the FBI for her protection. She was not, however, in protective custody for very many days in January and February 1976. The first time Special Agent Price conversed with Myrtle Poor Bear about the shootings and the first time she stated anything about the events of June 26, was on 19 February 1976 when she was driven to the Rapid City FBI office and reportedly interviewed there by Special Agents Price and Wood. The result of this interview was the *first* extradition affidavit, signed by Myrtle Poor Bear on 19 February 1976 (4540, 4541, 4544, 4525, 4526).

In her first affidavit of 19 February 1976, Myrtle Poor Bear stated she overheard Leonard Peltier and several others begin planning how to kill BIA or FBI agents who might come into the area. This alleged scheme was being put together during the second week of June 1975. According to this affidavit, Peltier was "mostly in charge" of the planning. Approximately a day before the agents were killed, Peltier told Poor Bear that he knew FBI agents or BIA officers would soon be coming into the area to serve a warrant on Jimmy Eagle, so people should get ready to kill them. Myrtle Poor Bear was told to have her car filled with gas and ready for an escape, but she left the Jumping Bull area and did not return. She did not, according to this first affidavit, meet Leonard Peltier again until August 1975, on the Rosebud Reservation. There they allegedly discussed the killing of the two agents; Peltier confessed he had shot them, lost his mind and kept pulling the trigger. However, and this is important, this first affidavit exhibited that she was *not* an eyewitness to the killing of the agents. Therefore, this affidavit was not sent to Canada and not made public until the defense acquired it accidently (4449, 4551).

Myrtle Poor Bear signed a *second* affidavit on 23 February 1975 that was identical to the first except for one important section. The second affidavit changed her assertion that she left the Jumping Bull area to the following: "I was present the day Special Agents of the FBI were killed. I saw Leonard Peltier shoot the FBI agents." Special Agent Price testified that when Poor Bear signed the second affidavit, he was aware of the discrepancy in the two testimonies. However, since he and Wood were meeting Poor Bear frequently on another matter, he could not exactly say how this change came about (4501, 4539, 4540).

The day after Myrtle Poor Bear signed this second affidavit, Special Agent Edward Skelly, at the request of Price and Wood, interviewed her. Myrtle Poor Bear informed Skelly she was allegedly living with Leonard Peltier in the Jumping Bull area since May 1975. She overheard Leonard Peltier and the others who were living at or near the Jumping Bull residences planning to kill either BIA officers or FBI agents sometime prior to 26 June 1975. On the day of the shootings she observed an FBI car drive into the Jumping Bull area. Leonard Peltier called her outside, telling Ricky Little Boy to give her a rifle, which he did. She heard shots; arriving next to the agents' cars, she saw that Leonard Peltier was holding a rifle while one of the agents lying near the cars on the ground proclaimed, "I surrender." The body of this agent jumped each time it was hit; at that point she could not stand it any longer so she began to run away. Peltier called her to come back and attempted to stop her. She then fired a shot at Ricky Little Boy, who was pursuing her. Her car was hidden under some trees and bushes to be used as a escape vehicle (4468, 4475, 4478, 4479, 4484).

Special Agent Edward Skelly had not asked Myrtle Poor Bear for her automobile registration, driver's license, the year and make of the car, the color of the car or where the car was hidden—all of which would have helped corroborate her story. Nor did he ask for a description of Ricky Little Boy or any other kind of identifying information. He "overlooked" this even though, according to her story, Ricky Little Boy was at the Jumping Bull area immediately prior to the shootings, and he would have been an important eyewitness. Myrtle Poor Bear did, however, identify Bob Robideau and Dino Butler as having participated in shooting the agents (4486, 4489, 4490).

Moreover, during this interview, Myrtle Poor Bear allegedly informed Skelly about another criminal event: two nights prior to the shooting when Peltier was away for the evening, she was raped by Jimmy Eagle and approximately eight other men. However, Skelly did not ask Poor Bear for a description of Eagle nor for the names of the eight others involved, nor a physical description of any of those individuals. Even though the Major Crimes Act provides that if certain offenses, including rape, are committed on Indian reservations, the FBI is to investigate these offenses, Skelly admits, "I did not initiate any investigation whatsoever." One of the individuals "may have been" Dino Butler, according to Poor Bear. However, neither Butler nor Eagle was ever charged with rape, an investigation was never begun, even though they both were in jail and available for questioning at the time (4491, 4493, 4494).

Special Agent David Price testified he had received important information from Canadian Justice Department attorney William Halprin that the second affidavit had not included enough details about the killing of the agents and that " . . . it would have to be redone." As a result, on 31 March 1976, five weeks after Myrtle Poor Bear signed the second affidavit, she signed a *third* affidavit. The contents of this affidavit alleged the following: On the morning of 26 June 1975, Myrtle Poor Bear was in the big house in the Jumping Bull area and with her was a woman by the name of Madonna Slow Bear as well as an old woman cleaning a gun whose name she could not recall. Before noon, Peltier called out to her, "They're coming." Peltier and Poor Bear then went outside the house, and Peltier talked with three or four other Indian males who were standing near a bright-colored truck-type vehicle with windows on the side. (Price testified that during this interview he knew Peltier was associated with a red and white van.) Myrtle Poor Bear next observed two FBI cars. One was either yellow or gold with a white top and the other green. She and Madonna Slow Bear approached these cars, finding Peltier, Jimmy Eagle, Robideau and an unnamed Indian male standing there. One of the agents threw his handgun to the side and said that he surrendered. Another agent was lying face down on the ground by the car, and she could see blood coming from underneath him. Peltier stood in front of the agent who was leaning against the car and holding his left shoulder while Peltier pointed a rifle at his head. Myrtle Poor Bear tried to run from the area, but Madonna Slow Bear grabbed her by the hair, keeping her from running away. She was turned around against her will to face Peltier and the others. Peltier's rifle jumped, she heard a shot, and the agent's body hopped into the air and landed face down on the ground. She broke away from Madonna Slow Bear, ran up to Leonard Peltier and pounded him on the back. She then turned and ran away, leaving the area. As she left, she heard more shots coming from the vicinity of the agents' automobiles. She reached the creek bottom where Ricky Little Boy was in charge of the horses to be used in the escape (4543, 4542, 4548, 4551, 4569, 4570, 4573, 4574, 4575).

During this interview Myrtle Poor Bear alleged this time she had been raped on the reservation by Dick Marshall and several of his friends, and not by Jimmy Eagle and eight other men (4568, 4569).

On the stand at Fargo Price was asked whether he had any questions regarding Madonna Slow Bear and if he was concerned about obtaining the wrong name. Price replied he knew Madonna Slow Bear from Oglala. When the defense brought Madonna Slow Bear to the stand, Special Agent David Price was unable to identify her. Moreover, Madonna Slow Bear testified at the Fargo trial that no FBI agent had ever questioned her regarding her presence at the Jumping Bull area during the shootings. Further, she testified the first time she had seen Myrtle Poor Bear was the previous evening in Rapid City when they boarded the same airplane to travel to Fargo (4584, 4580).

Contradicting her affidavits, Myrtle Poor Bear testified at the

Fargo trial that she had never seen Leonard Peltier before she entered the courtroom. Furthermore, she was not at the Jumping Bull area on the Pine Ridge Reservation on 26 June 1975; she never lived with Leonard Peltier, and the first time she had ever met Madonna Slow Bear was the night before on the plane. She added that Special Agents Price and Wood informed her about the killings on 26 June 1975 and showed her a photograph in the Federal Building at Rapid City, telling her it was Leonard Peltier (4588, 4590, 4597).

Special Agents Price and Wood escorted Myrtle Poor Bear twice to the Jumping Bull area. While she received this tour, the agents told her "to remember where Harry Jumping Bull lives." She had not known Dino Butler, Bob Robideau, Ricky Little Boy or Madonna Slow Bear but rather heard their names from the agents (4607, 4610, 4611, 4612, 4626).

Myrtle Poor Bear further testified that though she had signed two of the three affidavits at the courthouse in Rapid City, no one read the contents of them to her and she had not read them herself. She signed the affidavits because Special Agents Price and Wood told her to. Upon reading the affidavits she stated on the witness stand that the contents of the affidavits were not true. After reading the 302 report of her interview with Special Agent Edward Skelly, she stated that she never said the things purported and that the contents of the 302 were false. She did not see anybody killed on 26 June 1975 (4592, 4593, 4594, 4595, 4623, 4624, 4625, 4613).

Poor Bear testified she spent "a lot" of hours with the two agents, *them* telling her about the shootings. She was very frightened by the government, and when asked if anyone ever said anything to make her afraid, she replied, "The agents are always talking about Anna Mae . . . they just would talk about that time she died" (4598, 4599).*

On the way from the airport to the city of Fargo, defense attorney Elliott Taikeff rode in the same automobile as Myrtle Poor Bear, and at first she refused to speak with him. He continued this story to Judge Benson and the prosecutors in a conference at the bench:

> . . . and finally she told me that the reason she didn't want to talk is that she was afraid she was going to be killed; and I asked her, "Who are you afraid of?" and she said, "The agents," and I said, "Why are you afraid of the agents" and

*As noted earlier Anna Mae Aquash was threatened by the FBI and later found dead with a bullet hole in the back of her neck. The FBI autopsy claimed she died of exposure.

she said that they told her that they were going to do the same thing to her that happened to Anna Mae Aquash (4601).

Myrtle Poor Bear further testified that the agents (Price and Wood) had offered to give her a new name and to send her to a different city or state. They additionally threatened her with prison, stating she could be incarcerated for about fifteen years for "court conspiracy." In a direct threat to her, Special Agent Wood told her "that they could get away with killing because they were agents" (4614, 4615, 4616).

The relationship between Myrtle Poor Bear and the FBI can be summed up in the following exchange:

Q: (Elliott Taekeff) Miss Poor Bear, will you please tell us whether Agent Price ever threatened you?

A: (Myrtle Poor Bear) Yes, he did.

Q: What did he say to you?

A: He told me that they were going to plan everything out and if I didn't do it I was going to be hurt.

Q: Did anybody else ever say that to you from the FBI?

A: Bill Wood (4650).

This ended the Myrtle Poor Bear offer of proof.

The defense offered Myrtle Poor Bear's testimony in an attempt to demonstrate how the FBI intentionally and falsely constructed a case against Peltier by introducing certain pieces of evidence through particular witnesses, but that these pieces were flawed. Poor Bear testified that none of the evidence was known to her; she did not know the defendant; she was never at the Jumping Bulls. Yet she signed affidavits claiming she was cognizant of all of the above. Norman Brown had testified he was threatened by the FBI to give certain evidence which duplicated much of Myrtle Poor Bear's story, a story she denies any knowledge of. Moreover, Michael Anderson also testified to some of the same facts. This coincidence of testimonies suggests that the FBI manufactured rather than discovered its case (4652).

The testimony in the offer of proof (by FBI agents, Madonna Slow Bear and Myrtle Poor Bear) was important for two reasons: First, it rebutted and contradicted, through circumstantial evidence, certain key pieces of evidence which had been introduced against Leonard Peltier. Second, Poor Bear's testimony demonstrated a pattern of misconduct on the part of FBI agents. All of this then, the defense argued, should be heard by the jury so that they "may consider whether they are prepared to find a moral certainty that another human being should spend the rest of his life in a prison under these circumstances." Prosecutor Lynn Crooks replied that this was simply an attempt to put the FBI in general on trial for "some supposed misdeeds that the paranoid defense team has thought up" (4653, 4654).

Judge Benson then ruled on the offer of proof. Myrtle Poor Bear was, according to Benson, obviously under "great mental stress." Since neither Myrtle Poor Bear nor the three FBI agents who interviewed her (Wood, Price and Skelly) were called to the stand as *government* witnesses, Judge Benson came to the following deduction:

> The court concludes that credibility of this witness for any purpose is so suspect that to permit her testimony to go to the jury would be confusing the issues, may mislead the jury and could be highly prejudicial. The offer of proof therefore is denied (4657, 4658).

He further concluded that her testimony was "irrelevant" and she was not a "believable witness" (4665). The following day Benson "clarified" his ruling on the offer of proof in the following manner:

> If the witness as she testified yesterday were to be a believable witness the Court would have seriously considered allowing her testimony to go to the jury on the grounds that *if believable by the jury* the facts she testified to were such that they *would shock the conscience of the Court* and in the interests of justice should be considered by the jury (4707-4708) (emphasis added).

"However" Benson went on, "for reasons given on the record yesterday the Court concluded the danger of confusion of the issues, misleading the jury and unfair prejudice outweighed the possibility that the witness was believable" (4708).

Here we see how the federal government will judge a witness believable in one situation and unbelievable in another. When the Federal government wanted to extradite Peltier, Myrtle Poor Bear's testimony was believable; however, when she exposed FBI misconduct her testimony was suddenly irrelevant and unbelievable.

An Afterward on Poor Bear's Affidavits

At Leonard Peltier's appelate oral argument in St. Louis in April 1978 Evan Hultman responded to questions from the Judge that he knew the affidavits the FBI coerced Myrtle Poor Bear into signing were false. Part of that exchange is as follows:

Judge Ross: But anybody who read those affidavits would know that they contradict each other. And why the FBI and the Prosecutor's office continued to extract more to put into the affidavits in hope to get Mr. Peltier back to the United States is beyond my understanding.

Mr. Hultman: Yes.

Judge Ross: Because you should have known, and the FBI should have known that you were pressuring the woman to add to her statement.

Mr. Hultman: Your Honor, I personally was not present at that stage. I read the affidavits *after they had been submitted*, so I want this Court to know that.

Judge Ross: The Government—

Mr. Hultman: . . .It was clear to me her story didn't check out with anything in the record by any other witness in any other way. So I concluded then, in addition to her incompetence, first, that secondly, there was no relevance of any kind. Absolutely not one scentilla (sic) of any evidence to do with this case. And it was then that I personally made the decision that this witness was no witness. . .

Judge Ross: But can't you see, Mr. Hultman, what happened in such a way that it gives some credence to the claim of the—

Mr. Hultman: I understand, yes, your Honor.

Judge Ross: —the Indian people that the United States is willing to resort to any tactic in order to bring somebody back to the United States from Canada.

Mr. Hultman: Judge—

Judge Ross: And if they are willing to do that, they must be willing to fabricate other evidence. And it's no wonder that they are unhappy and disbelieve the things that happened in our courts when things like this happen.

Mr. Hultman: Judge Ross, I in no way do anything but agree with you totally.[5] (emphasis added)

No legal action has been brought against the FBI by the Justice Department.

In the above exchange, it is clear Evan Hultman attempted to disassociate himself from the affidavits. He stated that he read the affidavits *after* they had been submitted. However, FBI documents uncovered through the Freedom of Information Act indicate this was not true. According to an FBI investigation of the preparation and submission of the Poor Bear affidavits to Canada, the decision was made by Canadian Prosecutor Halperin "with the concurrence of special prosecutors Evan L. Hultman and Robert Sikma that only two of the three affidavits were used in the extradition proceedings." Contrary to Hultman's answer to Judge Ross, the FBI contends he took part in the submission of the Poor Bear affidavits to the Canadian government. He therefore had to have read them *before* they were submitted. Amnesty International, an organization known for its work and campaigns for human rights around the world published a 1981 report entitled *Proposal for a Commission of Inquiry into the Effects of Domestic Intelligence Activities on Criminal Trials in the United States of America*.[6] The report outlines the history of the Myrtle Poor Bear incident in relation to the extradition and prosecution of Peltier. It goes on to recommend that the United States government establish an independent commission to conduct an inquiry into the events.

The .223 Casing and AR-15 Rifle

A .223 cartridge casing, allegedly found in the trunk of Special Agent Jack Coler's automobile, was "perhaps the most important piece of evidence" to the government's case in the Fargo trial. The government contended that this casing was ejected by the killer's gun, an AR-15, which they maintained belonged to Leonard Peltier. We will look at the inconsistencies in testimonies connected with these two important pieces of evidence, the .223 casing and AR-15 rifle.

Inconsistencies by Cunningham and Lodge

In this section we will see that the FBI had contradictory reports from its agents about 1) who discovered the .223 cartridge casing, 2) whether it was actually inventoried on the day of the shooting, and 3) when it was removed from the car and by whom.

The .223 cartridge casing was vitally important in the United States government's case for the extradition of Leonard Peltier from Canada in 1976. For these extradition proceedings Special Agent Cortlandt Cunningham, Chief of the FBI Firearms and Toolmarks Division, signed an affidavit under oath in the Spring of 1976. This affidavit had been prepared in the Rapid City FBI office and sent to Cunningham in Washington, D.C. for him to sign. Part of paragraph 6 of this affidavit reads as follows:

Also in the said 1972 Cheverolet Biscayne automobile I found one.223 cartridge case in the trunk which I took into my possession and placed in an envelope marked "Items recovered from trunk, Jack R. Coler automobile" (2113, 2114).

On the witness stand in Fargo, Special Agent Cunningham testified that the above affidavit was *not* correct and that he had *not* personally found that casing (2114). This gave rise to the following exchange in which both Judge Benson and Prosecutor Robert Sikma would speak for the witness:

Q: (John Lowe) When you read that paragraph 6 did you understand when you read it, did you comprehend that, representing to anybody that read the affidavit you gave under oath that you found the .223 cartridge in the trunk?

A: (Cortlandt Cunningham) I did not know there was any significance, which I answered previously, to that particular paragraph and any of the rest. I do not; the significance of that paragraph at the time I signed this affidavit was not apparent to me.

Q: Your Honor, I am saying I know he's not answering my question and I ask that the Court direct him to be responsive. I'm not asking whether it's significant. I'm asking whether he knew when he read that paragraph that it was holding out to the reader of the affidavit that he found that round in the trunk. Am I entitled to an answer to that question?

The Court: Do you understand the question?

The Witness: I do not know, sir.

Mr. Lowe: Shall I restate it or would the reporter repeat it back?

Mr. Sikma: Your Honor, he's answered the question now.

The Court: I think he may have answered it. Reporter will read it back.

The Question was Read Back.

The Court: And his answer was "I did not." So I think that answered the question (2125-2126).

In his 302 report dated 1 July 1975, of the initial search of Coler's car, Cunningham did not mention this .223 cartridge casing in a complete listing of recovered objects.

FBI fingerprint specialist Winthrop Lodge testified that on 29 June 1975, he examined Special Agent Jack Coler's automobile for fingerprints before turning it over to Special Agent Cunningham later that day. During this examination Lodge allegedly found the .223 cartridge in the trunk of the car, tagged it, examined it for latent fingerprints and found none, and handed it over to Special Agent Cunningham. This .223 casing is mentioned on the last page of the notes Lodge made during his examination of the automobile (3012, 3013, 3079, 3080).

Lodge likewise examined Special Agent Williams' automobile on 27 June 1975 and the red and white van and 1967 Ford Galaxie (both found in "tent city") on 30 June 1975 but did not make notes during his examination of these automobiles (3112, 3113, 3114, 3118, 3119, 3120).

Further testimony by Lodge revealed once again the unreliability of FBI evidence. At first he testified the items found in Coler's automobile for evidence had not been removed from the vehicle. Shortly after he stated, "Yes sir. Most of the items were actually taken out of the automobile." A few minutes later he finally admitted, "all evidence was inventoried and removed from the vehicle" (3126, 3127, 3130).

Following his examination of Coler's automobile, he allegedly turned *all* evidence over to Cunningham. In Lodge's words, "As far as I recall everything, the automobile and the contents, were turned over to Mr. Cunningham." No receipt was given to Lodge acknowledging what were the entire contents of Coler's car. Finally, Lodge would later once again testify, "not everything was turned over to Cunningham. . . since some of the items were carried back to Pine Ridge and turned over to the agent personally in charge of the evidence." Lodge, of course, could not recall or specify which items of evidence he had turned over to Cunningham and which ones he had taken to Pine Ridge (3137, 3138, 3162, 3163).

Inconsistencies by Hodge

The key witness concerning the .223 casing and AR-15 rifle was SA Evan Hodge, a specialist in the Firearms and Tool Marks Identification Unit of the FBI. He connected the .223 casing found in Coler's trunk with the AR-15 rifle. In this section we will analyze several important issues concerning Agent Hodge's testimony and lab reports. Specifically, we will look at 1) the sequence of events surrounding the testing of the AR-15 rifle which is inconsistent with Hodge's testimony at the Fargo trial, and 2) the reliability of the gun test allegedly performed by Agent Hodge on this AR-15 rifle.

As we noted earlier, on 10 September 1975 an automobile transporting Bob Robideau, Norman Charles, Michael Anderson, Jean Bordeau, Kamook Banks and Bernie Nichols exploded on a turnpike near Wichita, Kansas. Agent Michael Gammage of the Tobacco and Firearms Division of the FBI in Wichita, testified he found an AR-15 rifle in the wrecked automobile. He subsequently delivered this AR-15 to SA Evan Hodge at the FBI headquarters in Washington, D.C. on 12 September 1975. Part of the gunbarrel had been destroyed, and its firing mechanism was practically melted by the fire following the explosion (3233).

This weapon and two others were later returned to the Wichita FBI office accompanied by a report prepared by Special Agent Hodge and dated 31 October 1975. In this report, Hodge specifically stated that none of these weapons could be connected with the Pine Ridge murder scene. While testifying in Fargo, Special Agent Hodge affirmed he had written this October 31 lab report (3342, 3388). According to him, he had not begun examining the .223 cartridge casing which was received in July 1975 until around the end of the year or the beginning of 1976. He eventually signed an affidavit (10 February 1976) under oath that connected this .223 casing to the Wichita AR-15 (3235, 3388).

While testing a cartridge casing against a rifle, Hodge told the jury, there are two ways this can be performed. One way is through a firing pin impression test, which is based on an analysis of the dent at the butt of the cartridge casing which is made when the trigger is pulled. This test is normally decisive and conclusive. A second method is through an extractor marking test which is based on scratches acquired when a spent casing is expelled. This testing method is significantly less reliable than the firing pin impression test (3248).

Agent Hodge informed the jury that in order to determine whether a casing had been fired from a particular weapon, "to the exclusion of all others," microscopic comparisons of firing pin impressions and breach face marks would have to be made (3247-3248). However, Hodge stated that a *firing pin comparison test was inconclusive* in this case (AR-15 and .223) since there was "a lack of marks on the bolt face and the condition in which I received it" (3235, 3247).

According to Hodge, the Wichita AR-15, "because of its condition, could not be fired." However, Hodge was able to remove the bolt from this AR-15 and place it in another AR-15 rifle and test fire it. Hodge continued,

This I did and compared the markings, microscopic markings placed on the cartridge cases that I fired using the bolt of Government Exhibit 34A [Wichita AR-15] with Government Exhibit 26—I'm sorry, 34B [.223 casing found in Coler's trunk] (3234).

Hodge went on to tell the jury that an extractor testing was inconclusive and even a positive comparison of markings

does not necessarily mean that the cartridge case has been fired in that gun because the markings can be placed on the cartridge case without actually firing that cartridge case. In other words, put the shell in and then throw it out of the gun without pulling the trigger will often leave this type of mark on the cartridge case (3248).

Utilizing this less definitive extractor marking test on the "most important piece of evidence" Hodge testified that the .223 casing found in Coler's trunk was "positively identified" as having been loaded into and extracted from the Wichita AR-15 (3247).

However, new documents uncovered through the Freedom of Information Act exhibit some problems with the testimony of Special Agent Evan Hodge.

As early as 3 July 1975 Special Agent in charge of the investigation began requesting comparisons between any weapons, casings, and bullets seized and submitted in the case. On 21 July 1975 a shipment of cartridge cases were sent from Rapid City to the Director in Washington, D.C. Included in this was the .223 casing from inside the trunk of Coler's car.

Hodge testified, as we stated above, he received the .223 casing on 24 July 1975 but did not analyze it until December or January (3233-3234, 3388). However, FBI documents reveal that the shipment which included this .223 casing was "under continuing examination" in early August 1975.

Two months after the .223 casing was received in Washington, two AR-15's were submitted to the FBI lab: a damaged weapon from Wichita and a .223 caliber colt AR-15 from Rosebud.

On 27 September 1975, the Rapid City FBI office became very interested in a thorough ballistics comparison between the Wichita AR-15 and ammunition components found at the scene and asked specifically that the FBI lab compare cartridge cases found in the 1967

Ford with the Wichita AR-15. Five days later Rapid City learned from Washington, D.C. that the comparison between the casings seized at the Jumping Bulls and the AR-15 from Wichita proved *negative*. As the teletype observed:

> Referenced Bureau teletype October 2, 1975, indicated .223 casings not identifiable with AR-15 rifle located in vehicle which exploded on Kansas turnpike September 10, 1975. Laboratory requested to compare *all* .223 casings with AR-15 rifle located Al Running property September 11, 1975 . . . (emphasis added)

Indeed, other documents than the one above also indicate it is highly unlikely that Hodge just failed to study the "critical casing" for several months as he testified at Fargo. On 21 October 1975, Special Prosecutors asked the FBI Lab to answer the following questions:

1. Whether or not the FBI Laboratory has slugs and casings of a type which have not been matched to any weapon presently in the FBI's possession.

2. Whether or not the FBI has submitted weapons believed to have been used on June 26, 1975 but for which we have no slugs or casings.*

Shortly after the Prosecutors' request, on 7 November 1975, the Rapid City office asked the Laboratory to complete its analysis of the Wichita AR-15 so it could be "returned for discovery hearing to Wichita no later than five p.m., November 14, 1975."

All of this evidence clearly casts doubt on Hodge's claim that the casing in Coler's trunk was ignored until two or three months after the comparisons reported in late October. These documents also support the earlier report that none of the ammunition components submitted to the lab from the scene was fired by the AR-15 from Wichita.

Most importantly, however, are Hodge's own notes (to the October 31 report) of his comparison between seven .223 casings (found by SA Hughes) and the Wichita AR-15. As we noted above, Hodge testified that a *conclusive* firing pin test could not be performed on the

---

*The above teletype is the only portion of a longer document that was provided; the laboratory's response was also not provided to Peltier's defense attorneys under the Freedom of Information Act suit.

Wichita AR-15 because of "a lack of marks on the bolt face" (3247). However, the more conclusive firing pin test not only could have been performed, indeed, according to Hodge's notes it *was* performed on the Wichita AR-15. Hodge performed a firing pin as well as an extractor test on this AR-15 and came to the conclusion that the seven .223 casings found by agent Hughes were not fired by the Wichita AR-15.

Other AR-15s and Related Events

In this section we will look at some testimony that reveals 1) the existence of other AR-15's recovered on the Rosebud Reservation in South Dakota and near Ontario, Oregon, 2) what weapons and ammunition components the government considered important and therefore presented to the jury, and 3) evidence which points to other weapons as possibly being the fatal weapon.

The AR-15 found near Wichita is one of three AR-15's about which testimony was presented at the Fargo trial. The government introduced *only* this burned AR-15 into evidence and presented it as Leonard Peltier's gun, even though he was not present when the automobile exploded on 10 September 1975.

Two FBI agents from New York City and one FBI agent from South Dakota testified in Fargo about an arrest and raid they participated in on the Rosebud Reservation in South Dakota. According to them, a total of 50-60 agents assisted by helicopters and the military, wearing flack vests and fatigue jackets and carrying shotguns, handguns and M-16's were involved in an overall raid on the reservation. On 5 September 1975 these agents invaded both Al Running's residence and an area known as Crow Dog's Paradise, both on the Reservation (2576, 2579, 2580).

A handgun (Smith and Wesson .357 Magnum with an obliterated serial number) was allegedly found in a reddish-orange and white International Scout registered to a Leroy Casados. Both the government and defense agreed that this .357 Magnum was the revolver Ron Williams had on 26 June 1975. There was, in addition, a loaded magazine for an AR-15 found in this vehicle. Other weapons and ammunition components were found in the area, including an AR-15 and some .223 casings. Both the defense and government agreed that Leonard Peltier had not been at Al Running's property or Crow Dogs Paradise on 5 September 1975 (2606, 2602, 2607).

On 14 November 1975 a station wagon and a motor home were

stopped by the police on a highway near Ontario, Oregon. Detailed information was presented by government witnesses regarding items of evidence found in these vehicles, which included fingerprints of Leonard Peltier who was allegedly present but escaped. The government was allowed (over objection by the defense) to exhibit in front of the jury a number of weapons allegedly found in the two vehicles. One photograph showed a group of weapons allegedly found in the vehicles which did not include an AR-15. However, during both direct and cross examination, FBI agents and Oregon State Troopers testified an AR-15 had been found (2478).

The following teletype accompanied the AR-15 that was sent to the D.C. FBI lab on 17 November 1975:

> Bureau should note past investigation has indicated AR-15 and a Ruger .44 magnum have been used by Bureau fugitive Leonard Peltier during pertinent RESMURS period and *that AR-15 may be actual weapon utilized by him to kill SA's Coler and Williams* (emphasis added).

What is interesting is that the FBI had by this date already concluded that Peltier had killed the agents, even though only limited evidence existed to prove this. It is evident that he was targeted early on.

When Special Agent Steven Hancock of the Portland, Oregon FBI office testified about the AR-15 found in the motor home, his responses were manifestly inconsistent. On direct examination he affirmed the AR-15 had not been included in the photograph of the group of weapons because it had been removed. During cross examination he stated the AR-15 had not appeared in the photograph because it had not yet been found. Further, Hancock testified he personally had made an individual photograph of the AR-15, which he in turn handed over to the U.S. Attorney's office along with the other photograph. The government did not show this photograph to the jury and it was not to be found among their exhibits (2464, 2486, 2474).

Why did the government "hide" this AR-15 from the jury? The reason, as we will see, was because this AR-15 did not match with the .223 shell found in Coler's trunk. And Peltier was in Oregon but not in Wichita where an AR-15 was found that allegedly did match this .223 casing.

During the trial the government displayed eleven charts depicting each weapon and ammunition component which *the government* considered relevant to its case against Leonard Peltier. Special Agent Evan Hodge both examined the items depicted and prepared the charts for presentation, with the advice and assistance of Mr. Sikma, the prosecutor (3291, 3292).

Each of the eleven charts portrayed a particular weapon and the ammunition components which, according to the government, had either definitely or possibly been fired from that weapon. There were no charts depicting either the Rosebud AR-15 or the Oregon AR-15, nor were there charts portraying the six other weapons related to the case and found by the FBI.

According to the government Dino Butler had fired an M-1 rifle on the day of the shooting. Special Agent Hodge put together a chart displaying this weapon and the ammunition components which, according to him, had definitely or possibly been fired from this weapon. This chart, however, did not show thirteen spent 30-06 cartridge casings which had been found at the Siers residence and which, according to Hodge's laboratory reports, had been fired by Dino Butler's M-1. Hodge further did not mention these fired casings to the jury (3301).

According to the government, Norman Charles had fired a .303 British caliber Lee Enfield rifle on the day of the shooting. Special Agent Hodge displayed a chart depicting this weapon and the ammunition components recovered which, according to him, had definitely or possibly been fired by that weapon. This chart did not, however, display a fired .303 cartridge casing which had been found at the Siers house. According to Hodge's laboratory reports, these casings had been fired from Norman Charles' .303 British Caliber Lee Enfield rifle. Hodge further did not mention this fired cartridge casing to the jurors (3340). There was also a .303 casing found inside the red Scout; however, there were insufficient microscopic markings to compare it with any of the guns.

There was no chart depicting a Springfield U.S. rifle which the FBI had recovered in another case and which had, according to Hodge's laboratory reports, fired a cartridge case that had been found at the Siers residence. Hodge did not mention this cartridge casing to the jurors (3302).

Moreover, there simply were no charts depicting "a whole lot of ammunition components" which, according to Hodge, could not be identified or connected to any of the above mentioned guns but which had been found at the site of the shooting (3296).

The government had also prepared for the jurors a large chart of the Jumping Bull area on which they attached pictographs of all items of evidence at the location where these items had been found. This provided the jury with a graphic summary of the evidence. Many of the items recovered at the Siers house did not appear on this chart.

Of the three AR-15s found in connection with this case, only the burned one from Wichita was discussed. The .223 casing found in Jack Coler's trunk had allegedly been fired from this AR-15, as had other casings found near the log house in "tent city." Hodge testified it was also possible this AR-15 could have fired bullets, fragments of which had been found in the ground under the agents' bodies.[7] The government and defense agreed to a stipulation regarding these fragments; the fragments had been tested for the presence of blood and none had been found. Further testimony by Hodge also established these bullets could have been fired from an M-16, a .222 Caliber Remington Rifle, a .225 Caliber Winchester Rifle, and "a whole variety of centerfire .22 caliber rifles." Ammunition components which could have been fired from practically any of these weapons were found in the Jumping Bull area (3317, 3313, 3314).

Testimony likewise confirmed .223 ammunition can be fired from M-16's, the Remington bolt action rifles, the Ruger Mini-14's as well as AR-15's. Hodge testified that many FBI agents carry M-16's, and these rifles use civilian as well as military ammunition. However, Hodge received only four weapons used by law enforcement officers at the firefight for laboratory inspections: Special Agent Coler's shotgun, his .308 rifle and pistol, and Special Agent Williams' pistol (3325, 3278, 3279).[8]

The pathologists testified that the agents had been killed by *high velocity weapons*. According to the government, Peltier was firing an AR-15, a high velocity weapon, on the day of the shootings. However, FBI agents had testified that within a 10 yard radius of Special Agent Coler's car, only four cartridge casings had been found. The government attributed three of the casings to the agents' weapons; the fourth casing was the .223 discussed by Hodge. The AR-15 casings eject *automatically*, flying three to fourteen feet away within an arc of 120 degrees (2948, 3330).

However, as we have said, there were no casings to be found (except the one .223) around the crime scene which were attributable to an AR-15. The government argued Peltier picked up his expended casings before leaving the scene, i.e., in the middle of a firefight! The defense presented photographs taken on 26 June 1975 near Jack Coler's car showing an abundance of tall grass, which would make it inconceivable that even if Peltier had attempted to pick up his casings, he would have been able to find them all. Testimony had placed Peltier and Dino Butler in the treeline area near the junked cars. Although 30-06 casings were found there, no .223 casings had been found. The 30-06 casings are much larger and therefore would have been easier to find than .223 casings.

Requirements for a possible murder weapon would consequently appear to be (1) a high velocity weapon and (2) a weapon which does not eject automatically. Three weapons meeting these conditions were found in the Jumping Bull area; (1) A .303 British Enfield bolt action rifle found in tent city, (2) a Springfield bolt action rifle found at the Siers residence and (3) a 303 British Caliber Lee Enfield rifle attributed to Norman Charles. Only the last gun was discussed and presented to the jury.[9]

Moreover, Special Agent Hughes had testified he personally found seven .223 cartridge casings. FBI laboratory reports declared that these cartridges were found in the crime scene area. However, these same reports showed there was *no* gun found, including the AR-15 which the government introduced into evidence, which could match the fired shells. Thus, other weapons were at the scene of the June 26 crime, but they had not been accounted for (2966).

The main points of this section can be summarized as follows:

• The .223 casing found in Coler's trunk was the government's most important piece of evidence.
• The government argued this casing was fired from an AR-15, the murder weapon.
• Special Agent Cortlandt Cunningham, Chief of the FBI Firearms and Toolmarks Division, signed under oath a *false* affidavit used in the extradition of Leonard Peltier. This affidavit stated erroneously he found the .223 casing.
• FBI fingerprint specialist Winthrop Lodge allegedly made notes while examining Coler's car but curiously did not make notes while examining all other cars involved in the case.
• Lodge's overall testimony was highly inconsistent and contradictory.
• Special Agent Evan Hodge reported on 31 October 1975 the AR-15 could not be connected with the Pine Ridge Murder Scene. In a report of February 10, 1976, Hodge suddenly connected this AR-15 to the .223 casing.
• Considering the evidence, the testimony by Hodge was very untrustworthy, and he possibly perjured himself.
• The government did not present as evidence
    1) the Rosebud or Oregon AR-15's

    2) six other weapons related to the case found by the FBI

    3) the cartridge casings found at the Siers residence

• It is highly probable that the murder weapon was a high velocity rifle which did not eject automatically.

• Three weapons meeting this criteria were found in the Jumping Bull area, yet only one was discussed and presented to the jury.

• Other weapons were at the crime scene area on June 26, yet they had mysteriously vanished.

On the Circumstantial Evidence

During the five weeks of testimony, at the Fargo trial, Judge Benson would not allow the jury to (1) take notes, (2) consult the trial transcripts, or (3) discuss the case among themselves or with others. The evidence presented was voluminous, approximately 5300 pages of transcripts. It was often complex, and, as we have seen, repeatedly contradictory and inconsistent. Moreover, in an involved trial like this one, the jury's attention was often diverted from the material facts to be proved—in this case to the prosecution's advantage. The long and highly complex trial, combined with the constraints imposed on the jury by the Court, made it impossible for them to recollect adequately even the most crucial elements of testimony.

Moreover, what made it even more difficult for the jury was the fact that this was a *circumstantial case,* meaning the government had to rely on circumstantial evidence to attempt the conviction of Leonard Peltier.* As Lynn Crooks stated in his closing argument,

> I submit that . . . we have submitted strong circumstantial
> evidence which indicates that Leonard Peltier did in fact fire
> the fatal shots; (4974)

Even though, as Crooks pointed out, "We have not been able to produce an eyewitness to the actual killings. . . . we have got all sorts of circumstances, however, which fill that hole" (4973). And the Appellate Court stated in its review of the case, "The evidence against Peltier was primarily circumstantial."

---

*Circumstantial evidence is evidence that does not bear directly on the fact in dispute, but on various accompanying circumstances. The Judge and the jury then conclude, on the basis of all the evidence, the occurrence of the fact in dispute. Thus, a circumstantial case is one where a web of circumstantial evidence forms a *tendency* toward accepting or refuting the occurrence of the fact in dispute. In the case of Leonard Peltier, as will be shown, the evidence points directly to the latter case.

The government was not obligated to prove Peltier pulled the trigger. The "law" only required they substantiate that he was somehow *responsible*. What the government meant by responsibility was aiding and abetting in the murder of the agents. According to Crooks, " . . . anyone who commits an offense against the United States, who aids, abets, counsels, commands, reduces, or procures its commission, is punishable" (4973).

Consequently, the important question we want to scrutinize in this section is: Did the government prove, through the use of circumstantial evidence, that Leonard Peltier was responsible for the murder of agents Coler and Williams? We will answer this question by looking at the government's argument and what the Appellate Court, in its review of the case, determined was the strongest circumstantial evidence against Peltier. We will see in this section that first, the circumstantial evidence against Peltier is both highly inconsistent and contradictory, and therefore, totally unreliable. Second, as a result of this, in order to argue the theory that Peltier committed the murders, one would have to (1) ignore important pieces of evidence, and (2) then make use of others in different ways to fit the needs of the theory. Consequently, third, the evidence leaves us with no more than some unanswered and troubling questions.

The Peltier Van Theory

The government, primarily through the testimony of Michael Anderson and Norman Brown, but also several FBI agents, attempted to piece together a Peltier Van Theory, which allegedly described what happened on the morning of 26 June 1975. The Appellate Court, in its review of the case, accepted this theory. The Court listed eight pieces of circumstantial evidence that it considered to be "strongest evidence that Peltier committed or aided and abetted the murders."

The first listing reads as follows: "(1) The *van* that the agents followed into the Jumping Bull Compound was occupied by Peltier, Norman Charles and Joseph Stuntz" (emphasis added). The Court uncritically accepted the testimony of Michael Anderson (775). Summarizing the evidence in his closing argument, Lynn Crooks stated,

> Shortly before noon Special Agent Williams spoke by radio to Mr. Coler. He spoke concerning a red and white vehicle that he was going to chase or was moving next to . . . (4981)

> The red and white vehicle had stopped and it looked like they were going to fire at them. This again was overheard

by several agents: Waring, Hughes, Adams, some of the others (4982).

It was these two transmissions which, according to the government, corroborated Michael Anderson's testimony (4982). The Appellate Court once again accepted uncritically the testimony of Anderson and listed it as number four in its list of the "strongest" circumstantial evidence.

> 4. Michael Anderson, one of the AIM members who was firing at the cars from one of the houses in the Jumping Bull Compound, testified that after both sides had been shooting at one another from a distance, and at least one of the agents had been wounded, he saw Peltier, Robideau and Butler down at the agents' cars. Peltier at the time was holding an AR-15. Shortly after he saw the three down at the agents' cars, he began to walk back to Tent City, a distance of about a quarter mile. When he arrived at Tent City, Peltier, Robideau and Butler were already there, as was Williams' car. FBI agents who later searched the area recovered Williams' badge and billfold on the ground near the junction of the roads leading to the houses and Tent City. It was at this junction that Peltier's van had stopped shortly before the firing commenced.

It was the government's argument that the two agents were killed at this time by Peltier, Butler and Robideau. As Crooks stated in his closing argument,

> As I said earlier, it appears that as these three men came down, they committed the murders. Apparently Special Agent Williams was killed first. . . . Leonard Peltier then turned, *as the evidence indicates,* to Jack Coler lying on the ground helpless. He shoots him in the top of the head (4996) (emphasis added).

As we have seen, this circumstantial evidence does not hold up to close scrutiny. It does, however, leave many unanswered and troubling questions.

The government and defense stipulated that the death of the agents took place at approximately 12 noon, give or take fifteen minutes. Therefore, 11:45 a.m. to 12:30 p.m. is the key time in this case, since we must also take into consideration the escape of the killer(s). The first radio transmission was at approximately 11:50 a.m. and by

12:10 p.m. or possibly 12:15 p.m., judging by the radio transmissions, the agents were apparently either dead or dying.

Four FBI agents had testified they overheard communications by Agent Ron Williams around noon on 26 June 1975. Agent Adams testified overhearing, "looks like there's some guys around that house. It looks like they're getting into that *pickup*. It looks like they're going to take off . . . I hope you've got alot of guys . . . looks like they're going to shoot at us . . . we've been hit" (72–73). Agent Waring testified he heard "there was a red and white vehicle traveling near them and there appeared to be a number of Indians in the vehicle; the Indians appear to have rifles; that he was being fired on by these individuals" (1836–37). BIA officer Robert Ecoffey had testified he heard from "someone" the agents chased a red vehicle, van or pickup (4460). Neither Agents Hughes nor Skelly had testified overhearing a radio transmission about a vehicle. None of the agents had testified to overhearing a radio transmission about the vehicle stopping.

Yet the government's argument, as exemplified in Crooks' summary, ignores Agent Adams and Officer Ecoffey's testimony regarding type and color of the vehicle. It modifies Agent Waring's testimony (therefore adapting it to Michael Anderson's testimony) and then proceeds to argue that this modified version of Waring's testimony was in fact what was heard over the radio by Agents Adams, Hughes and "some of the others." Clearly, this was not in accordance with the evidence.

At approximately 11:55 a.m. one of the agents was already wounded, and at 12:06 p.m. we know Special Agent Adams arrived. At 12:18 there was a transmission which stated that Special Agent Gary Adams was on the scene, and he observed a red pickup leave the Jumping Bull Hall area, preceeding north, and Pine Ridge police were instructed to stop this particular pickup. Further, Adams made a transmission at 1:26 p.m. to the effect that another red pickup stopped at the log house with only the driver but that it left with three people in it.

These two transmissions represent very significant facts in this trial. The 12:18 pickup left the Jumping Bull area within minutes of the time the agents were murdered. How many people were in that pickup? Who were they?

Regarding the 1:26 pickup, two individuals were taken from the vicinity of the log house. What were they doing there? What if anything did all of these people in both pickups have to do with the agents? There was a .223 cartridge casing fired by an AR-15 found by the log house. Is there any connection between the individuals who left in these two pickups and the firing of that weapon?

Why the great sensitivity about the red pickup? Did those red pickups carry away people who murdered the two agents? Those directly involved? Why did the government consistently use the word "vehicle" in their questions even though the answers were always "pickup?" Why the concentration on Leonard Peltier's van? Could it be that this fits the government's scenario and the red pickup does not? What about all the documents indicating a confused understanding of *three* red vehicles: the pickup, Scout and jeep?

In his testimony, as we have seen, Michael Anderson had contradicted himself on all major points of evidence. Testimony of others allegedly at the scene in turn contradicted Anderson's testimony. For instance, Wilford Draper stated on the stand that Anderson was in the camp immediately preceeding the shooting, a time Anderson testified to being at the Siers house. (1127) Norman Brown had testified he was talking to Joe Stunz in camp when the shooting began (1426).

Angie Long Visitor testified the van in fact belonged to Sam Loud Hawk, a relative of her husband. Later, while being questioned by the prosecution, she would state that Sam Loud Hawk was known as Leonard Peltier. Under cross examination by the defense, she would state Sam Loud Hawk never used the name of Leonard or Leonard Peltier (2668, 2672, 2727).

The government's argument, however, conceals the inconsistencies in the above testimonies of Anderson, Draper, Brown and Long Visitor.

Michael Anderson's most important and disputed statement was that he had seen Leonard Peltier, Dino Butler and Bob Robideau down by the agents' cars with their weapons. He did not testify he saw the three men shoot the agents nor did he hear gunfire at the time. Michael Anderson had been asked specifically about each time he had looked down at the agents and their cars. He had testified to looking down four times and his testimonies were highly contradictory.

Norman Brown testified he left the area of the houses *with* Michael Anderson (1496, 1497). They went to a location near tent city and remained there for approximately 2 hours until they were told of Joe Stuntz's death (1512). According to testimony by law enforcement officers, Joe Stuntz had been killed around 2:15 p.m. (1855–1857, 1994–1996). Norman Brown testified that around the time when he left the area of the houses, he looked down at the agents and their cars for the last time, and both agents were firing (1495, 1503). According to Brown's testimony, then, it would appear the agents were killed after Brown and Anderson had *left* the area of the residences.

Thus, the government's argument conveniently disregards the discrepancies in Michael Anderson's and Norman Brown's testimony. Instead, it expands on Anderson's testimony by saying that Peltier, Robideau and Butler had committed the murders. Moreover, it states that Peltier did in fact murder Coler and probably murdered Williams. In fact, no evidence to substantiate these charges had been presented.

Under cross examination Anderson made some interesting changes in his testimony. His alleged four sightings of Coler and Williams were confused and contradictory as was his alleged observation of Peltier, Butler and Robideau by the agents' cars. He also stated under cross examination that he remained inside the Siers house until the agents drove past, then he ran down to tent city.

Anderson, we recall, during his interview with the FBI had asked for an attorney, but one was never called. He was told, "If you don't talk I'll beat you up in your cell." Anderson understood that if he did not give the FBI the answers they wanted, he would be hurt. He therefore complied with their wishes and subsequently testified at the trial that he saw Leonard Peltier down by the agents' cars.

In the first interview Anderson had stated he was in tent city at 11:30 a.m. and "Peltier was at the Jumping Bull's residence on the 26th, the day of the shooting." The first time he looked down at the FBI cars the agents seemed dead.

During the second interview, however, his story changed. He gave a complete statement, which included the information that at 10:00 a.m. he was in tent city. At this time he heard gunfire and left the tent area for the top of the hill. Interestingly, all of Anderson's pre-trial statements placed him in tent city at the start of the shooting, and not, as he testified at the trial, on top of Wanda Siers' house where he allegedly saw the red and white van chased by the agents. The charges pending against him were dropped.

Brown was served with a subpoena, taken by car to Pierre, South Dakota, put in a private plane, flown to Fargo and locked in a hotel. He asked three times for an attorney and each time none was offered him. On 22 September 1975, threats were made to both his mother and him, "If you don't cooperate you will not walk the earth again." He went in front of the Grand Jury and perjured himself by testifying he saw Peltier, Butler and Robideau down by the cars.

Are these testimonies believable in the sense of "eyewitness" accounts of Peltier's involvement in the murders of Coler and Williams?

The .223 Casing and AR-15 Rifle

The circumstantial evidence involving the alleged murder weapon included the following details. FBI agents testified they found a .223 cartridge casing in the trunk of Coler's car. According to the government, this casing was extracted from the weapon the government claims was Peltier's, that is, the AR-15 found in the exploded car in Wichita. Anderson and Brown testified they observed Peltier carrying an AR-15 (788, 1446), a high velocity weapon. According to the pathologists, the agents were killed by a high velocity, small caliber weapon (635, 593, 623). The Appellate Court, uncritically accepting the testimony of Bloemendaal, Noguchi, Anderson, and Hodge, listed this circumstantial evidence in the following manner:

> 5. According to the doctor who performed the autopsies, the agents were shot with a high velocity, small caliber weapon. Peltier's AR-15 . . . was the highest velocity weapon fired that day. No other person was seen by any trial witness on June 26 with an AR-15. Peltier carried his AR-15 out with him when he and the other participants of the shootout escaped from the reservation and fled to the Rosebud Reservation, where they remained for some time before splitting up. Robideau, Charles and Anderson went south after leaving Rosebud. Anderson testified that he loaded their car with weapons, one of which was an AR-15, before they left South Dakota. On September 10, 1975, the car exploded on the Kansas Turnpike, and police recovered from the car the AR-15 which the government contended Peltier used on the day of the murders.
>
> 6. Ammunition components linked ballistically to the same AR-15 were found at the crime scene. The ballistics expert was unable to fire the AR-15 because it had been damaged in the explosion on the Kansas Turnpike. However, he was able to remove the bolt from it, place the bolt in another AR-15, and test fire the replacement AR-15. The expert testified that a .223 cartridge casing found in the trunk of Coler's car had been loaded into and extracted from the AR-15. He also testified that a .22 caliber copper bullet jacket found in the ground underneath the bodies of Coler and Williams had rifling impressions consistent with the rifling of the barrel of an AR-15. There was no testimony to indicate that either Robideau or Butler was seen the afternoon of the murders with a weapon that fired .22 caliber bullets.

As with the Peltier Van Theory, the circumstantial evidence surrounding the .223 casing and AR-15 does not hold up once it is thoroughly investigated. Instead, it leaves many unanswered and troubling questions.

There were several inconsistencies by Cunningham and Lodge regarding who discovered the .223 casing, whether or not it was in fact inventoried on the day in question, and when it was removed from the car and by whom. Do these facts indicate a cover-up or just plain incompetence on the part of the FBI?

The key witness concerning the "critical casing" and the AR-15 was SA Evan Hodge. FBI documents reveal a sequence of events surrounding Hodge's testing of the AR-15 to be inconsistent with his testimony at the Fargo trial. Did Hodge perjure himself? Is the gun test Hodge testified to performing reliable? What about the evidence indicating Hodge did in fact perform a successful firing pin impression comparison on the Wichita AR-15?

A careful search was conducted in a 40 yard diameter area around Agent Coler's car, the scene of the murders. However, only one casing was found, a .223. The agents were killed, according to the pathologists, at close range. What happened then to the expended cartridges? The government argues the killers picked them up. The defense argues the grass was so high it would have been impossible to find every single spent casing. How is it possible the agents were shot at close range and there are no cartridge casings on the ground? Similarly, there was no mention of casings from the weapons of the agents and law enforcement people who assaulted the area that same afternoon.

The murder weapons might not have been semiautomatics, but were possibly either lever or bolt actions. FBI laboratory reports show that a spent casing from a .303 British Enfield *bolt action* rifle was found near the Wanda Siers' home. Yet it was not introduced into evidence by the government and it was not recorded on their charts displayed to the jury. There was a 30-06 cartridge casing fired from a Springfield *bolt-action* rifle found at the Wanda Siers' residence, yet neither casing nor rifle was in evidence. And finally, there was another .303 British Enfield *bolt action* found in the vicinity of "tent city" which was not presented as evidence.

The two .303 British Enfields and the Springfield bolt action rifle are possible murder weapons since they fire high velocity cartridges and do not eject them automatically. Why weren't these guns investigated as murder weapons? Had they been, what would have happened to the government and FBI version of what happened on June 26?

It is true, bullet fragments had been found in the ground under the bodies of the agents. However, Special Agent Hodge testified these were .22 ammunition. He had not been able to further identify them. In other words, he could not be specific enough to say they were .222 or .223 ammunition. Hodge's testimony also established these fragments could have come from six types of weapons as well as a variety of centerfire .22 caliber rifles. In fact, according to Hodge, the AR-15 was the *only* weapon actually capable of firing those fragments that the jury saw. Government and defense had signed a stipulation stating the fragments had been tested for the presence of blood and none had been found (3245, 3313–3317).

Dr. Robert Bloemendaal testified that it was the *last* gunshot wound that SA Williams received which killed him. Bloemendaal's initial autopsy finding, however, indicated Williams was killed by the *first* bullet. Did Bloemendaal therefore perjure himself in Fargo? How could Williams state over the car radio "I'm hit" if he was killed by the first bullet? Initially Bloemendaal reported that Williams was *possibly* killed by a high velocity bullet. What made him change his mind between that finding and his testimony in Fargo? Rather than question the alleged radio transmissions, the Bureau employed another pathologist, Dr. Thomas Noguchi, because they considered Bloemendaal incompetent. Were Noguchi's tests reliable? Did Noguchi lie on the stand?

Other Circumstantial Evidence

Corporal R.C. Tweedy of the Royal Canadian Mounted Police testified at the trial that when Peltier was arrested in Canada for the murder of the two agents, Peltier advised him "that the two agents were shot when they came to a house to serve a warrant on him" (for the 1972 attempted murder charge in Milwaukee, Wisconsin) (3405, 3417). The Appellate Court listed this "evidence" in the following manner:

> 3. Peltier had reason to believe that the agents were looking for him, rather than Jimmy Eagle. He stipulated at trial that there was an arrest warrant outstanding, charging him with attempted murder. Upon his arrest in Canada months later for the murders of the agents, Peltier remarked that the two agents were shot when they came to arrest him.

However, once again, this circumstantial evidence does not hold up to close inspection. According to the charge, Peltier was involved in a fight with two off-duty police officers. The officers claimed Peltier had made an attempt on the life of one of them. Subsequently, he was charged with attempted murder. However, as it turned out, this was a fabricated charge. Nine months after the Fargo trial, in January 1978, Peltier was acquitted by a jury in Milwaukee of this charge. At this trial, defense witnesses testified Peltier had been severely beaten by the off-duty police officers. One of the officers affirmed that for three days following the incident his hands had been too swollen for him to work. Was Peltier so worried about this attempted murder that he murdered FBI agents in order to avoid arrest? Possibly, if Peltier was a pathologically deranged and violent individual. However, all evidence concerning Peltier's character and personality depicted him as the opposite. For example, Jean Day stated at the trial,

> He was respected alot. People, you know, listened to what he said, and I don't know more than that because the people, for you to gain respect in the community like that, is one of the highest honors you can have; and they knew Leonard was not a violent man for the mere fact that there was times, you know, when Leonard could have gotten angry at any one of us in the group, and he never did. He may try to find other means of taking care of things. . . . He devoted himself towards the people (3531).

And Ethel Merrival agreed, stating that Leonard Peltier was "clean in character, clean in appearance, very kind to children, nobody scared of him on the Reservation. He is welcome into our homes." And moreover, "he is devoting his life to a cause that he believes in, civil rights" (3913–3914).

The statement that the agents were shot when they came to arrest him is far from incriminating, and in fact lacks much substance. For example, did Peltier hear from someone else that the agents were shot when they came to arrest him? The statement in and of itself is far from being adequate evidence, let alone when we consider all the other "circumstantial evidence."

Moreover, Peltier had information that the agents were looking for Jimmy Eagle. Charles, Anderson and Draper had been picked up by Williams and Coler the night before the firefight, mistakenly thinking one of them was Jimmy Eagle. Peltier was informed of this incident.

There is some circumstantial evidence regarding Wilford Draper. However, when we look at it closely, it fails to point the finger at Peltier. The Appellate Court, in its listing, noted that Peltier, Robideau and Butler were overheard discussing the murders the evening of the escape. Uncritically the Court accepted Draper's testimony in the following manner:

> 7. Wilford Draper, a member of the escape party that left Tent City the evening of the murders, testified that he overheard Peltier, Butler and Robideau discussing certain details of the murders on the evening of June 26, 1975.

First, there were many problems with Draper's overall testimony. Draper testified in Fargo that Peltier was not in tent city one hour before he heard shooting. At the Cedar Rapids trial, Draper stated on the stand that Peltier was in tent city 30–45 minutes before the shooting took place. Draper also testified in Fargo that Anderson was in tent city when the shooting began.

Some of his testimony he gave to the grand jury was false, and parts of his Fargo testimony referred to something an agent told him happened rather than what he actually saw himself.

Draper stated on the stand in Fargo that the FBI "tied me to a chair and handcuffed me." The FBI interviewed him for hours. He provided the story the FBI wanted. Was Draper coerced? Does his testimony also call into question Anderson's testimony that he was on Wanda Siers' house and observed the agents chase in Peltier's red and white van?

Second, Draper's testimony at trial referred to above, is in fact contrary to the Appellate Court's interpretation. Referring to the Butler-Robideau trial transcript, U.S. Attorney Evan Hultman asked the following question in Fargo:

> Q: Mr. Draper, in response to the question at the time in which we are referring, is it not a fact that your response was:
>
>> The night we were walking to Morris Wounded's house I heard Dino and Bob and Leonard talking about the agents. Leonard said something like, "I helped you move them around the back so you could shoot them." Maybe he was talking about Butler or Bob. I don't know who he was talking about that night.
>
> End of response.
>
> Do you remember making that response?
>
> A: Yes
>
> Q: Was that response at that time to the best of your knowledge a *true response on your part?*
>
> A: *No* (1061–1062) (emphasis added).

And finally, there was some circumstantial evidence regarding the events in Oregon. Oregon State trooper Kenneth Griffiths testified that on the night of 14 November 1975, he was operating radar on the shoulder of an interstate highway a few miles northwest of Ontario, Oregon. According to his testimony, he saw a motor home and a white stationwagon go by. He had read an FBI teletype about two such vehicles which might contain federal fugitives for whom there was an all points bulletin. He followed the vehicles and radioed their license numbers to police headquarters. He received a confirmation and radioed for assistance. Another state trooper, Clayton Kramer, responded and stopped the stationwagon. Griffiths stopped the motor home and parked his car about fifteen feet behind it. He approached the motor home cautiously, carrying his shotgun. He asked the people inside to come out. Some women and children and a man came out. The man was tall, close to six feet and weighed about two hundred pounds. He had dark hair and looked Mexican. He gave Griffiths a common Mexican name. Griffiths told them all to lie down on the shoulder of the highway. Suddenly, the motor home accelerated and at the same time the tall man ran away and jumped over the 5–5½ foot barbed wire highway fence. The women and children were standing between Griffiths and the escaping man. Griffiths heard a shot and saw a flash. He fired two shots at the disappearing man, who he maintained had fired at him. On the stand in Fargo, Griffiths was asked if he could "see an individual in the courtroom who *resembles* the individual who fired at you and escaped over the fence?" Griffiths response was, "He's the defendant" (emphasis added) (2218–2223, 2230, 2231, 2237, 2252, 2271).

Trooper Kramer, meanwhile, had stopped the stationwagon and was standing about three hundred and fifty feet behind the motor home. He testified he heard the shot (which occurred just prior to Griffiths' shots) from the area where trooper Griffiths was and had heard a bullet whiz over his head (2285–2286, 2300).

According to Griffiths, another police car arrived. Griffiths then proceeded after the motor home and found it about one half mile down the highway on the median strip with its engine running and the door closed. After assistance had arrived, a teargas round was fired into the window to force out any occupants. The trooper approached and entered the vehicle. No one was found (2233–2236).

Under the passenger's seat of the motor home trooper Edward Hanson and Sergeant William Zeller allegedly found a paper bag containing Jack Coler's Smith and Wesson .357 Magnum. Sergeant Zeller testified that he had found a single identifiable fingerprint on the paper bag which had allegedly contained this revolver. This fingerprint was matched to Leonard Peltier (2345, 2357, 2507).

As a result of this evidence, the government's argument was that the tall, Mexican looking individual was Leonard Peltier. This was substantiated by Peltier's thumbprint on the paper bag allegedly containing Coler's .357 revolver, as well as Griffiths' testimony that the escaping man "resembled" Peltier. It was therefore Peltier who ran from the scene and who fired at officer Griffiths just prior to jumping the fence (5014).

The Appellate Court uncritically adhered to the government's argument.

8. Peltier was stopped by police months later in the State of Oregon. He fled the scene, turning to fire on one of the police officers. The motor home in which he was riding was searched, and Special Agent Coler's revolver was found in a bag bearing Peltier's thumbprint.

However, there is more to the story that both the government and Appellate Court ignore. First, there were no fingerprints on the .357 revolver found in the paper bag which matched Leonard Peltier (2362). Second, only one fingerprint on the paper bag had been matched to Peltier, and according to FBI fingerprint specialist, Eugene Mulholland, there was no way of knowing the age of that print. In fact, Mulholland testified that a fingerprint could remain on a piece of paper for years (2547–2548). Third, no one, including trooper Griffiths could positively identify the tall man as Peltier (2271). Fourth, trooper Kramer, who stopped the stationwagon, had heard the first shot (not from Griffith's gun), come from the area of Griffiths' and the accelerating motor home, not the fleeing man (2285–2286, 2300). And fifth, a .357 revolver, with one shot fired from it had been found near where the motor home was abandoned (3850). This revolver had a fingerprint on it of one of the individuals riding in the stationwagon (2550), thus calling into question the idea that this revolver was discarded by someone other than those in the motor home.

This *ignored* evidence indicates a different story than that argued by the government. In fact, a much stronger argument can be made that the above discarded gun was the one which fired the shot heard by trooper Kramer. This gun was probably fired from the motor home as it accelerated, later to be thrown to the side as the occupants escaped. How else can we explain the fact that trooper Kramer heard a bullet whiz over his head? If the fleeing man shot from the side of the highway, in a perpendicular manner, the bullet would have proceeded *across* the highway, not parallel with it and over trooper Kramer's head.

All of the strongest circumstantial evidence brought against Peltier has by now been challenged, except for one. The remaining piece of evidence the Appellate Court felt was strong is the following:

> 2. At the time Peltier had access to information that *he was being followed by FBI agents*. One of the occupants of the van, Norman Charles, had been picked up, along with two other AIM members, Anderson and Draper, by Coler and Williams the day before. The three had been transported to Pine Ridge in Williams' car, and were later released after the agents were informed that none of them was Jimmy Eagle (emphasis added).

However, it is clear that this is an unsupported assumption on the part of the Court. The evidence the Court cites, as we have seen above, does not in the *least* indicate that Peltier was being followed. On the contrary, Peltier had "access to information" that it was Jimmy Eagle who was being followed and looked for by the agents. There was no evidence at the trial that the agents even knew Peltier was on the reservation.

In short, there was not sufficient evidence presented at the Fargo trial to warrant a guilty verdict. There was nowhere near enough competent and valid evidence for any jury to find Leonard Peltier guilty beyond a reasonable doubt. In fact, as we have seen, critical portions of the evidence were insubstantial and totally unreliable.

In this light, take note of the following instructions given to the jury by Judge Benson:

> The jury will remember that a defendant is never to be convicted on mere suspicion or conjecture.

> The burden is always upon the prosecution to prove guilt beyond a reasonable doubt. . . .

> A reasonable doubt exists whenever, after careful and impartial consideration of all the evidence in the case, the jurors do not feel convinced to a moral certainty that a defendant is guilty of the charge. So, *if the jury views the evidence in the case as reasonably permitting either of two conclusions—one of innocence, the other of guilt—the jury should of course adopt the conclusion of innocence* (emphasis added).

Once we consider all the coerced testimony, the suppression and fabrication of evidence, and the inconsistencies and contradictions in the government's circumstantial case, we are forced to ask ourselves a final troubling question:

Was justice or the status quo served in the trial of Leonard Peltier?

Leonard Peltier's Statement

On Saturday 16 April 1977 the jury began its deliberations. Four hours later, they sent two notes to Judge Benson requesting a rereading of the testimony presented by Michael Anderson regarding his activities at the Wanda Siers' home during the shootout and testimony regarding statements allegedly made by Leonard Peltier at the time of his arrest in Canada. Judge Benson summoned the government and defense teams to Chambers, stating: "My position will be that unless counsel on both sides agree, I am not going to read or submit a portion of the transcript to the jury." The defense strenuously objected to Benson's decision. Taikeff stated, "I have been trying cases for a little more than nine years. I have never anywhere in my state and in my district found the Judge who was unwilling, or had an experience with a Judge who was unwilling, to read or have the court reporter read testimony back to them when they asked for it. It is a novel idea for me." The government opposed the defense and agreed with Judge Benson. Judge Benson responded to the jury's request by instructing it to rely upon its recollection of the witnesses' testimony during the trial (5266-5273).

The jury resumed deliberations on Monday, April 18. Around 3:30 p.m. that day they reached a verdict, finding Leonard Peltier guilty of two counts of murder in the first degree (5281).

On 1 June 1977 Leonard Peltier, in court awaiting sentencing, made the following statement to Judge Benson:

"There is no doubt in my mind or my people's minds you are going to sentence me to two consecutive life terms! You are, and have always been prejudiced against me and any Native Americans who have stood before you, you have openly favored the government all through this trial and you are happy to do whatever the FBI would want you to do in this case.

"I did not always believe this to be so! When I first saw you in the courtroom in Sioux Falls, your dignified appearance misled me into thinking that you were a fairminded person who knew something of the law and who would act in accordance with the law! Which meant that you would be impartial and not favor one side or the other in this law suit; that has not

been the case and I now firmly believe that you will impose consecutive life terms solely because that's what you think will avoid the displeasures of the FBI. Yet neither my people nor myself know why you would be so concerned about an organization that has brought so much shame to the American people. But you are! Your conduct during this trial leaves no doubt that you will do the bidding of the FBI without any hesitation!

"You are about to perform an act which will close one more chapter in the history of the failure of the United States courts and the failure of the people of the United States to do justice in the case of a Native American. After centuries of murder of millions of my Brothers and Sisters by white racist America, could I have been wise in thinking that you would break that tradition and commit an act of justice? Obviously not! Because I should have realized that what I detected was only a very thin layer of dignity and surely not of fine character. If you think my accusations have been harsh and unfounded, I will explain why I have reached these conclusions and why I think my criticism has not been harsh enough:

"First, each time my defense team tried to expose FBI misconduct in their investigation of this law suit and tried to present evidence of this, you claimed it was irrelevant to this trial. But the prosecution was allowed to present their case with evidence that was in no way relevant to this law suit—for example, an automobile blowing up on a freeway in Wichita, Kansas; an attempted murder in Milwaukee, Wisconsin, for which I have not been found innocent or guilty; or a van loaded with legally-sold firearms and a policeman who claims someone fired at him in Oregon state. The Supreme Court of the United States tried to prevent convictions of this sort by passing into law that only past convictions may be presented as evidence if it is not prejudicial to the lawsuit, and only evidence of the said case may be used. This court knows very well I have no prior convictions, nor am I even charged with some of these alleged crimes; therefore, they cannot be used as evidence in order to receive a conviction in this farce called a trial. This is why I strongly believe you will impose two life terms, running consecutively, on me.

"Second, you could not make a reasonable decision about my sentence because you suffer from at least one of three defects that prevent a rational conclusion: you plainly demonstrated this in your decision about Jimmy Eagle and Myrtle Poor Bear aspects of this case. In Jimmy's case, for some unfounded reason that only a Judge who consciously and openly ignores the law would call it irrelevant to my trial; in the mental torture of Myrtle Poor Bear you said her testimony would shock the conscience of the American people if believed! But you decided what was to be believed and what was not to be believed— not the jury! Your conduct shocks the conscience of what the American system stands for!—the search for the truth! by a jury of citizens. What was it *that made you so afraid to let that testimony in. Your own guilt of being part of a corrupt pre-planned trial to get a conviction no matter how your reputation would be tarnished? For these reasons, I strongly believe you will do the bidding of the FBI and give me two consecutive life terms.*

"Third, in my opinion, anyone who failed to see the relationship between the undisputed facts of these events surrounding the investigation used by the FBI in their interrogation of the Navajo youths: Wilford Draper, who was tied to a chair for three hours and denied access to his attorney; the outright threats to Norman Brown's life; the bodily harm threatened to Mike Anderson; and finally, the murder of Anna Mae Aquash—must be blind, stupid, or without human feelings so there is no doubt and little chance that you have the ability to avoid doing today what the FBI wants you to do—which is to sentence me to two life terms running consecutively.

"Fourth, you do not have the ability to see that the conviction of an AIM activist helps to cover up what the government's own evidence showed: that large numbers of Indian people engaged in that fire fight on June 26, 1975.

"You do not have the ability to see that the government must suppress the fact that there is a growing anger amongst Indian people and that Native Americans will resist any further encroachment by the military forces of the capitalistic Americans, which is evidenced by large number of Pine Ridge residents who took up arms on June 26, 1975, to defend themselves. Therefore, you do not have the ability to carry out your responsibility towards me in an impartial way and will run my two life terms consecutively.

"Fifth, I stand before you as a proud man; I feel no guilt! I have done nothing to feel guilty about! I have no regrets of being a Native American activist—thousands of people in the United States, Canada and around the world have and will continue to support me to expose the injustices that have occurred in this courtroom. I do feel pity for your people that they must live under such an ugly system. Under your system, you are taught greed, racism and corruption—and most serious of all, the destruction of Mother Earth. Under the Native American system, we are taught all people are Brothers and Sisters; to share the wealth with the poor and needy. But the most important of all is to respect and preserve the Earth, who we consider to be our Mother. We feed from her breast; our Mother gives us life from birth and when it's time to leave this world, she again takes us back into her womb. But the main thing we are taught is to preserve her for our children and our grandchildren, because they are the next who will live upon her.

"No, I'm not the guilty one here; I'm not the one who should be called a criminal—white racist America is the criminal for the destruction of our lands and my people; to hide your guilt from the decent human beings in

America and around the world, you will sentence me to two consecutive life terms without any hesitation.

"Sixth, there are less than 400 federal judges for a population of over 200 million Americans. Therefore, you have a very powerful and important responsibility which should be carried out impartially. But you have never been impartial where I was concerned. You have the responsibility of protecting constitutional rights and laws, but where I was concerned, you neglected to even consider my or Native Americans' constitutional rights. But, the most important of all—you neglected our human rights.

"If you were impartial, you would have had an open mind on all the factual disputes in this case. But, you were unwilling to allow even the slightest possibility that a law enforcement officer would lie on the stand. Then, how could you possibly be impartial enough to let my lawyers prove how important it is to the FBI to convict a Native American activist in this case? You do not have the ability to see that such a conviction is an important part of the efforts to discredit those who are trying to alert their Brothers and Sisters to the new threat from the white man, and the attempt to destroy what little Indian land remains in the process of extracting our uranium, oil, and other minerals. Again, to cover up your part in this, you will call me heartless, a cold-blooded murderer who deserves two life sentences consecutively.

"Seventh, I cannot expect a judge who has openly tolerated the conditions I have been jailed under to make an impartial decision on whether I should be sentenced to concurrent or consecutive life terms. You have been made aware of the following conditions which I had to endure at the Grand Forks County jail, since the time of the verdict:

1) I was denied access to a phone to call my attorneys concerning my appeal;
2) I was locked in solitary confinement without shower facilities, soap, towels, sheets or pillow;
3) the food was inedible; what little there was of it;
4) my family—brothers, sisters, mother and father—who traveled long distances from the reservation, was denied visitation.

"No human being should be subjected to such treatment; and while you parade around pretending to be decent, impartial, and law-abiding, you knowingly allowed your fascist chief deputy marshal to play storm-trooper. Again, the only conclusion that comes to mind is that you know and always knew you would sentence me to two consecutive life terms.

"Finally, I honestly believe that you made up your mind long ago that I was guilty and that you were going to sentence me to the maximum sentence under the law. But this does not surprise me, because you are a high-ranking member of the white racist American establishment which has consistently said,

"In God we Trust," while they went about their business of murdering my people and attempting to destroy our culture.

"The only thing I'm guilty of and which I was convicted for was being Chippewa and Sioux blood and for believing in our sacred religion."

Judge Benson's reply to Leonard Peltier's statements consisted of the following: "You profess to be an activist for your people, but you are a disservice to Native Americans."

Leonard Peltier was subsequently sentenced to two life terms to run consecutively.

Leonard Peltier's conviction was appealed to the Eighth Circuit Court of Appeals in St. Louis in 1978. In the middle of this first level appeal, it was revealed that William Webster, one of the three judges on the panel, had been chosen to head the FBI. William Webster continues today as director of the FBI.

Webster is well known to American Indians. In 1973, the Wounded Knee Legal Defense/Offense Committee* sued the FBI, presenting documented evidence of beatings, attacks and illegal surveillance on the Committee during the Wounded Knee occupation. However, in court, "the judge who refused to enjoin the illegal activities of the FBI was none other than William Webster."[8] Another lawsuit in 1974, this one regarding the illegal election of Richard Wilson as tribal chairman of Pine Ridge, ended up in the Court of Appeals. The plaintiffs prevailed in a 2 to 1 decision. The dissenting opinion however was written by William Webster.[11] Further, in 1976, several Wounded Knee convictions had been appealed to the Eighth Circuit Court. Attorney Ken Tilsen explains what happened to them:

> The U.S. Court of Appeals, again in a 2 to 1 decision, reversed those judgments and they reversed those judgments because of the interference with the First Amendment which was implied in applying the Civil Obedience Act to the acts of people who were attempting to bring food and medicine and otherwise to get to Wounded Knee. And again there was a vicious objecting dissent, saying that First Amendment rights had nothing to do with the events at Wounded

*This organization has provided legal representation for criminal charges in connection with Wounded Knee II and subsequent events, including the trial of Leonard Peltier.

Knee. And the judge who again made that bitter dissent was William Webster.[12]

During the trial of Leonard Peltier, a U.S. Marshall had an argument with John Trudell, one of the leaders of AIM. Trudell allegedly swore at this Marshall during a recess and was subsequently sentenced to 60 days in prison for contempt of Court. Trudell appealed his conviction and appeared in front of none other than William Webster. Webster upheld Trudell's contempt citation. Because of this and his other repressive activities as a federal judge, Webster was rewarded with the directorship of the FBI.[13]*

Peltier's appeal centered around government intimidation of witnesses and perjuring of evidence, and Benson's decision regarding the offer of proof of Myrtle Poor Bear and the testimony concerning the AR-15.

The Court of Appeals, however, upheld Peltier's conviction. Yet, as we have seen, the court's decision was based on a certain understanding of the events at the Jumping Bulls on 26 June 1975. The Court summarized these events in the following manner:

> Shortly before noon on June 26, Special Agent Williams, driving a 1972 Rambler and Special Agent Coler, driving

*In a *Time* article (30 January 1978:22) it was reported that Judge William Webster was approached by Attorney General Griffin Bell during the summer, 1977, concerning the FBI and its directorship. At the time of this meeting, Judge Frank Johnson had received the nomination for the position. The article stated, "What would his answer have been, Bell wondered, had Webster been asked to head the bureau instead of Alabama Federal Judge Frank Johnson? 'I don't know', replied Webster, 'I have never thought of myself in that role.' " Subsequently, on 29 November 1977 Johnson withdrew his name from the nomination. On 12 December 1977, Webster, along with two other judges of the Eighth Circuit Court of Appeals, heard oral arguments on the appeal of Leonard Peltier. Thus, the potential FBI director-nominee sat on the appeal of one of the FBI's most important cases which entailed arguments surrounding FBI fabricated and coerced evidence used to convict Peltier. Both federal law and the American Bar Association Standards require a judge to disqualify him or herself from sitting on a case where there is even the appearance of bias or prejudice. It is evident that on 12 December 1977, Webster must have considered himself at least a possible nominee for the directorship, and should have followed the above standards. However, a full month transpired between the oral argument and a 12 January 1978 visit with President Jimmy Carter before Webster felt that presiding at Peltier's appeal warranted his withdrawal from the matter.

a 1972 Chevrolet, entered the Harry Jumping Bull Compound on the reservation. The agents were following three individuals riding in a *red and white van* that had entered the compound shortly before them. The *van* stopped at a fork in the road leading to Tent City. The agents stopped at the bottom of the hill. Williams advised Coler on the radio that the occupants of the *van* were about to fire on them (emphasis added).

The Court of Appeals went on:

. . . only five shell casings attributable to the agents guns were ever found at the scene. Both agents were wounded by bullets fired from a distance. . . . These wounds were not fatal. The agents were killed with a high velocity, small caliber weapon fired at point blank range.

According to the Appeals Court the evidence against Peltier was strong enough to warrant a conviction. A petition was also filed with the Supreme Court, but review was denied on 10 March 1979.

The Court, FBI, and Legal Repression

Why did the prosecution ignore the inconsistencies and contradictions that were inherent in their circumstantial case? Why did they go to such great lengths to argue that Peltier was the killer when in fact the evidence was so unreliable and untrustworthy? Why were certain FBI memoranda withheld from the defense? Why did the FBI fabricate evidence, coerce testimony, and possibly commit perjury? We cannot simply dismiss all of this as irresponsible incompetence. What has in fact emerged in the trial of Leonard Peltier is a *pattern of misconduct*; a pattern not related to incompetence but rather to the very organizational goals of the Justice Department itself.* In this section we concentrate on why this pattern of misconduct occurred.

The state response to collective behavior organizing to resist cor-

---

*I find it difficult to believe that experienced U.S. attorneys merely failed to catch the inconsistencies. If we consider (1) the amount of research that goes into a trial of this nature as well as (2) the prosecutors' *conscious* decision not to provide the defense with FBI memoranda that would possibly help clear up these inconsistencies and contradictions, one might well conclude that the attorneys *consciously* chose to ignore them in order to proceed with the prosecution of Leonard Peltier.

porate expansion contains two essential, but inherently contradictory aspects. First, and most important, it must disrupt and disorganize the behavior threatening corporate expansion. The state must respond as quickly as possible to that form of collective action which either immediately threatens, or has a growing potential of threatening, the future profit of the corporate giants. In short, the state will repress the activity as soon as possible. However, the state cannot merely overtly repress behavior which is considered a menace to profit-making. It must also legitimize that repression. This brings us to the second major aspect of the state response to collective resistance. If the state merely engages in outright repression, it runs the risk of destroying its hegemony, which relies on people believing that the state is a neutral arbiter. Such a strategy could lead to an *increase* in the political composition of the organized movement. The state is therefore confronted with a highly conflicting and contradictory situation. It must first of all act in the short-run to allow corporate expansion. Yet at the same time it must consider its long-term interests of maximizing its legitimacy. The state is compelled to maintain a legalistic image if it is to limit political, collective resistance in the future.[14]

The state solves this inherent problem by appealing to the legal system. This enables the state to dispose of threatening political behavior while simultaneously legitimizing its repressive acts. Through the legal system and formal codes of law the authority of the state is legitimized. It claims to be applying universal codes impartially and not singling out specific groups for special and arbitrary treatment. But as Anatole France ironically notes, "It is the majestic equality of the . . . law which forbids both rich and poor from sleeping under the bridges of the Seine."

What is important here is that legitimacy dwells in a sense of the legal order as an autonomous unit containing formal codes and procedures to which even the rulers are subject. This legitimacy principle sets certain limits, then, on the state's short-run ability to end collective resistance as quickly as possible. The legal system (especially substantive and procedural forms to be applied both to the government and the governed) "sets definite constraints on the ability of political elites to dispose efficiently" of collective resistance, "constraints which they can ignore only at the risk of endangering their long-run legitimacy and interest in minimizing" a growing political movement. Nevertheless, the "immediate pressures" to end collective resistance "unavoidably dictate serious abrogations of the" law.[15] The immed‑ interest to allow unencumbered corporate expansion by repr‑

threatening collective behavior inevitably leads to alarming violations of the law.

The FBI

The FBI is charged with the first aspect, repression, and studies show that it does this with uncommon vigor. A Report to the House Committee on the Judiciary by the Comptroller General in 1976, entitled: *FBI Domestic Intelligence Operations—Their Purpose and Scope,* found that in 1970 the FBI initiated the Key Extremist program (the American Indian Movement is considered an extremist group by the FBI) to obtain intelligence on the day-to-day operations of various "extremist group leaders."[16] This program was necessary because "certain vocal individuals were traveling extensively" and engaging in "disruptive acts." An FBI internal memorandum stated that "we should cover every facet of their current activities, future plans, weaknesses, strengths, and personal lives to neutralize the effectiveness" of the extremist group leaders. It was imperative, according to another FBI memorandum, that "continued consideration must be given by each office to develop means to neutralize the effectiveness of each" extremist group leader.[17] Reports on leaders were to be submitted every ninety days, and another memorandum from FBI headquarters to all Special Agents in charge urged the use of "initiative and imagination" to achieve "the desired results."[18] Consequently, according to the report, "FBI officials said a principal way to neutralize individuals was to show that they were violating Federal, State, and local statutes."[19] And as we have seen in this chapter and the previous one, the FBI will fabricate and suppress evidence in order to tie the leaders up in the courts and prison. The FBI also encouraged agents to lie; one FBI memo stated that "it is immaterial whether facts exist to substantiate the charge. If facts are present, it aids in the success of the proposal but . . .disruption can be accomplished without facts to back it up."[20] Thus we see that the objective of FBI intelligence operations dictates they "get the leader" of the resistance movement, even if it entails the outright violation of the law.*

---

*Indeed, the recent publication by Amnesty International discussed earlier investigated the fabrication of evidence, coercion of testimony, and use of informants by the FBI in specifically the case of Elmer Pratt of the Black Panther Party and Leonard Peltier and Richard Marshall of the American Indian Movement. The report concluded that "solid grounds" exist for an independent inquiry to determine the extent of FBI misconduct leading to

The state is inevitably lead into a situation where its agents are forced to break the law. Leonard Peltier and the grassroots movement he is a part of were organizing to resist the continued expropriation of their land and sovereignty. As a result, the FBI, through illegal actions, disrupted the leadership of that resistance.

The murder of two agents (Williams and Coler) at Pine Ridge was the necessary element to "tie the leader" of that movement "up in the courts." This event supplied the state with the opportunity to nullify the leadership of a maturing, organized, political resistance, struggling to save traditional Indian and treaty-guaranteed land from corporate exploitation. The trial of Peltier can only be seen in this light. The evidence indicates in fact that the FBI and government attorneys were more concerned about nailing Peltier than finding the killer(s) of their comrades.

First of all, testimony indicates the FBI suborned the perjury of Anderson, Draper, Brown and Myrtle Poor Bear. Second, the evidence indicates they (1) fabricated evidence, i.e., Poor Bear's affidavits and possibly (2) perjured themselves, i.e., Special Agent Hodge. Third, the FBI and prosecuting attorneys refused to follow up several important leads and thus critically evaluate the contradictions in their theory. They collaborated concerning what evidence should be presented to the jury, and in so doing the government willingly excluded from their investigation certain important events such as the two red pickups which left the murder scene and the possibility that the murder weapon was a lever or bolt action rifle. And finally, and most important, the government possibly suppressed crucial exonerating evidence concerning (1) pathologist reports, (2) the .223 casing and AR-15 rifle, (3) the red and white van issue, and (4) other individuals at the scene during the firefight.*

In short, the goal of the FBI only tangentially included any efforts to discover and prosecute the killers of their fellow workers, but was

the wrongful conviction of minority political activists. Specifically regarding AIM, the report concluded:

> Amnesty International . . . notes with concern that while engaged on its intelligence work in relation to AIM the FBI has appeared willing to fabricate evidence . . ., (withhold) information from defendants which should have been disclosed and infiltrated the defense team of individuals indicted on a serious charge.[21]

*See the writ of habaes corpus filed by Peltier's attorney for evidence concerning other individuals possibly involved in the firefight.

primarily directed at locating, prosecuting, convicting, and imprisoning—in short, neutralizing—an important leader of the American Indian Movement.*

The Court

The Justice Department then provided the "evidence" to attempt the conviction of Leonard Peltier. *Both* Judge Paul Benson and the defense were mislead since not all evidence was available to them. As such, Benson's decisions regarding, for example, matters of evidence, must have reflected this manipulation. Nonetheless, many of Benson's decisions aided the prosection in obtaining a conviction of Leonard Peltier. Some of the more important decisions made by Benson which served the prosecution's case were:

1) ruling evidence of FBI misconduct irrelevant;
2) ruling the testimonies surrounding the offer of proof of Myrtle Poor Bear could not be heard by the jury;
3) not allowing into evidence important FBI 302's;
4) denying himself as well as members of the jury an opportunity to make the sighting test;
5) allowing the photographs of the murder scene and the autopsies to pass freely among the jurors;
6) not allowing the jury to take notes and reread important parts of the trial transcripts.**

Leonard Peltier was found guilty by the jury not because he was guilty, but because crucial aspects of the trial were manipulated to favor the prosecution and, consequently, cause a conviction. The pros-

---

*I am not saying *all* FBI agents and prosecuting attorneys involved in this case were not concerned with the deaths of Williams and Coler. However, a number of government officials—it seems from the evidence—were far more concerned with obtaining the conviction of an *important* leader of the American Indian Movement than with helping to bring about justice.
**In its opinion the Court of Appeals upheld Benson's decisions on points 1, 2, 3 and 6. Points 4 and 5 were dealt with by the court. Regarding point 2, the Myrtle Poor Bear offer of proof, the Appeals Court stated:

> While the more prudent course might have been to allow the defense to present the evidence, we find no abuse of discretion in the trial court's exclusion of the testimony of . . .Myrtle Poor Bear, in light of its low probative value, the potential for further delay in the trial, and the danger of unfair prejudice to the government.

ecution was allowed for five weeks to present all kinds of emotionally biased and prejudicial evidence. Though Benson approved the prosecution's evidence, he cut the defense's planned several weeks of testimony to two and a half days and limited examination to those events specifically connected to the killings, and then not all of them.

The collaboration between the FBI and the Justice Department regarding false prosecutions, cover-ups and the manipulation of the judicial apparatus is nothing new. Evidence exists showing that the FBI and Justice Department have colluded to 1) conceal hundreds of incriminating documents in civil rights trials, such as that of Fred Hampton; 2) perjure themselves, e.g., Wounded Knee and Vietnam Veterans against the War Trials; 3) destroy and conceal evidence associated with assassination plots, e.g., Dr. Martin Luther King; 4) destroy evidence indicating illegal activities in pursuit of "subversive" groups, e.g., Weather Underground; 5) cover up their role in assassinations, e.g., Malcolm X, Fred Hampton; 6) lie to judges, e.g., Socialist Workers Party cases, 7) conceal damning evidence from the Church Committee on Intelligence, e.g., the American Indian Movement.[22]

In addition to "wrongdoings" in legal proceedings, the FBI and Justice Department have many times worked in secret with judges to insure that their goals were carried out. I quote at length from the influential National Lawyers Guild's *Documentary Look at America's Secret Police:*

> Judge Irving Kaufman worked directly with the Justice Department and the FBI to assure that the Rosenbergs would be executed, and later joined with them to spread pro-government propaganda about the case; the current Chief Judge of the Northern District of Illinois, James Parsons, while a District Court Judge, made derogatory public statements concerning the Nation of Islam and the BPP at the instigation of counter-intelligence agents; former Chief Judge William Campbell intervened in the Chicago 8 Conspiracy trial to assure J. Edgar Hoover that a defense subpoena for surveillance documents would be quashed, and secretly passed information from Judge Hoffman to the FBI concerning possible contempt citations against the defendants and their lawyers. Hoffman also met secretly with FBI agents and U.S. Attorney Thomas Foran to discuss these contempt citations. In the *Hampton* trial, Judge J. Sam Perry met

secretly with both the FBI and police lawyers to discuss documents which were to be turned over to the Panther plaintiffs. Perry also wrote ex parte letters to then Attorney General Levi praising the conduct of FBI agents and their attorneys who had withheld important documents, and told the Assistant U.S. Attorney investigating charges of misconduct to let the court dispose of the matter at the end of the trial. An Appeals Court Judge, Wilbur Pell, who issued a stinging dissent protesting the ordering of a new trial in the *Hampton* case, turned out to be a former FBI agent himself, and a long time member of the Society of Former Special Agents, which was fundraising to defend FBI Special Agents, charged with misconduct while the judge was hearing the case.[23]

A Case of Legal Repression

Does the story of Leonard Peltier repeat this past history? Is it in fact an account of legal repression? The state employed legal procedures—while covertly violating those procedures—to legitimate its repressive acts. This resulted in effectively breaking up the leadership of a growing grassroots movement. It was hardly, however, a conspiracy, a plot on the part of state agents to control American Indians for the ruling class. Rather, state functionaries (FBI agents, prosecuting attorneys, etc.) are basically bureaucrats whose primary concerns are advancing their careers and promoting the interests of their agencies. Those who do the dirty work of repression share a basic acceptance of contemporary social and economic norms and consequently view the system as natural and good. High-ranking agents of the state come from class backgrounds where they have received more "benefits" from the existing system. Their training emphasizes loyalty as an ultimate virtue. Their charge is to defend the familiar status-quo. They take existing societal conditions as given and dissent as unwarranted. Consequently, behaviors which threaten contemporary relations are deemed bad. These legal officials can simultaneously avow the virtue of law and order and then break laws and impose chaos in order to repress dissent because they see dissent itself as anti-social, beyond the civilized arena where law should be taken seriously. As Jerome Skolnick has put it:

> Nonconformity comes to be viewed with nearly as much suspicion as actual law violation, correspondingly, the police

value the familiar, the ordinary, the status quo, rather than social change. These views both put the police at odds with the dissident communities with whom they have frequent contact and detract from their capacity to appreciate the reasons for dissent, change, or any other form of innovative social behavior.[24]

Thus organized efforts to inhibit corporate expansion tend to be viewed by the FBI as a "conspiratorial" plot of authoritarian individuals.[25]

In the case of Leonard Peltier we must look further for an adequate explanation. Systems which, in the final analysis, maintain non-whites in positions of subordination by functioning according to operating rules that seem impartial on the surface, are properly understood as being institutionally racist. There is a structural and racial inequality built into our *criminal* justice system. What the law defines as "criminal behavior" (street crime) and therefore who it defines as criminal (the poor and non-white), looks fair and unbiased on the surface yet works to the detriment of the poor and racial minorities. The criminal justice system does not concentrate its efforts on the "white man's crimes," such as price fixing, false advertising, pollution, defrauding consumers, unsafe working conditions, and many more, which have been shown to be more harmful, momentous, and extensively damaging to society than street crimes. As a result, actors in the criminal justice system have come to see racial minorities and the lower classes as the "scum of the earth," as the criminal and dangerous classes; in short, as inferior human beings. In repressing this group anything goes. The majority of those who work in the system then (like FBI agents, judges and prosecutors) because of its very structure, reflect this racism.

Moreover, all racial minorities—blacks, chicanos, and Native Americans—are encouraged throughout life to adapt to white society, to become white. To the extent the individual does, he/she is considered "well adjusted." White society views such people as living examples of the progress being made by society in solving the "race problem." But what about the individuals and groups who do not want to disassociate themselves from their race, their culture, their community, and their heritage? What about those individuals and groups who want to maintain this and will struggle to defend it. *They are repressed by white society and its racist institutions* because they are seen as misleading otherwise satisfied individuals who have allegedly "risen above the race question."

Government functionaries have a faith, then, in their role of restoring and preserving social stability. They attempt to bring order to what for them is a precarious society and, therefore, play a key role in promoting a program of repressive law and order.

The mystification of state functionaries and their service to the capitalist system results from "the ideological understandings they have internalized and their structural and class [and race] determined motivations." In short, as "producers of ideology," state functionaries are "often more mystified" than members of the lower classes and minority groups "as to the social processes in which they are involved."[26] As Lichtman puts it;

> . . . human action can be understood neither independently of the meaning which the actor gives it, nor simply identified with his own interpretation. Recognition of the false conciousness of the actor is necessary to comprehend the nature of his acts. Activity has an objective structure which is often discrepant with its intended meaning.[27]

Yet legal repression by the state does more. Not only does it help disrupt the leadership of a political movement by mystified state functionaries, it also provides the state with a mechanism for future ideological social control.

Repression by the legal system accomplishes this latter mission in two important ways. First, by securing the leader "tied up in the courts," the legal system affects the consciousness of not only other participants in the movement, but also friendly spectators outside the movement. The state defines the leader as "criminal," and so paints a politically conscious American Indian (in the case of Peltier) as a dangerous individual. This affects the image of the organization as a whole. Second, once the legal process is set in motion, the attention of the public is diverted from the political nature of the resistance. The legal system effectively confines arguments to whether the proscribed behavior was "beyond a reasonable doubt" committed by the individual in question. Public debate, as a result, is focused on the "trial" of the accused. The substantive issues surrounding the "crime" are pushed aside and seen as inapplicable to the determination of guilt. By processing individuals through formal legal structures, the conflict is transformed into one over "facts." The overall reasons as to "why" the event occurred are secondary to whether or not the individual in question committed the act.[28] As a result, the criminal justice system is effectively depoliticized, and the state secures control while masking its own criminal and generally politically motivated behavior.

Potential opposition to the institutional structure is *legitimately* neutralized by the criminalization process. Through the procedure of individualizing the problem, threatening political activity may be effectively curtailed. Individuals or groups whose political actions threaten the existing state of affairs may be depoliticized by a state-imposed criminal definition of the group, its activities, or its leader. The politicality of the judicial apparatus is most blatant during criminal adjudication. And it is specifically the criminal trial which can be employed to eliminate political opposition deemed a threat to the existing social order. This specific strategy has historically been used against political activists in the United States. The history of political trials in this country demonstrates the use of criminal prosecution for political ends. Leon Freidman, in his history of political trials in the United States, notes that throughout this history, the legal system has offered a "tempting opportunity for those in power to damage enemies, tarnish their image, and isolate them from potential allies by casting them as criminals." The criminal trial, according to Friedman, has been used as a mechanism to "frame-up" political opponents, since "authorities press the case with uncommon vigor (ignoring all evidence to the contrary) to show how criminal their adversaries are."[29] Some examples of this kind of repression are the murder trials of Industrial Workers of the World leader Big Bill Haywood in 1907, of Tom Mooney (labor leader) in 1916, the famous anarchists Sacco and Vanzetti in 1921, and the Chicago 8, Wilmington 10, BPP, and the trials of AIM leaders, Russell Means, Dennis Banks, and Richard Marshall.

The trial of Leonard Peltier follows in the footsteps of these political ordeals. The case of Leonard Peltier not only continues this history, it also exposes once again the idea of a "politically insulated prosecutor," a "neutral judge and jury" and a "normal trial" as a myth, only serviceable to the state. But the trial of Leonard Peltier, and in fact all political trials, are important for another reason. If subjected to intense scrutiny, political trials expose certain aspects and dimensions of a society—the illegal activities of agents representing the state itself—that are usually hidden under the cloak of justice. The essential function of the state is *not* to alleviate the conditions giving rise to dissident political activity, but through the legal system to *repress* the activity, maintain order, and restore society to the pre-activity condition by *legitimizing* the repression. In short, the legal system contains people (FBI agents, judges, prosecutors) in institutional roles attempting to cope with conflicts generated by contradictions in the larger political economic organization of society. As a result, the state uses the courtroom to maintain ideological hegemony (consequently obscuring the larger contradications) while, simultaneously, its own agents utilize numerous extralegal and illegal methods to ensure legal repression.[30] In short, the legal system effectively depoliticizes political activity by resorting to repression and legitimation. It represses the activity through the law enforcement apparatuses and then legitimates that repression by appealing to the rule of law.

In the final chapter, we will specifically investigate "why" this event took place and thus what Leonard Peltier and this grassroots movement were resisting. Before we turn to those important issues, however, the following chapter examines what has more recently happened to Peltier in his current status as a political prisoner on his own land.

Four

AN ASSASSINATION PLOT?

On 26 July 1979 Leonard Peltier was recaptured after he escaped from Lompoc Federal Prison. Substantial evidence, as we will see below, exposes a plan, possibly by the government, to murder Peltier while in prison. Since he was aware of this plot, he felt no choice but to escape the prison walls for his life. However, evidence about this plot was once again suppressed during the escape trial, and the jury heard nothing about it. As in Fargo, repression persisted. The Fargo trial was the result of an attempt through the normal functioning of the state to place Peltier behind bars where his voice would no longer be heard. This chapter reveals a government scheme to still the voice that even imprisonment could not silence.

On 20 July 1979, Leonard Peltier, Bobby Garcia and Dallas Thundershield escaped from Lompoc Federal Prison in California. These men were assisted from outside the prison by Roque Orlando Dueñas. Dallas Thundershield was shot in the back and killed while surrendering to prison employee, William Guild, during the escape. Peltier, Garcia and Dueñas were indicted on 1 August 1979, for a variety of offenses, including escape, conspiracy to commit escape, and assault of a federal officer with firearms. Peltier was additionally charged with possession of a weapon by a felon.

The story which follows describes in detail the events leading up

129

to that indictment and thus the escape trial of Leonard Peltier. The narrative is based on factual material which Peltier's defense attorney, Bruce Ellison, attempted to offer into evidence at the trial in U.S. District Court, Los Angeles, 14 November 1979 before Federal Judge Lawrence Lydick. The Court refused to allow the evidence claiming it was "insufficient" and therefore "irrelevant."

Standing Deer

The overall plot to murder Leonard Peltier begins with an American Indian male by the name of Standing Deer, also known as Robert Hugh Wilson. On 29 October 1976, Wilson was sentenced to 25 years in federal prison, to be served at the Marion federal prison in Marion, Illinois. The reason for his confinement at Marion is revealed in several prison documents. A "Medical Record of Federal Prisoner in Transport" (from Chicago MCC to Marion) states that Wilson was diagnosed as having an "assaultive personality." According to the report, he "has assaulted every officer who has ever attempted to apprehend him" and consequently, "Wilson is considered by the FBI to be the most dangerous individual apprehended in this district."[1] As a result of Wilson's "negative and assaultive behavior," his "history of escapes" and his overall "extremely dangerous" personality, Wilson was classified for the behavior modification unit (control unit) at Marion federal prison, on 4 November 1976.[2]

In addition to Wilson's violent behavior, prison medical records indicate that he had a history of severe back problems. Specifically, Wilson's problems have been diagnosed by prison doctors as being a form of "degenerative disc disease of the L5-S1" as well as "osteophyte formation of the I4-5 vertebral bodies." Since Wilson was in a state of "chronic lower back pain," medication was prescribed.[3]

In September 1977 Wilson was transported to Texas in order to stand trial there. This traveling, in combination with his incarceration, aggravated his back problems to the point where he was hospitalized in the early months of 1978. On 17 March 1978, while in the hospital, Wilson was approached by the prison doctor, J. Plank, who suggested that Wilson help Chief Correctional Supervisor Captain Carey "in keeping an eye on Leonard Peltier." In Wilson's words:

> On March 17, 1978 I was confined in the prison hospital in the federal prison at Marion, Illinois. On that date, I was told by the Marion prison doctor, J. Plank, that I would not receive medical treatment for my injured back until I

agreed to cooperate with the Chief Correctional Supervisor
R.M. Carey in keeping an eye on Leonard Peltier.[4]

Wilson at this time however refused to cooperate.

Six days later (March 23) Wilson requested his medical records
transferred to Oklahoma since he would, the following month, be
attending trial there.[5] Wilson had been indicted in Oklahoma for seven
felonies which included an assault with the intent to kill a police
officer, several bank robberies and auto theft. On March 29 Dr. Plank
discharged Wilson from the hospital and he was placed in "the hole"
under guard.[6] Two days later Wilson requested a wheelchair so he
could attend an Institutional Discipline Committee (IDC) hearing
which he was to appear before. The hearing was scheduled for 3 April
1978, yet his request was denied by Dr. Plank stating "Wilson does
not need a wheelchair" and "is capable of walking." Wilson subsequently failed to appear at the hearing since without a wheelchair he
was unable to walk the distance and climb the stairs necessary to
attend.[7]

He was convicted in abstentia. Two days later, Wilson again
requested a wheelchair and immediate medical treatment since he was
in severe pain. His request to Dr. Plank states briefly:

> I am in severe pain in my lower back and left leg. I am
> barely able to walk. I was brought to the hole in a wheelchair
> on 3-29-78 by Lt. Jones, MTA Elliot and four other guards.
> My condition remains the same and I still need the wheel-
> chair in order to attend IDC meetings as I am unable to
> negotiate the stairs. I request medical treatment immedi-
> ately.[8]

Doctor Plank refused his request. Wilson continued to ask different
individuals for medical assistance, specifically for a wheelchair so that
he could get around. Repeatedly, nothing was offered. On April 12,
Wilson was informed his medical records would *not* accompany him
to Oklahoma where he would be facing a long trial. By April 19,
Wilson had exhausted practically all alternatives, although he did write
prison hospital administrator Anderson, describing his worsening condition and need for immediate medical treatment.

> I am in severe pain in my lower back and left leg. I have
> a hard time getting to and from the shower. My knee locks
> and I have lower back spasms and cramping which cause
> me to fall to the ground. I can not climb the stairs in the

unit and I need a wheelchair. I request medical treatment immediately.[9]

Wilson's condition steadily worsened to the point where he could no longer walk even short distances. In early May, while attempting to walk twenty feet from his cell to the shower, he fell down and was unable to get up. Several inmates called for help from the guards, but no help came. Wilson's recreation partner, Eddie Griffin, helped him to his cell where he was practically immobile.[10]

It had been seven months since he had contact with sunshine and fresh air. He continually asked for medical aid; especially for a wheelchair so that he could go outside during recreation hours, but none was forthcoming. On May 10, Officer Eaks informed Wilson he was wanted in front of an IDC for a hearing. He was unable to attend, however, because once again his request for a wheelchair was denied. After the hearing Captain Carey came to Wilson's cell inquiring about his physical ailments. According to Wilson's sworn affidavit there was more to it than just medical necessities:

> . . . R.M. Carey came to my cell door in the hole and asked me if I was now ready to cooperate in return for medical treatment. I told Carey that I would talk about it if he would see to it that I was given medical treatment immediately.[11]

Medical Treatment Arrives

Two days later Dr. McMillan came to Wilson's cell. In a report of his examination, Dr. McMillan stated that Wilson should immediately be "transferred to the hospital for local anesthesia and hydrocortisone injections in the tender area plus physiotherapy and medicine," as well as a bone scan.[12] On 15 May 1978 Wilson was taken by wheelchair to the prison hospital. He was asked to sign a medical release form but refused until an outside doctor approved the treatment planned.[13] Consequently, no treatment was administered on either that day or the next.

On May 16, the Longest Walk* in support of Leonard Peltier and other political prisoners arrived at Marion Federal Prison. Due to

---

*The Longest Walk, which began in California and ended in Washington, D.C., was a march of Native people and their supporters whose purpose was to dramatize violations of treaties and the effects of those violations on Native Americans.

public pressure generated by the Walk, several people were allowed to visit Peltier. The day following (May 17), Captain Carey and an unidentified "civilian" in a light brown suit came to Wilson's hospital room to discuss the "neutralization" of Leonard Peltier. In Wilson's words:

> On May 17, 1978, Chief Correctional Supervisor R.M. Carey and a civilian came to my hospital room. The civilian said that if I would cooperate with them in "neutralizing" Leonard Peltier, they would (1) provide immediate medical treatment, (2) get me paroled from the federal system to the State of Oklahoma, and (3) have seven (7) indictments pending against me in Oklahoma City dismissed. I agreed to cooperate.[14]

Wilson responded privately, in his personal diary, that he would reveal the plan to Leonard Peltier; he hoped that Peltier would not act in a way that would cause Wilson problems. Wilson felt that if he refused to cooperate, another individual would be sought who probably would not expose the plot on Peltier's life to him. Therefore, Wilson thought it best to cooperate while covertly explaining the plan to Peltier.

Shortly after Captain Carey and the civilian left, Dr. McMillan appeared at Wilson's bedside and immediately began treatment with Etrofon, linament and hot packs. These treatments continued through May while Wilson remained in the hospital. On 24 May 1978, Bonnie L. Streed, Records Control Supervisor at Marion was notified by Oklahoma County Sheriff Lieutenant Larry D. Hayes that the state of Oklahoma had removed its detainers on Wilson.* The Lieutenant requested the return of the warrants to Oklahoma.[15] On 1 June 1978 Bonnie Streed informed Wilson that Marion had complied with the state of Oklahoma's request.[16] Wilson continued to receive medical treatment in the hospital through the month of June.

On 17 June 1978 Wilson made the following request: "My attorney, Mr. Alvin Bronstein will be in Marion to visit me, . . . (so) I will require the assistance of a wheelchair in order to get out to the visiting room." For the first time in months, this request was granted.[17]

---

*A detainer is a hold order filed against a person incarcerated by another jurisdiction. This order empowers another jurisdiction to take an individual into custody to answer another criminal charge upon release from current confinement.

At the end of June 1978 Wilson was released from the hospital. On 4 July 1978 during a barbecue at the prison yard, Wilson had a conversation with Leonard Peltier, and explained to him "everything about the meeting with R.M. Carey and the civilian. Leonard Peltier told me to continue to pretend cooperation for my own safety and his. He decided that so long as they thought I was acting in their behalf they would not be likely to hire another assassin whose identity we would not know."[18]

The blond-haired civilian had suggested to Wilson that he develop strong ties with Peltier by joining a cultural prison group to which Peltier belonged. Immediately upon his release from the hospital, Wilson became actively involved and within a short time became the organization's chairperson.[19] He emerged as the leading spokesperson for the group, continually requesting such things as (1) the right to hold religious services in the chapel, (2) the right to have the sacred pipe in their possession, (3) the right to receive instructions from their medicine man, and (4) the right to hold services as often as other religious groups.[20]

On 15 September 1978 Wilson was informed that the Oklahoma charges pending against him had been formally dismissed.[21]

On 9 November 1978 Wilson, as chairperson of the Native American Culture Group, was called to the office of R.L. Williams, staff advisor to the group. Not only did he meet with Williams but also the civilian who "hired" him on May 17.

> The civilian told me that both me and Leonard Peltier would be transferred to USP Lompoc; that I would leave before Christmas for Leavenworth prison; Leonard Peltier would follow my departure by sixty (60) days bound for USP Lompoc; that I was to wait in Leavenworth until another Indian was situated in Lompoc who would help me neutralize Leonard Peltier; that if I had to stay over thirty (30) days in Leavenworth I would be taken care of by the Chief Correctional Supervisor in order to make my wait as comfortable as possible.[22]

That evening, Wilson informed Peltier of the conversation with the civilian. Peltier expressed great dismay since the plan change meant another unknown Indian prisoner was involved. Moreover, the plan could conceivably be changed again in the near future. Since Wilson and Peltier were being separated, Peltier would probably not know about any alteration in the scheme.[23]

Standing Deer and Peltier Separate

On 21 December 1978 the two separated; Wilson was transferred to the federal prison at Leavenworth.[24] The trip from Marion to Leavenworth aggravated Wilson's back condition causing him to be hospitalized. Four days later Wilson and a guard had an argument over an "aspirin." Wilson threatened the guard and was immediately taken to the "hole."[25]

A disciplinary hearing concerning the incident was then scheduled for December 27. Since Wilson was unable to walk, he requested a wheelchair to attend the meeting. The request was denied. Consequently, he failed to appear, was found guilty and sentenced to return to the Control Unit at Marion Federal Prison.[26]

This sentence was never carried out, however. A few weeks after the IDC hearing Associate Warden Lipman visited Wilson in solitary. Lipman explained to Wilson he would not be transferred to Lompoc for a while and would remain at Leavenworth until his transfer. Rather than being sentenced to the control unit at Marion or solitary at Leavenworth, Wilson was in fact *promoted* and given a job as clerk in the Chief Correctional Supervisor's office at Leavenworth. In other words, the most dangerous man ever apprehended in the Northern District of Illinois, who had assaulted every law enforcement officer who ever attempted to apprehend him and who had just been found guilty of threatening a guard was given a position enabling him free access to all prison documents and freedom to move about the prison.[27] Moreover, Wilson asked for and was granted (without the usual three month waiting period after such a request) a single cell in a cellhouse next to a good friend, Stephen Berry. This was the first time in prison Wilson had ever had either a job or housing arrangements of his own choice.[28]

Peltier Arrives at Lompoc

Around this same time (early February) Leonard Peltier was transferred from Marion to Leavenworth. He remained at Leavenworth for some time and then was brought to Lompoc Federal Correctional Institution by 10 April 1979.

Two days after Peltier arrived at Lompoc, the prosecutors in Oklahoma City formally moved to have the seven felony charges against Wilson dismissed. Although government documents at Marion exhibited dismissal of the charges in September 1978, they were not formally dismissed until April 1979.[29]

On 24 May 1979, Charles Richards, an individual known to have engaged in numerous violent acts against members, supporters and relatives of members of the American Indian Movement arrived at Lompoc, FCI.* Richards immediately attempted to befriend Peltier, an unusual practice for an anti-AIM "goon." Richards constantly talked with Peltier, had meals with him and spent time with him during recreation hours. Richards, moreover, while in Lompoc FCI, changed his name to Richardson in an attempt to hide his real identity. Peltier, however, found out who "Richardson" really was and immediately cut off contact with him.

Peltier Escapes

During this period Peltier was working in a detail which maintained the grounds directly in front of a major tower, a job earlier assigned to him. About a week later the prison administration ordered Peltier transferred to "the inside grounds," an assignment in a secluded area not visible from any tower.[30] This new work area, according to several prisoners, was an ideal location for a murder since it was effectively isolated from watchful eyes. By August 1979 seven individuals had already been murdered at Lampoc, indicating the high risk Leonard Peltier was facing.[31]

Upon learning the true identity and history of Charles Richards, Peltier believed the threat of death facing him was real and imminent. Consequently, he began to plan his escape. He could not turn to prison officials for help since the Bureau of Prisons had been implicated through Captain Carey. Further, the various prison transfers that had occurred "went to plan" and his change in work assignments all added up to an assassination plot. In short, Peltier was "persuaded" by these events that the only way to save his life was to flee the prison. Thus, on 20 July 1979, Peltier, with the assistance of Bobby Garcia and Dallas Thundershield, fled the prison.

A Few More Facts .

Did prison and other government officials know of the escape? Did government officials try to murder Peltier during the escape? Let's look at a few facts.

*Charles Richards was known to the residents of Pine Ridge as Charles Manson.

Roque Dueñas (a friend of Peltier's who was from Washington) was not allowed to visit Peltier in mid-June, even though Dueñas had no criminal record. Normally, under these circumstances, getting on a prisoner's visitation list is easy. Prison officials were aware, however, that he was visiting with Peltier by going to see another prisoner at the same time Peltier was seeing his fiancee, Carlotta Kaufman. On 18 July 1979, two days prior to the escape, after a visit, Dueñas left his wallet behind. The contents of the wallet were checked by prison officials who discovered two bills of sale for a .223 cal. mini-14 and a .45 cal. pistol, two weapons found outside the prison walls after the escape. The officials later gave the wallet to two women who came for it, without asking their names. After pleading to aiding and abetting Peltier with the escape from outside the prison, Rogue Dueñas was released from custody without even probation.

On the evening of the escape, a meeting was held for the Native American prisoners and numerous guests. Actor Max Gail has stated that unlike the previous meeting he had attended, security was very lax. In fact, he and others were given a careless search, were not asked for identification, and when he arrived, he learned another man was already at the meeting using his name. No questions were asked by prison officials about this. Why the informal atmosphere?

William Guild, an ex-guard working at the prison's power facility, responded to the escape and shot in the back the first long-haired Indian he saw as the man raised his hands to surrender. This individual was Dallas Thundershield,* who from the rear looked similar to Peltier. Did Guild think he was killing Peltier? Only Guild fired a weapon at close range at a prisoner, even though others had the chance. Moreover, according to testimony of William Guild at the trial in Los Angeles, he *knew* the route the escaping men would take.

Regarding Robert Wilson, an interesting bit of evidence is available. On 25 June 1979, Wilson received *extra good time* for his excellent work at the CCS office in Leavenworth prison. A memo signed by the Warden of Leavenworth states the following:

> Inmate Wilson has been assigned as the CCS Clerk since February 1979 and has exceeded all requirements of the job. In addition to very high quality of daily work (seven days

---

*This individual was included in the escape at approximately five minutes before Peltier and Garcia left the prison.

a week) he frequently puts in additional time in the evenings to insure smooth operation in this office. Wilson provides helpful suggestions that aid the efficient discharge of the CCS Clerk's duties.[32]

Even though his recommended "meritorious good time" became effective 1 July 1979, Robert Wilson was fired from his job on 20 July 1979 only a few hours before the escape attempt.[33]

It is my contention that prison and government officials knew of Peltier's escape. How else can we explain why a convicted murderer of two FBI agents successfully escaped the walls of a U.S. federal penitentiary? With today's penal technology it's hard to imagine. Moreover, why was Peltier, a "convicted murderer," moved to a medium federal institution? How is this event related to what has happened to other leaders of movements who have challenged the status quo? For example, what about all the members of the American Indian Movement who the Indian Treaty Council say have been murdered by either the FBI or BIA police? What about Anna Mae Aquash? Was she murdered by members of the FBI? What about Martin Luther King? The FBI did everything they could to "neutralize" him, even threatened to expose his personal life if he did not commit suicide.[34] And finally, what about Mark Clark and Fred Hampton? Both were murdered when Chicago police, aided by the FBI, raided a Black Panther Party apartment in 1969. The night of the raid Hampton was drugged by William O'Neal, an FBI informer who infiltrated the Black Panther Party and was Hampton's body guard. FBI documents show that O'Neal was paid $30,000 for the information he revealed, and was given a bonus of $300 after Hampton was murdered.[35]

Has the FBI turned over a new leaf? Or does the evidence indicate that Leonard Peltier was being led up the same old path?

Peltier was captured five days after the escape, and the prison escape trial began on 14 November 1979. At the trial the above evidence was not allowed to be presented to the jury. Bruce Ellison, Leonard Peltier's attorney, attempted to use the "Duress and Coercion" defense, arguing to the jury that Peltier escaped to save his life. This however was denied by Judge Lawrence Lydick. As a result, on 22 January 1980 Peltier was convicted and given the maximum sentence, seven years, on charges of prison escape and illegal possession of a weapon and acquitted on charges of conspiracy and assault of a federal officer. Bobby Garcia was given the maximum five year sentence on the escape conviction.

Approximately eleven months after the two were convicted for the escape, (13 December 1980) Bobby Garcia was found dead in his cell at the Federal Prison in Terre Haute, Indiana. All inmates in his cellblock were removed so that no one but prison officials could view his body. The government-performed autopsy determined that Garcia had hung himself. They claimed to have found eight drugs in his body, all various types of barbituates. Oddly enough, two days prior to Garcia's death, a close friend received a letter from him which indicated throughout that he was in good spirits and looked forward to his release and return to work. Furthermore, other acquaintances (both inside and outside the prison) stated perplexedly that "Bobby just wasn't the type of person to hang himself, and he wasn't into drugs." The government autopsy was performed very quickly and the body embalmed as soon as possible, greatly hindering an independent autopsy.

Roque Dueñas and his nephew Kevin Henry went fishing on Thursday 1 October 1981 at 9 p.m. On the following Friday, at 2:15 a.m. their boat was found upside down about 200 yards from the shore; approximately half of their six-hundred foot fishing net was wrapped around it. Kevin Henry's body was found, the cause of death being drowning and possibly being hit by a blunt object. As this book goes to press, the body of Roque Dueñas still remains missing. This disappearance occurred near the Narrows Point in the Tacoma Sound of Washington State. Thus, all individuals (Dallas Thundershield, Bobby Garcia and Roque Duenas) who helped Peltier escape are now either dead or missing.

Peltier's conviction was appealed to the U.S. 9th Circuit Court. The three-judge appeals court reversed the escape conviction, ruling that U.S. Judge Lawrence Lydick erred in denying Peltier the opportunity to ask a government witness questions pertaining to his personal bias against Peltier. The Court also "suggested" that the lower court permit the assassination plot evidence at the ordered new trial. The chances of retrial seem remote, however, as the evidence would put on court record—and therefore expose—government misconduct. Most likely the government will drop the charge.

Five

CORPORATE EXPANSION
& INDIAN SURVIVAL

In this final chapter we look specifically at why the events surrounding 26 June 1975 occurred at Pine Ridge. Our information thus far inevitably has led us to political-economic motivations. Consequently, we begin by examining the "energy crisis" and its relationship to depleting oil reserves and thus to big oil. Next we turn to the relationship between the state and big oil, and the move by the corporate giants to exploit non-petroleum energy resources found on Indian lands. Third, we shift our investigation briefly to describe the growth of major corporations in this country (railroads, coal, cattle, oil, etc.) between 1860 and 1890 and their effects on American Indian peoples, land and culture. Finally, we close with a look at how these developments are all related to the resistance at Pine Ridge, specifically the plans that Leonard Peltier, AIM and the traditional people have been trying to impede. We hope to make clear how the judicial apparatus and procedures have been masking over and mystifying these plans by big business.

Mother Earth and Oil

Our country consumes approximately one third of the world's petroleum. Overall, the world consumes 30,000 gallons of petroleum

141

every second and "about 10,000 gallons a second are consumed some-where in the United States." Between 1975 and 1979, the annual *increase* in consumption of oil in the U.S. ranged between 5.5 and 8 percent.[1] The reason for this increase is that our capitalist economy is energy-based. Our transportation systems, our production processes based on synthetics and petrochemicals, and our outright refusal to engage in conservation insures the continuance of this consumption rate. The abundance of both domestic and imported crude oil over the past one hundred years has enabled big business to expand at an increasing rate. Yet we are now in a time of transition to what has recently been called "the post-petroleum era," and many studies reveal the veracity of this label.

The *Oil and Gas Journal* in December 1975 estimated proven world crude oil reserves at 658 billion barrels.[2] One year later their estimate had dropped to 599 billion barrels,[3] so that if worldwide consumption remained stable, the amount in recoverable reserves would run dry in ten years! Other sources, though not so pessimistic, do not give the oil supply much more time.

One ecologist notes that there are only enough ultimately recover-able reserves of petroleum to provide each individual with five hundred barrels. What this boils down to is that

> an American with a large automobile that averages ten miles
> per gallon and that is driven ten thousand miles per year
> requires just over forty barrels of oil per year. At this rate,
> an individual's share of remaining oil would be exhausted
> in just twelve years.[4]

A far more sophisticated study of the availability of resources in the future by Richard Barnet of the Institute for Policy Studies con-cluded that "at some point in this generation and possibly in this decade the oil era is coming to an end. This does not mean that it will all disappear, but the demand for oil will exceed *available* supply."[5]

Barnet, however, was simply echoing what big business has been stating for several years. According to the Workshop on Alternative Energy Strategies, which included representatives of capital from fifteen countries, the available supply of oil will "fail to meet increasing demand before the year 2000, most probably between 1985 and 1995, even if energy prices rise 50 percent above current levels."[6] The work-shop, held at M.I.T., was directed by Carrol L. Wilson, former pres-ident of Climax Uranium Co., a current member of the Trilateral Commission, director of the World Coal Study, former president of

Metals and Controls Corporation, and member of the Atomic Energy Commission.[7] Wilson has stated that the world "must drastically curtail the growth of energy use and move massively out of oil into other fuels with wartime urgency. Otherwise, we face foreseeable catastrophe."[8]

The Trilateral Commission itself has indicated a concern equal to Wilson's. The Commission was founded by David Rockefeller, Zbigniew Brzezinski, and others in 1973, the year the OPEC nations raised the prices of crude oil. Approximately 300 members, drawn from international business, banking, government, academia, media and labor make up the commission whose purpose, as Holly Sklar explains, is to

> . . . engineer an enduring partnership among the ruling classes of North America, Western Europe, and Japan— hence the term 'trilateral'—in order to safeguard the interests of western capitalism in an explosive world. The private Trilateral Commission is attempting to mold public policy and construct a framework for international stability in the coming decades.[9]

The Commission analyzed the energy situation around the world and concluded that the demand for oil will, by the early 1990s, begin to surpass supply. The report went on to recommend that the oil companies "boost prices now" in order to discourage consumption (and insure a long-term source of steady income for big oil) and move to alternative supplies such as coal, shale and uranium.[10]

Even though there is strong evidence that the "energy crisis" is a creation of the oil companies,[11] there is no doubt that the supplies of petroleum *available* to Western corporations are diminishing. Although large reserves are found in the Third World (Latin America has 166 billion barrels, Africa has 160 billion, although in each case over seventy-five percent is still in the ground), they are not easily found or extracted. Moreover, big oil refuses to invest in "unstable" areas, countries that are considered part of the "explosive world" where wells may become nationalized under popular pressures for social change. Further, the diminishing supplies open to Western oil companies are becoming increasingly expensive. In 1974 alone, Exxon and Mobil spent one billion dollars looking for new reserves off the coast of Florida. Five companies spent one hundred and fifty million drilling in the Gulf of Alaska. In both cases, drilling ceased without a find.[12]

What "energy crisis" boils down to is the fact that big oil faces a future problem of small returns on *their* investment; it is financially hazardous, in their eyes, both to dig new holes and to invest in "unstable" Third World countries. Furthermore, if available supplies were to be tapped at current consumption rates, they would most likely run dry in the next twenty years or so.[13] In that sense, then, petroleum reserves are diminishing.

Consequently, the oil companies face a crisis, based both on depleting *available* oil reserves and dubious prospects for return on immediate and future investments. The solution to this crisis, according to big oil, politicians, academia, and the Trilateral Commission is non-petroleum energy resources.

Big Oil, The State and Non-Petroleum Energy Resources

The oil companies are shifting their investments to alternative energy resources for obvious reasons: owners of the big oil companies are in business to make profits and consequently expand. In order to stay in business, each corporation must continuously look for ways to at least protect, if not increase, its profits. They do this by cutting costs and finding new markets and products. When supplies of petroleum are abundant and easily accessible, oil companies will of course continue to invest in the search for and extraction of available reserves since this will result in overall profitability. However, when resources are scarce and expensive, the owners of big oil (and other corporations as well) search for new areas to "establish business" and thus invest.

The essence of capitalism is expansion of both markets and profits. If corporations were unable to continually grow, the necessary surplus needed for re-investment would decline drastically, and the corporation would go bankrupt. As Jeremy Rifkin states:

> As long as nonrenewable (and renewable) resources remained relatively cheap in relation to other production costs—labor and capital—capitalist corporations had no choice but to exploit them without concern for depletion because it served to boost returns on investments and the immediate profit picture of their respective enterprises.[14]

The picture, however, has changed drastically. In short, we can see the coming of the post-petroleum era, as energy corporations invest heavily in non-petroleum energy resources. Since 1973 the oil giants have been buying up the coal and uranium reserves in the United States, taking over some smaller firms and driving others out of business. For example, in 1979, energy companies owned approximately 100 billion tons of coal reserves. Of this, 57.5 billion tons were controlled by 12 of the top 13 oil companies. Moreover, six of the fifteen national coal producers are now owned by major oil companies.[15] The control of uranium is even worse. In 1977, the major oil firms clearly dominated the uranium market, owning almost seventy-seven percent of all the available reserves. The following is the percent of uranium reserves owned by some of the top oil firms.

Kerr McGee	33.5%
Gulf Oil	18.5
Conoco	5.8
Getty Oil	4.6
Exxon	4.0
Atlantic Richfield	3.6
Phillips Petroleum	2.8
Standard Oil-Ohio	1.2
Tenneco	
Texaco	
Standard Oil-Indiana	2.0
Union Oil	
Total	76.5%[16]

The important point, however, is that the majority of non-petroleum energy reserves in this country are on Indian lands. Both the Council of Energy Resources Tribes (which comprises 24 tribes in ten western states), as well as the Department of Energy, estimate that American Indians control 33% of the low sulphur strippable coal reserves in this country.[17] Regarding uranium, "North American Indian tribes own reserves of uranium so vast that if taken as a whole, they would be the fifth largest uranium owning nation in the world."[18] Approximately 80% of all uranium reserves in the United States are found on Indian land.[19] However, as of 1974, less than 1% of the uranium leases already made to oil companies, and 36% of coal leases, were producing energy. As Michael Garitty states, "that leaves a lot of resources just waiting to be torn from the grounds of reservations," not only from land already leased to big oil, but also from Indian land yet to be leased.[20] And the state of course is helping big oil find those sources of energy so that big oil can maintain its profit margins at the expense of depleting the Indian Nations' natural resources, and in many instances, rendering the Indian land base uninhabitable.

Big oil and the state have been looking toward Indian lands for "energy development" because reserves are abundant, and extraction as well as the rights to mineral deposits and labor, are all relatively inexpensive. For example, there is still an abundance of coal reserves in Appalachia, yet energy companies are, as we will see, interested in strip-mining, particularly in the Great Plains and Rocky Mountain areas; strip-mining is cheap (partly because it's not labor intensive) and moving west provides an escape from the United Mine Workers. As a result, profits soar.

Such a situation is essentially built into the U.S. system of Indian Affairs. The Interior Department, of which the Bureau of Indian Affairs is a part, also contains the Bureau of Land Management, National Forest Service, and other agencies, each committed to its own particular vision/mission in terms of use and allocation of "public" (federal) lands. In most cases, particularly in the era of James Watt, priority goes to so-called resource development in cooperation with private sector (corporate) interests. Even assuming the BIA truly attempted to exercise its trust responsibility in behalf of the tribes—which, demonstrably, it generally does not—it would quite likely lose out to conflicting and dominant elements internal to the Interior Department itself. Indian interests are thus clearly and systemically subordinated to "the greater good" at the most fundamental level.

The state helps the oil monopolies find areas to invest through, specifically, the Department of Energy which, for example, administers the National Uranium Resource Evaluation Program. This enterprise examines and analyzes the entire nation for potential uranium sites. The project was funded at $33 million in 1977 and in just two years received $78 million.[21] In fiscal year 1980, Union Carbide was paid almost $3 million by the Department of Energy for uranium exploration in South Dakota.[22] The state also provides, among other things, information and aid to big oil through subsidizing research and development as well as publishing research reports out of the U.S. Geological Survey and the Departments of the Interior, Agriculture and Energy. Before we look at how the state assists corporate capital to find energy resources on Indian lands, let's turn to the history of the relationship between the Plains Indians and corporate desire for Indian land and resources.

The Great Plains Indians and the Corporation: 1860-1890

In the 1860s the indigenous people of the Great Plains controlled the potential railroad and existing wagon routes westward and to the

Gulf of Mexico; some grazed cattle over land which contained coal and oil, and in many circumstances, they did not want to give up their traditional communal values, and therefore resisted capitalist expansion. However, in the end, the Plains Indians lost out in the struggle to retain much of their natural resources and traditional way of life.

The Minnesota Sioux (Santee Dakota) uprising of 1862 was just one form of this resistance. According to Washburn:

> The Sioux Indians of Minnesota and the Dakotas occupied the last area and lived in the last time when Indians of North America dealt on a plan of political and military equality with the United States. Yet they were crushed militarily during the Civil War and the years immediately following, forced on to increasingly restricted reservations, and coerced into the unnatural life of agriculturalists and dependents on annuities grudgingly doled out to them by their conquerors.[23]

After making treaties with the U.S. for fifty years, the Santees were forced to live on a reservation 50 by 10 miles, little more than a tenth of their original 30 million acres. For the land, they received "money, goods and food"; increasingly, however, these remunerations meant cheaper money, shoddy goods, and unbearable food. These conditions combined with the continued "encroachment on their greatly reduced reservation,"[24] caused the Santee to announce that they would no longer allow whites to pass through their country by either land or water. Whites ignored the Indian grievances and the latter rebelled, but in the end U.S. arms were successful. Approximately 1800 Santees were captured, 306 condemned to death and eventually, 38 hanged.[25]

This Minnesota uprising was the beginning of large-scale Northern Plains tribal resistance to white encroachment. The Indians were resisting migrants and railroad companies who cut trails to the west and who took over land needed for laying tracks. These groups encroached on tribal hunting grounds, the Indians' source of livelihood, and resulted in Indians being forced to settle on ever smaller areas of land. The "Indian Wars" were clearly caused by the need for these tribes to "protect their lives, lands and food supplies (buffalo) from willful destruction," which was resulting from migration and the rise of capitalist corporations.[26]

For example, in the early 1860s, the Southern Cheyennes were pressured (in direct violation of the Treaty of Medicine Lodge) off the bulk of the western Kansas and eastern Colorado buffalo range. They were shunted onto a small reservation in southeastern Colorado within which subsistence was less than marginal. As a consequence, a number of younger men shifted north to the open range of the Lakota, raiding southward against white settlements and supply routes.

In retaliation, the Third Colorado Volunteers, under Methodist minister and sometime Colonel John M. Chivington, slaughtered the *peaceful* Cheyennes of Black Kettle and White Antelope at Sand Creek (within the Colorado reserve) on 29 November 1864. As has been noted elsewhere:

> The Sand Creek Massacre, the My Lai of the day, poisoned relations between whites and Indians and...The entire Plains area was soon turned into a battlefield. Not only the Cheyennes and the Sioux, but virtually all the tribes of the Plains went to war.[27]

Following Chivington's example, Lt. Colonel George Armstrong Custer repeated the butchery of Black Kettle's people in 1868 at the big bend of Oklahoma's Washita River. The scattered remnants were then annihilated on the Sappa Creek in Kansas as they attempted to flee the southern plains altogether. The Comanche too were slaughtered in their sleep, at the hands of Texas Rangers, at Palo Duro Canyon. By 1870, the tribes of the south had been decimated and herded into barren reservations in western Oklahoma.[28]

On the northern plains, the Lakota, Northern Cheyenne and Arapahoe held out somewhat longer, defeating the U.S. Army in the field in 1867-68 and forcing the government to sue for peace. The resultant Fort Laramie Treaty was a virtual guarantee of tribal sovereignty and assured the Indian perpetual control over:

> unceeded Indian Territory from which whites are excluded, stretching from the Missouri River west to the Powder River hunting grounds into the Wyoming Big Horn Mountains and from the Canadian border South into Nebraska...[29]

In the next six years, however, the Treaty was broken repeatedly. In 1874 General George Armstrong Custer intruded onto the Indian land to confirm the presence of gold, which his regiment found in the Black Hills of South Dakota. By 1875 there were 400 U.S. Army

Figure 2:   SIOUX LAND CESSIONS

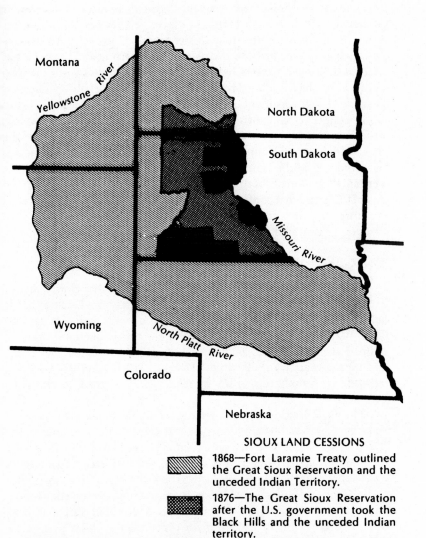

Montana

Yellowstone River

North Dakota

South Dakota

Missouri River

Wyoming

North Platt River

Colorado

Nebraska

SIOUX LAND CESSIONS

1868—Fort Laramie Treaty outlined the Great Sioux Reservation and the unceded Indian Territory.

1876—The Great Sioux Reservation after the U.S. government took the Black Hills and the unceded Indian territory.

1889—Great Sioux Reservation broken into smaller reservations for the various Sioux bands.

1975—Reservation land signed over to the U.S. government since 1975.

Source: Ortiz, Roxanne Dunbar, *The Great Sioux Nation: Sitting in Judgement on America* (Moon Books/International Treaty Council: New York-San Francisco, 1977). With modification by Ward Churchill.

troops and a 75-wagon geological expedition carrying "several thousand gold-hungry miners . . . scouring the Lakota's sacred hills."[30] In 1876, the Lakota, Cheyenne and Arapaho gathered at Little Big Horn in Montana, "the largest gathering of native peoples ever to have taken place in the hemisphere—that Custer stumbled upon."[31] The Lakota and their allies, led by Gall, Two Moons, Dull Knife and Crazy Horse, reacted to the trespassers by wiping out Custer and 204 of his men because they had "violated the sanctity of the Black Hills."[32] The next year the U.S. government once again ignored the treaty and passed an act in Congress that confiscated Lakota lands in Nebraska, Wyoming, Montana, North Dakota and South Dakota and officially annexed the Black Hills for gold mining.[33] By 1886, the Great Sioux Nation had been reduced to the central western part of South Dakota and only a very small section of southwestern North Dakota passed in 1877 by an Act of Congress that confiscated the Black Hills region and the unceded territory. By 1889 it was only five reservations in western South Dakota, as indicated in Figure 2.[34]

The Railroads Move In

The Civil War stimulated industrial growth of the United States. The need for railroads to carry troops and supplies from battle to battle helped create a new social and political-economic order. When the Civil War broke out in 1860, there were thirty thousand miles of railroad track; by 1862, only two years later, immigrant labor had laid approximately 110,000 miles of track.[35] The first transcontinental railroad was completed in 1869 by two companies, the Central Pacific and the Union Pacific.[36]

The Civil War also established the economic basis and many of the techniques by which the overall self-sufficiency and autonomy of the Plains tribes was destroyed over the coming decades. While they were not Plains Indians (they had been relocated to eastern Oklahoma's woodlands from the Southeast during the Jackson era), the experience of the Cherokee during the 1860s is instructive in this connection. During and after the war, the tribe was defrauded of approximately $2 million by government procurement officers and similar parties. By 1865, the tribe, along with a number of others on reservations in that area, was so destitute that it (and they) were ready to treat with the government for relief under virtually *any* terms. A treaty conclave was thereupon set up specifically for the purpose of connecting tribal leaders with corporate lobbyists, most of whom represented railroad interests. Staged at Fort Smith, Arkansas, the meeting lasted some twelve days during which discussions centered upon the centrality of corporate development and railroads to the future prosperity of the tribes.[37]

At the treaty conclave, the U.S. government asked the Cherokees to provide a home for tribes residing in Kansas so that Indian lands could be transferred to two railway corporations, a move which would diminish the land in "Indian Territory" and strengthen the grip of Kansas-based corporate power.[38] Several treaties were signed at Fort Smith; however, further negotiations were moved to Washington for the "Five Civilized Tribes," the Cherokees, Creeks, Choctaws, Chicasaws, and Seminoles. These negotiations lasted through the summer of 1866, when the Interior Department officially stated that the railway charter and land-grant bills which had passed the Congress, and were "part of the same transaction," were designed to establish railroads on Indian lands.[39]

The establishment and extension of the railroad system was the crucial aspect of the development of industrial capitalism in the United States. Not only was it a business of its own, it also acted as an "accelerator" for other emerging industries. And not only did the railroads "enlarge the market for manufactures," but their existence and extension "underwrote new construction work, facilitated and encouraged the filling up and mature settlement of the trans-Appalachian region, and provided the farmer with better connection with the cities and export centers." Both the states and the national government recognized the importance of railroads and as early as 1830 began to subsidize them. While several states gave cash gifts and the right to eminent domain to entrepreneurs, the federal government built many miles of railroads and then *gave* them to private capitalists.[40]

The U.S. government granted the Union Pacific and Central Pacific railways up to $48,000 for every mile of track they built, providing the owners with an easy method to accumulate profits, occasionally of scandalous proportions.*[41] According to Shannon,

*For example, the directors of the Union Pacific organized themselves into a construction company called the Credit Mobilier. Then they awarded the Credit Mobilier, or themselves, the contract for building the railroad. In this way, "the directors of the Union Pacific had ingeniously contracted with themselves at prices which rose from $80,000 to $90,000 and $96,000 a mile, twice the maximum estimates of engineers so that the total cost eventually was $94,000,000." Since railroad construction was very profitable at the time, it allowed for large-scale thievery, and the "Robber Barons" of the

through the use of land grants in the 1860s, the state made sure that

> the railroads got over 134,000,000 acres directly from the
> federal government, in addition to nearly 49,000,000 acres
> through the intermediary of the states or, as in Texas, from
> the state itself. By a very conservative estimate, this con-
> stituted a gift of a net value of $516,000,000 while some-
> what prejudiced calculation set the sum at $2,480,000,000.
> In addition, the railroads were given some 840,000 acres
> by local governments, individuals and the like, its valuation
> being figured at $232,000,000 . . . If to this there be added
> the $48,000,000 permanently accruing to the Union Pacific
> and its affiliates from federal loans, the large but incalculable
> value of stone, timber, and other building materials from
> government lands, all the bonuses voted by local govern-
> ments to encourage railroad building, and all the other
> governmental favors received, the magnitude of public char-
> ity to the corporations begins to become apparent.[43]

Furthermore, the United States government by passing the Homestead
Act in 1862 had earlier transferred control of another 100,000,000
acres from the Indians to white homesteaders.[44] The railroads going
west transported people to "settle" the land; returning east, they
brought coal, oil, timber and hides to the flourishing capitalist industries. As Josephson stated, "From the hills and behind cover the
red-skinned natives watched the march of invaders . . . cut through
their prairies like bands of pain, to grip them forever."[45]

In the rush for profits at the expense of the indigenous people,
the railroads were built. Two or three railways were built where only
one was needed. The railroads were pushed through Indian country
to exploit the land with its excellent soils, waterways, minerals, hides
and forests. The possibilities for financial gain, so imperative to cap-

---

Union Pacific ended up pocketing $50,000,000 for building their railway.
One of the organizers of the scheme was Sakes Ames, a director of the Union
Pacific and a Republican congressman from Massachusetts. Others involved
were James Garfield, who later became president, and Henry Wilson and
Schwyler Colfax, both vice-presidents under President Grant.[42] Capitalists
"cleaned up" on the people's money and were given 183 million acres of land
and accessories stolen from the Indians.

italism, were at the forefront of the genocide of the indigenous people. As we will see below, the railways were the catapult for the expansion of capitalism and the subsequent exploitation of the resources of the Native Americans' varied lands.

The American idea of freedom during this period was "the natural right of every citizen to satisfy his acquisitive instinct by exploiting the national resources in the measure of his shrewdness."[46] It was the Robber Barons, mostly railroad speculators such as Jay Gould, Jim Fisk and Dan Drew, who struggled for economic domination of U.S. society in the shrewdest ways possible. Prior to the rise of such industries as steel, agricultural machinery, and oil, "the epic villains in American history in the period from 1870 to 1900 were, John D. Rockefeller excepted, railroad men."[47] The consequences of their illegal and predatory acts were the oppression and super-exploitation of the masses in general and the genocide of the Native American nations in particular.

More specifically, the genocide of the Plains tribes was the result of four major processes. The first was the penetration of tribal political economies by fur trappers, traders and buffalo hunters who undercut the insularity of intertribal existence, initiated the extermination of entire species of wildlife, and pointed out the vast potential wealth of the west to Eastern merchants and speculators. Second, the penetration of the railroad into or near the unceded Indian territories radically increased the rate of white influx as well as the outflow of hides and other byproducts of animals on which the tribal economies largely rested. Increased transportation offered by the railroads facilitated the large scale development of mineral and coal mining operations within tribal areas during the 1870s, vast cattle concerns in the 1880s, and the emergence of the oil industry in the 1890s. This radical disruption of the environment constituted the third process. The fourth was the transformation of the overall physical environment due to the proliferation of farms and farm communities which had literally engulfed the Plains by 1900.

The construction of the railroad ushered in an ephemeral occupation by whites who contributed greatly to the destruction of Native American life. Their purpose was buffalo hunting, and individuals got rich by wiping out the herds which were the Plains Indians' sole sustenance. In 1492, there were between 50 and 125 million buffalo in the United States.[48] Slaughter for profit increased apace and between 1872 and 1874, for example, 3,700,000 buffalo were destroyed, only 150,000 killed by the Indians.[49]

The railroads dramatically accelerated the destruction of the buffalo by hiring sharpshooters to kill the animals to provide meat for construction crews as well as by providing a necessary conduit for shipping hides to Eastern leather manufacturers. The latter process is of particular note because millions of animals were slaughtered rapidly, not for food, but merely for the skin (which had become an Eastern fad). The carcasses were simply left to rot where they fell.[50] At one point, two thirds of the male population of Dodge City, Kansas, was engaged exclusively in buffalo hunting, a factor which indicates the economic importance of this practice in the West.[51] Individual hunters were killing as many as 2,200 buffalo per month during the halcyon days of the early 1870s; inevitably, by 1877, the buffalo had vanished from the Plains. The slaughter was so complete that, by 1895, only some 800 buffalo were known to exist.[52]

The buffalo were virtually eliminated as a species simultaneously to fuel the developing U.S. political economy of the Plains and to utterly destroy the basic economies of the various Plains tribes. Army generals such as Sherman and Sheridan viewed this process as primarily a military one; it was a conscious strategy perhaps unique in the annals of white/Indian warfare. The development of Euro-American economic institutions, however, inevitably carried with it the same essentially dialectical implications, regardless of the direct participation of the military. In this connection, we turn once again to the experience of the tribes of eastern Oklahoma as being illustrative of what was to become the fate of the Plains tribes in contemporary times.

Plains Tribes After the Railroads

The expansion of the railroads also led to the despoliation of land and disruption of Indian cultural patterns. Railroad companies removed timber from Indian lands "for construction elsewhere, buying from unlicensed traders, and refusing to pay for their ties."[53] Railroad companies attempted to deal with Plains Indians individually, thereby calling into question the communal land holding system where the whole tribe, rather than specific people, would benefit from a sale. Indian law allowed individuals to use timber to improve their own property, but restrained them from selling timber as individuals, since this right was reserved to the Nation as a whole. However, corporations consistently bought lumber from individuals rather than the group. The Indians continually protested this method. Yet it was highly profitable to buy from individuals rather than a Nation, and protesting

Indians only made it "clearer than ever that somehow the Indian economic system was an obstacle to the United States, which was moving to destroy it." In short, "to destroy common land tenure was viewed as the necessary preliminary to civilization."[54]

Coal was another resource which caught the eye of both the Robber Barons and white entrepreneurs. Railroads made the mines on the Indian lands available for exploitation. The Osage Coal and Mining Company, which shared officers with the Katy Railroad, engaged in extensive mining operations on Indian lands.[55] Clark gives one example of how these mines were made available to the "businessmen" of the day.

> The Choctaw Coal and Railway Company was the most persistent offender in executing fraudulent leases of coal lands. The union agent, Leo Bennett, reported that E.D. Chadick, acting for the company, had leased over one million acres of Creek land and even more in the Choctaw Nation. Chadick readily admitted that he had entered into illegal leasing agreements, but justified himself because he had found Indian law arbitrary in its regulation of mineral lands. The railroad company turned to Congress for relief, as did the holders of other illegally executed leases. An act of March 1, 1889, permitted the leasing of Indian lands for a period of ten years, and the Choctaw Coal and Railway Company was the beneficiary of a joint resolution which validated its thirty-year leases on eleven tracts of coal land.[56]

By 1901 there were thirty-nine United States coal corporations operating in the Choctaw Nation alone. These companies employed 4600 "non-citizens" and together mined almost one and one half million tons of coal a year. As a result of their participation in these mining activities and the accompanying assimilation process, by 1907 the Choctaw had vanished as a Nation.[57]

The growing coastal and midwestern cities needed food, and the "plains conditions were ideal for beef production"; therefore, "promoters recognized the economic possibilities" of cattle raising in the Midwest and began to invest in the industry, particularly meat packing. It was the railroads which "furnished transportation facilities to link the producer with the processor and the processor with the consumer," while the newly created refrigeration system on the trains extended "inestimably the possibilities for handling fresh meat." Many times the railroads owned and controlled meat-packing industries.[58]

Cattle, prior to the Civil War, were one of the major means of survival for Indians of Eastern Oklahoma. In an increasingly white-dominated country, herding was the only way for these tribes to fit into this newly imposed culture once their land was taken and their economies shattered.[59] Throughout the last half of the nineteenth century it was the cattle industry which the corporations exploited most extensively in Oklahoma "Indian Territory." Usually large eastern corporations fraudulently leased the land and ended up managing vast resources as well as helping in the rapid demise of Indian sovereignty.

Corporations did not negotiate leases directly with the tribes, but rather "had secret arrangements with individuals, who appeared at Indian councils mysteriously able to offer very large sums for grazing privileges for very large herds." After the arrangement was concluded, the lease was "quietly transferred to a large eastern corporation." Since there was an effort during this time (1880s) to eliminate corporate monopolies, corporations hid behind individuals or "associations" who carried out their business. The result was,

> a breakdown of tribal control of the cattle business, followed by infighting among Indian factions, accompanied by hesitancy of Indian and federal governments concerning jurisdiction, and climaxed by the ascendancy of the corporation, an institution well designed to manage vast resources and silence quarreling shopkeepers.[60]

Like the cattle industry, the railroads played a very important role in encouraging whites to settle in "Indian Territory" of Oklahoma since increased population and traffic would mean increased revenue. Many corporations (along with the railroads) formed an alliance with settler organizations (some of them also corporations) to urge the opening of Oklahoma "Indian Territory" to settlement.[61] The railroads extended and integrated the marketplace and accelerated the development of industrial capitalism in the United States, which in turn tremendously boosted the growth of cities. Between 1870 and 1886 a pattern of expanding and maturing industrial urbanization was firmly fashioned.[62]

Exploitation of the petroleum resources was the last corporate activity which had to deal with Indians as a sovereign and communal society. The stakes were high, and one of the leading capitalists of our time made his wealth combining railroad expansion and the transporting of oil.

The new Robber Baron was none other than John D. Rockefeller, the oil tycoon who exploited first the railroad and later Indian land in order to acquire his massive wealth. In 1870, Rockefeller, along with two others, combined their holdings to form a joint stock company named Standard Oil Company of Ohio. The oil company, like the railroads, the cattle industry, the settlement organizations, and the coal companies strengthened the corporation as a way of organizing economic activity—and spelled the end of Indian control over their resources.*

In the beginning, Rockefeller made deals with a number of principal refining companies and then conspired to drive out remaining companies by joining with the railroads to raise oil transportation prices for these competing refining companies. Josephson explains how this conspiracy worked:

> The refiners to be combined. . .were to have a rebate of from 40 to 50 percent on the crude oil they ordered shipped to them and from 25 to 50 percent on the refined oil they shipped out. The refiners in the Oil Regions were to pay *twice as much* by the new code. . .as the Standard Oil Company of Cleveland. But besides the rebate the members of the pool were to be given also a "draw back" consisting of part of the increased tariff rate which "outsiders" were forced to pay. Half of the freight payments of the rival refiner would in many cases be paid over to the Rockefeller group. Their competitors were simply to be decimated; and to make certain of this the railroads agreed—all being set down in writing, in minutest detail.[64]

Thus, Standard Oil was nourished with secret rebates while others simply starved. Standard Oil did business with Southern Pacific which carried Rockefeller's petroleum westward at favorable rates. By 1900 Standard Oil owned this railroad. In 1878 Standard Oil controlled at least four-fifths of the refining trade in the nation as well as all of the pipelines. By monopolizing the oil industry and fraudulently controlling prices and railroad rates, the "stupendenous holdings of the Standard Oil 'gang' greatly increased," so that by the turn of the century

*For example, although only 520 of 16,395 businesses in the State of Massachusetts were incorporated in 1870, they together held an astonishing $131,182,000 of the $135,892,712 total capital and employed 101,337 of the 166,588 workers.[63]

they contained "countless miles of railroads. . .in every state and city in America and its never-ended twistings of snaky pipe lines. . . ," while controlling the chief underground resources of the nation in iron and copper. Furthermore, by 1900 Standard Oil controlled 90 percent of the refinery output of the oil industry.[65]

Rockefeller and the Standard Oil Company consistently entered Indian lands to exploit them. With E.H. Harriman, a railroad baron, Rockefeller extracted oil from Indian land and then shipped it across to the burgeoning industrial eastern seaboard. They drilled on the Creek Nation and the Osage Nation in Oklahoma's Indian Territory.[66]

Not content with having "relocated" Indians to reservations west of the Mississippi since 1830, representatives of corporations were determined to destroy the overall tribal organizations that were standing now, once again, in 1884, in the way of commercial development. Not suprisingly, we find much evidence that corporate officials encouraged and promoted both the fracturing of tribal holdings and the dissipation of tribal governments to obtain control over Indian lands.

As early as 1818, members of the House of Representatives were encouraging allotment, and on December 5, Secretary of War, John C. Calhoun reflected this feeling in a speech stating that "the land that is Indian land ought to be divided among families; and the idea of individual property in the soil carefully inculcated."[67] It was only in the last quarter of the nineteenth century, however, that the assimilation of the indigenous people of the West into America's capitalist society began to take hold. This assimilation was achieved through breaking up reservations, destroying tribal governments and allotting the lands to individuals.

This supplanting of Indian existence in the western U.S. was the direct result of a concerted effort by a coalition of politicians and corporate elites to eliminate "dual sovereignty once and for all and open the region to white settlement. The corporate lobby pressing for this was known popularly as the Territorial Ring, and it should take its place beside the Tweed Ring, the Whiskey Ring, and the Gas Ring among the mysterious tokens of Gilded Age transformation of the world." Corporations basically felt that "as long as the tribes remained, profitable corporate enterprise was impossible."[68] Thus, by passing the General Allotment Act of 1887 (also known as the Dawes Act), the U.S. government quickly stepped in to guarantee the progress of the corporation and the destruction of Indian national identity and communal existence.[69] The four major provisions of the Allotment Act were:

(1) a grant of 160 acres to each family head and of 80 acres to each other single person under eighteen; (2) a patent in fee (simple) to be issued to every allotee but to be held in trust by the government for twenty-five years, during which time the land could not be alienated or encumbered; (3) a period of four years to be allowed the Indians in which they should made their selections after allotment should be applied to any tribe (failure of the Indians to do so would result in selections for them at the order of the Secretary of the Interior); and (4) citizenship to be conferred upon any other Indians who had abandoned their tribes and adopted the habits of civilized life.[70]

Since the Dawes Commission wrote the Act and was responsible for allocated land in Indian Territory, some of the members of this commission and who they represented cannot be ignored.

Pliny L. Soper, the U.S. District Attorney for the Northern District of Indian Territory, who was to represent Indians in disputes with corporations, was a stockholder in the Indian Territory Development Company (a trust company) as well as chief attorney for both the Cherokee Oil and Gas Company and the Frisco railroad company, corporations that were daily in court with Indians. Guy Cobb, Creek revenue inspector, was the major stockholder in the Tribal Development Company; P.S. Mosley, the Chickasaw tribal governor, was an officer of the same concern; Tams Bixley, Chairman of the Dawes Commission, was vice-president of Muskogee Title and Trust; and J. George Wright, Indian inspector for the Territory, was an officer in the same company, to mention only a few of the prominent.[71]

The ultimate consequences of the Allotment Act served capitalist expansion in three major ways. First, by allocating from 80 to 160 acres of land to families or individuals, the Allotment Act was specifically designed to make small, "individualistic" farmers out of the Indians by dividing up their communally held land and to convert Indian Territory to capitalist methods of production. Second, this act injured tribal unity and relations, which disrupted and disorganized possible Indian resistance to capitalist expansion. President Theodore Roosevelt called the act "a mighty pulverizing engine to break up the tribal mass," and Commissioner of Indian Affairs T.J. Morgan pointed out that the Act provided for "the entire destruction of the tribal relation; the Indians are to be individualized and dealt with one by one and not en masse. . ."[72] And finally, the Allotment Act made tremendous tracts of land available for capitalist exploitation. The members of the Dawes Commission "were enriching themselves by forming trust companies" through which they would lease allotted lands to oil corporations. Most striking of all, since members of the commission had had the land surveyed prior to allotment, they could withhold lands beneficial to corporations from allotment entry. For example, the Choctaw Coal fields were surveyed by the commissioners who discovered that 440,000 mineral-rich acres should be "segregated" from those regions registered for allotment. The end result was that an area of vast mineral resources was abducted from Indian land.[73]

At the time of the Act, the indigenous people owned 138 million acres. But from 1887 to 1934 (when the Indian Reorganization Act was passed, thereby ending forced allotment and approving some forms of tribal sovereignty and self-government) sixty million acres of the Indian land were declared surplus and sold to white capitalists. Furthermore, "of the lands allotted to individual Indians and held in trust for them by the government for twenty-five years, 27 million acres, or two-thirds of the land so allotted to individual Indians, were lost by sale between 1887 and 1934."[74] When the BIA examined the remaining lands, it found that *all* were either "critically," "severely" or "slightly" eroded. Not one single acre of the remaining Indian lands was judged free from erosion.[75]

Even after allotment, corporations experienced difficulty obtaining lease agreements for permission to exploit some Native American lands since many Indians resisted corporate intrusion. However, this was alleviated in 1898 with the passage of the Curtis Act. This Act, ironically titled "An Act for the Protection of the People of the Indian Territory, and for other Purposes," was basically enacted for the "other purposes." The bill gave complete control of mineral leasing on Indian lands to the Secretary of the Interior. Corporate owners celebrated obtaining complete control over "Indian Territory."

The Robber Barons and the railroads not only provided the driving force for corporate expansion but also, through their drive for such things as allotment, provided the "final solution" to the "Indian problem." The effect on the Plains Indians of the extension of railroads across this country was perceived as early as 1 November 1872, by

Francis A. Walker, Commissioner of Indian Affairs, in his annual report; "The progress of two years more, if not of another summer, on the Northern Pacific Railroad will of itself completely solve the great Sioux problem, and leave the ninety thousand Indians ranging between the two transcontinental lines as incapable of resisting the Government as are the Indians of New York or Massachusetts." The commissioner's insight was astute since eleven years later General William T. Sherman noted that peace with the Indian was the result of three important factors: "the presence of the army, the growth of settlements, and the completion of the transcontinental railroad, and that of the three factors the last was most important."[76]

Allotment took effect as Plains warfare came to a close at Wounded Knee, South Dakota in 1890. This massacre culminated in the slaughter of Indian men, women and children by the U.S. Cavalry, Custer's reconstituted Seventh Regiment. Michael Garitty explains why and how this event took place:

> Then came the Ghost Dance which prophesied the return of the slaughtered warriors and buffalo and told of a coming purification in which the whites would disappear and the earth would be new again. The government agents and the military saw the Ghost Dance as the beginning of an uprising. Sitting Bull was killed by BIA police and troops were sent into the reservations in another violation of the treaty of 1868. In December 1890 some of Sitting Bull's people who had fled their camp after his murder joined with Big Foot's Minneconjou Lakota. Together they sought Red Cloud's Oglala at Pine Ridge. They were intercepted by the restored Seventh Cavalry at Wounded Knee, about 18 miles from the Pine Ridge Agency. On 29 December 1890, after disarming the Indians, the Seventh Cavalry murdered all 300 Lakota men, women and children. The white press called it the last "battle" of the "Indian Wars."[77]

The mass murders of Wounded Knee signified the suppression and annihilation of Indian civilization as it had previously existed, a process which is being continued through to present day.[78]

Non-Petroleum Energy Resources and the Resistance at Pine Ridge

The continued encroachment onto Indian land by big business did not cease with Wounded Knee in 1890. It continues to this very

Figure 3: U.S. Corporate Interest in the Greater Sioux Nation

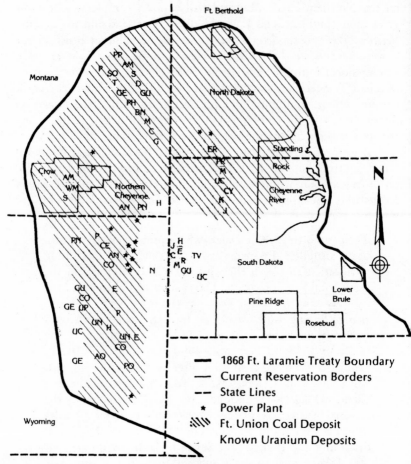

—		**1868 Ft. Laramie Treaty Boundary**
—		**Current Reservation Borders**
--		**State Lines**
★		**Power Plant**
░		**Ft. Union Coal Deposit**
		Known Uranium Deposits

AM	Amax	FO	Remont Oil	PP	Pacific Power
AN	American Nuclear	G	Getty Oil	PR	Power Resources
AO	Ashland Oil	GE	General Electric	R	Rio Alcom
B	Burwest	GU	Gulf Oil	S	Shell Oil
BN	Burlington Northern	H	Homestake Mining	SO	Sun Oil
C	Chevron	J	Johns Manville	T	Tenneco
CE	Commonwealth Edison	M	Mobil	TV	Tenn. Valley Autho
CO	Conoco	N	Nuclear Dynamics	UC	Union Carbide
CY	Cyprus	P	Peabody Coal	UN	United Nuclear
D	Decker	PD	Phelps Dodge	UP	United Pacific
E	Exxon	PH	Phillips Petroleum	W	West
ER	Energy Res.	PN	Pioneer Nuclear	WH	Westinghouse
F	Federal American	PO	Powerco	WM	Westmoreland

Source: Prepared by Ward Churchill from information provided by the Black Hills Alliance for Amelia Irvin, "The Black Hills 'National Sacrifice Area': A Study in U.S. Internal Colonialism," Minority Notes, Vol. 1, Nos. 3-4, Fall/Winter, 1980, U/Colorado at Boulder.

moment. Between 1936 and 1976, for example, more than 1.8 million acres of Indian owned land have been "taken by governmental action alone."[79] American Indians have resisted this every inch of the way and continue to do so. This resistance is what Leonard Peltier, the American Indian Movement and the traditional people of White Clay were all part of on 26 June 1975; as their brothers and sisters had done before, they organized to maintain their natural resources, land and culture. What was it that they were up against? Or, more appropriately, who and what were the "goons," the BIA police, and FBI protecting? Was it different from before?

In 1971, then Assistant Secretary of the Interior James R. Smith initiated the *North Central Power Study (NCPS)*. The study was conducted by a task force representing the major commercial energy suppliers in the Great Plains states as well as municipal "representatives".[80] What the task force was concerned with was the possibility of stripping the immense coal reserves in the northern Great Plains and building huge mine-mouth thermal generating plants right next to the fuel source. These generating plants would then, according to the study, deliver power throughout the Great Plains states by ultra-high voltage transmission lines. The study concluded that large scale development should be done since it was "economically attractive." Consequently, forty-two plants were proposed, twenty-one in Montana, fifteen in Wyoming (of which thirteen were to be 10,000 megawatts, five times larger than any plant existing today), five in North Dakota and one each in South Dakota and Colorado. The effects of such "energy development" on American Indians and their land would be devastating.

What the study revealed was a plan by the energy companies to rip up 250,000 square miles of the Great Plains by strip mining for coal. Machines called "draglines" 365 feet high, with buckets which can consume more than three greyhound buses in one scoop, dig up the earth to get at the coal. The coal in most areas is from 100 to 150 feet down, and thus the dragline consumes everything between it and the coal seam-rock, grass, soil, trees, roads, houses, etc. The dragline scoops out a full load of this "overburden" approximately every minute, and uses a staggering amount of energy.[81]

Strip-mining is environmentally damaging to the land in other ways. After mining, mineral sulfides in the sub-soil mix with moisture to form sulfuric acid. This and other pollutants unite with the "runoff" from eroded hillsides and flow into rivers and lakes, killing aquatic life. Furthermore, after the overburden has been removed and mining completed, it is practically impossible to restore the land and the surrounding ecosystem to its natural state. This is particularly true because western coal acts as a water-bearing layer in a dry area; once the coal is gone, so is the water. Contrary to what some believe, reclamation in the arid west is only a pipe dream.[82]

Once the coal has been mined it is to be used, according to the NCPS, in on location mine-mouth thermal generating power plants. The study concentrated on the construction of thirteen such power plants, 10,000 megawatts each, around Gillette, Wyoming.[83] To give you an idea of the size of these plants, consider the following:

> . . . as the last group of astronauts was returning from the moon to earth, and when they were still several thousand miles out in space, the only man-created thing they could see was a yellowish smudge emanating from the coal fired power plants near Farmington, New Mexico—the Four Corners power plants. *Together, this complex constitutes 2,085 megawatts.* (Emphasis added)[84]

Clearly, these gargantuan power plants will be extremely polluting. Coal cumbustion results in sulfur, nitrogen, ash and other elements escaping into the air and so into people's lungs and as acid rain over large areas downwind of the plants. Moreover, the highly dangerous fallout of these elements can be carried downwind for hundreds of miles before settling. The Four Corners plants pollute an area of 100,000 square miles.[85]

But probably the most important danger in the increased use of coal is the emission of large amounts of carbon dioxide into the atmosphere. Such an accretion of carbon dioxide will raise the earth's temperature by retarding the escape of heat into space. This creates a "greenhouse effect" by trapping the sun's heat in the lower atmosphere.[86] The effect on the earth of raising the temperature could be devastating. As Jeremy Rifkin points out:

> The entire ecological balance of the earth would be completely jarred. Among other consequences, the polar ice caps would melt, raising ocean levels worldwide, and causing almost all major port cities around the globe to drown. Dramatic changes in world temperature would result in the wholesale extinction of much of our existing plant and animal life. The speed of the change alone—seventy-five years or less—would eliminate the possibility of evolutionary adaptation.[87]

Still more, thermal-electric power plants such as those proposed under the NCPS, require large amounts of water because coal is burned to convert water into steam to rotate turbines which then generate electricity. However, where is all the water to power forty-two generating plants going to come from? The NCPS says water resources (rivers, reservoirs, etc.) that are filled by the Missouri River will be the source.[88] Yet the energy companies, according to one source, plan to use as much as "10 to 35 million acre-feet of water a year in the Northern Great Plains alone." However, the Missouri River has only approximately "18½ million acre-feet flowing through it each year."[89] This in the semi-arid Northern Plains where water is needed for drinking, irrigation, farming, livestock and municipal uses.

And finally, transmission. What the NCPS proposed was a transmission system to transport electricity from the mine-mouth thermal generating plants to, for instance, Minneapolis/St. Paul, Des Moines, Omaha, Kansas City and St. Louis. According to the study, "for best economy and minimum impact on the environment," 765 kilovolt lines would be used.[90] There's no doubt they will provide the best economy for a certain group of individuals, but how minimum would environmental impacts be?

The NCPS plans on beginning these lines at the plants located near Gillette, Wyoming (see Figure 4). As it is very expensive to turn or bend the lines, they will then radiate out in straight lines across South Dakota, Nebraska, Southern Minnesota, Iowa and Missouri. Moreover, the right of way for one line is wider than a football field is long.[91] One such line is already in existence in northwestern Minnesota, and the consequences are frightening. Residents who live along the line complain of such health problems as nose bleeds, fatigue, headaches, irritability, skin rashes and high-blood pressure since the line has been turned on. Moreover, the Minnesota farmers report a sharp increase in aborted calves, general infertility among livestock and a decrease in milk production since the line has been operating. Furthermore, grazing livestock consistently keep their distance when the line is transmitting.[92] But the line does more than endanger human and animal life in the manner described above. It has also been noted to

. . . blank out television sets, attract lightning . . . shrivel crops, inhibit the germination of seeds and prevent corn from reaching fruition. Metal irrigation systems can become deadly electrocutors. Fences and metal buildings can become

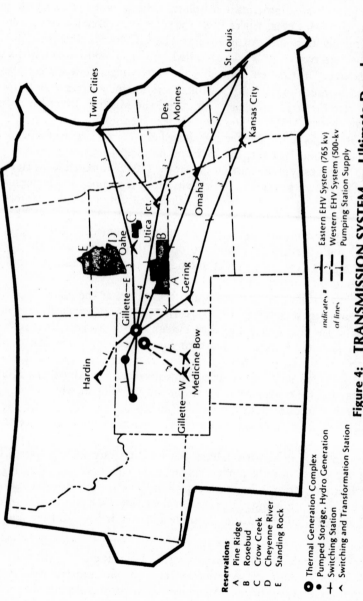

Figure 4: TRANSMISSION SYSTEM — Ultimate Development
Development Level: 10,000 MW West, 43,000 MW East

Reservations
A Pine Ridge
B Rosebud
C Crow Creek
D Cheyenne River
E Standing Rock

○ Thermal Generation Complex
● ○ Pumped Storage, Hydro Generation
✛ Switching Station
∧ Switching and Transformation Station

┼┼┼ Eastern EHV System (765 kv)
┼┼┼ Western EHV System (500-kv)
┼·┼·┼ Pumping Station Supply

indicates #
of lines

Source: North Central Power Study, (Billings:
Bureau of Reclamation, 1971), p. 20. Reservations adapted.

charged with dangerous static electricity. And studies indicate the utilities now have on the drawing boards lines of 1,000 and even 1,500 kilovolts.[93]

The fact that the majority of coal, overburden, water and topography—which these power plants and transmission lines will (and do) exploit—is on Indian land guaranteed by the 1868 Fort Laramie Treaty did not, of course, come to the attention of the task force. Nor did the environmental and human effects of such activities. It did, however, come to the attention of American Indians living on reservations adjacent to the power plant sites. On Pine Ridge, traditional people knew they would be both directly and indirectly victims of such a "plan."

Indirectly, the reservation would be affected by pollution since it is downwind from power plant sites in eastern Wyoming, Montana, western North Dakota and western South Dakota. Moreover, Pine Ridge relies for drinking and irrigation upon water from the Oglala Aquifer (primarily) and Missouri River (secondarily). The reservation lies downstream from many proposed diversion sites along the Missouri, a factor which would dramatically reduce secondary water supplies. Worse, industrial utilization of water from the aquifer would drain that source very rapidly. Small wonder, then, that Jimmy Carter was wont to declare the entire Pine Ridge area a "national sacrifice area."[94]

More directly, the proposals set forth in the NCPS greatly affect the residents of Pine Ridge. Looking at Figure 4 again, we see that four of the eastern power lines will radiate from Gillette, Wyoming, straight through the reservation and on to Omaha, Nebraska, bringing with them all the dangers experienced by Minnesota farmers. However, these dangers will be multiplied four times for the residents of Pine Ridge! In short, the plan set forth by the NCPS concerns the future of a vast area of Indian land, which, as the traditional and AIM people recognized, is on the verge of being virtually destroyed.

But the effects of coal production and electrical generation are only partially responsible for the grave concern among the Lakota people. Today, uranium is the new gold sought in the sacred Black Hills as well as underneath the Pine Ridge Reservation itself. In 1975, the state, through the U.S. Geological Survey and the U.S. Bureau of Mines, grasped hands with the Bureau of Reclamation in a search for non-petroleum energy resources in the Great Plains. The Geological Survey and Bureau of Mines were brought together to gather as much information as possible "on the geology, mineral and energy resources, and potential for economic development of certain Indian lands." One such area was the Pine Ridge Indian Reservation. A report published one year later indicated their labor had not been wasted. Pine Ridge Reservation was found to contain mineral resources of "oil and gas, uranium and a large variety of non-metallic commodities." The structural and stratigraphic traps where these minerals were to be found were described as being "unique," consequently providing "good exploration potential." Uranium was found to be "present over a wide area in the reservation." The government was excited because these deposits were in "favorable areas" for mining. In short, the Geological Survey concluded that "the numerous potential pay zones" and the "relatively shallow drilling depths . . . combine to make the Pine Ridge Reservation an attractive prospecting area."[95] However, once again, the health hazards surrounding the exploration for, and mining of, uranium were not investigated.

Exploration drills penetrate rock layers which cause uranium to seep into underground water reservoirs known as aquifers. This drilling immediately contaminates the underground water supply as well as the plants, wildlife and livestock that eventually drink from it. Drill holes also accelerate underground water movement, causing a lowering of the water tables, especially upsetting for well-users. Moreover, since the uranium of Pine Ridge is rather shallow, energy companies can be expected to strip-mine for it. This method is advantageous for corporations since it is the most productive for obtaining the ore. However, it is highly disadvantageous to those who work or live near the strip-mine as it releases more radiation into the air than underground mining or in-situ leaching. Moreover, the contaminants from the wastes emitted from uranium mining can cause cancer.[96]

Once the uranium ore is extracted from the earth it is processed in the "mill" where some of the uranium is removed from the ore. The uranium is then sent further along the nuclear chain. What is left at the milling site is tons of waste materials known as "tailings." These tailings contain 85% of the radioactivity in uranium ore, including radium and radon gas, and thus pollute surrounding water and air.[97] Furthermore, the strip-mining for uranium ore causes the overburden to become radioactive, disallowing any possibility of reclamation. Michael Garitty describes the results of the Jackpile mine, operated until 1980 by ARCO on the Laguna Pueblo in New Mexico. Stretching five miles long, this mine was the largest uranium stripmine in the country, and the waters on the reservation have,

. . . turned green by the discharged effluent. It is this water that the people must drink and give to their live-stock; stomach cancer is on the rise. Although the mine has been in operation for 25 years, not one foot of the Pueblo's land has been "reclaimed." The reason is simple: reclamation of radioactive soil is impossible. The mine has produced 80 million tons of uranium-308, devastating 2,800 acres of the Pueblo. Anaconda's "Bluewater" processing mill has left 75 acres (13 million tons) of tailings to the mercy of the desert wind and rain.[98]

Massive amounts of uranium surround and are also found in the sacred Black Hills, thirty miles west of the Pine Ridge Reservation. Uranium was discovered in the Black Hills in 1951 and since then some three and one half million tons of radioactive tailings have been produced from mining and milling there. In 1962, Edgemonts Mill (in the southern tip of the Black Hills) spilled 200 tons of tailings that washed downstream to the Angostura reservoir. Nothing was ever done about it.[99]

The North Central Power Study and the U.S. Geological Survey indicated to the traditional people at Pine Ridge that a new movement by big business had emerged. The corporation, once again, was in the process of encroaching upon Lakota land guaranteed these people over one hundred years ago in the 1868 Fort Laramie Treaty. Moreover, new dangers, in addition to the loss of land, were invading their lives and culture. A grassroots movement emerged, organizing to struggle for their very survival, resisting the "final acts of genocide." This movement, as we have seen, has been countered by a repressive administration headed by Dick Wilson and reinforced by a vigilante police force, and dedicated to corporate expansion and the destruction of traditional Indian values. Moreover, the Federal Bureau of Investigation supported Wilson and helped through its actions to disrupt and disorganize the growing grassroots movement.

The day the firefight occurred at the Jumping Bulls, Dick Wilson was in Washington D.C. negotiating with the Bureau of Indian Affairs (who had requested from the Geological Survey one year ago information concerning non-petroleum resources on the reservation) and Department of the Interior, about possibly "giving away" certain sections of the Lakota people's traditional homeland, part of the Pine Ridge Reservation. However, such a land giveaway could not occur with a massive challenge from the growing grassroots movement. Leonard Peltier was indicted and jailed for killing two agents during the firefight, and AIM and the traditional people had to divert their attention immediately from treaty rights to preparing an adequate defense. The FBI subsequently engaged in criminal acts to guarantee the conviction of Peltier. Consequently, the FBI and judicial apparatus effectively disrupted the growing grassroots movement *long enough* to allow the alienation of part of the traditional people's homeland. On 2 January 1976, just a little over six months after the firefight, then Tribal Chairman Dick Wilson felt safe enough to officially sign over one-eighth of the reservation land, the Sheep Mountain Gunnery range, to the Badlands National Monument.[100] In this area on the northwest corner of the reservation the U.S. Geological Survey had found quantities of uranium, gas, oil and gravel.[101]

However, once again, I reiterate that as far as evidence indicates, this disruption was not a conspiracy between the government and Dick Wilson. It just so happens that the goals of the Justice Department coincided with the needs of Wilson. Consequently, both Wilson and the government benefited from the death of the two FBI agents.

Approximately two and a half years after the firefight, while Peltier was in Marion Federal Penitentiary, a new study emerged, prepared once again by the Department of Interior. This study reaffirmed both the hopes of the NCPS and the fears concerning American Indian survival of the grassroots movement that AIM and the traditional people at Pine Ridge had begun. This study, *Water for Energy,* made public in 1977, concluded that there would be—if the proposals of the NCPS were followed through—devastating effects upon the ecosystem of the Great Plains *and* the American Indian societies residing there.[102] The study confirmed that such energy development would practically destroy the environment by creating "unavoidable adverse effects" on land, water resources, air quality, and the biological community and soils. Let's look closer at each of these.

The development and operation of the proposed coal mines would, according to the study, "disturb about 188,000 acres" in the next twenty years, with approximately 23,000 additional acres being disturbed each year. Thousands of acres "would be disturbed by development of coal preparation facilities, conversion and processing plants, transportation routes, pipelines, towns, reservoirs and transmission lines." The remaining acreage would be used as sites for industrial facilities. Furthermore, the influx of people to construct, operate and manage the mines and their accessories would considerably shrink the open space and change the rural lifestyle for those currently residing in the areas.[103]

Regarding water resources of the Great Plains, the study noted there would be, if the proposals were carried out, "unavoidable adverse effects on surface and ground water quality." Moreover,

> Ground water flows can be temporarily and/or permanently interrupted by mining, diminishing aquifer recharge and causing depressed water levels in wells and springs near the mining operation . . . water levels may recover, however, this process could take up to 10 years. During this period, municipal, domestic and livestock water supply needs would be unavoidably and adversely affected as there are seldom alternative sources of water available to users.[104]

Air quality, according to the study, will be degraded by such things as: 1) engine emissions and dust from new roads produced, 2) drilling sites and pit construction, 3) movement of surface vehicles, 4) "accidental" coal fires which "add toxic vapors and particles to the atmosphere" and finally, 5) the power plants, "despite pollution control equipment," will provide "the largest quantity pollutants which impact air quality."[105]

The biological community would be significantly affected. Vegetation would be lost for facility sites, roads, etc. Strip-mined land would result in "significant loss of native vegetation and wildlife habitat." Pollution would damage vegetation and would subsequently be "concentrated through the food chain to top carnivores" (bears, weasels, birds, etc). Consider still, the following:

> Populations of some wildlife species (pronghorn antelope, sage grouse, etc.) in the areas used for mining, industrial and support facilities would be permanently reduced because of the loss of suitable habitat. Competition for limited habitats would temporarily increase mortality rates of certain species.[106]

Moreover, the loss of grazing and cropland, combined with pollutants, would result in "livestock losses and reduce farm productivity" as well as lower overall vegetative productivity. And "concentrations of lead, mercury, and fluoride as by-products of coal burning" would fall on plants eaten by animals.[107]

In short, the study concluded that mining and power plant activity would "destroy vegetation, disturb soil, degrade water supply and pollute the air," and reclamation efforts "would be hampered by the severe climate, limited rainfall, short growing season, availability of suitable plant species, and the nature of surface materials" in the Great Plains.[108]

Members of AIM and the traditionals at Pine Ridge were correct when they attempted to stop this planned ecological disaster. The Department of the Interior, in its own study, demonstrated what Peltier and the traditional people were struggling against. As Peltier stated to Judge Benson prior to being sentenced,

> But the most important of all is to respect and preserve the Earth, who we consider to be our mother. We feed from her breast; our mother gives us life from birth and when its time to leave this world, she again takes us back into her womb. But the main thing we are taught is to preserve her for our children and our grandchildren, because they are the next who will live upon her.

Yet the *Water for Energy* study did not stop at ecological devastation. It also made clear what the next chapter in the genocidal campaign against American Indians in this country is to be. The report pointed out that energy development in the Great Plains would result in the indigenous people losing their "special relationship with land" because energy development will require a "shift from agricultural to mining/light industry/trade service economy." More to the point, "land use activity will begin to shift from agricultural to mineral extractive use." This will, as a result, end Indian "isolation" and contribute by bringing American Indians into the "mainstream of American life." In short, energy development will bring American Indians into a "closer relationship with American society" and cause the "disappearance or loss of tribal cultural heritage/values."[109] Hence, what the state is in fact advocating is the destruction of the relationship of land and its people—the very basis of a people's existence—and the final act of genocide.

Big oil and other energy corporations have wasted no time in moving in to exploit this situation. By June 1978, 700,000 acres of land in the state of South Dakota (the six westernmost counties) had been leased to big oil for energy resource exploration and mining.[110] Today at least twenty-five energy companies—most of them large— have made claims or received exploration permits on about two million acres for resources around the Black Hills and Pine Ridge.[111] The

Tennessee Valley Authority alone wants to construct seventeen nuclear power plants and to fuel them. TVA will build a processing mill and exploit 110,000 acres of leases in the Black Hills, the sacred *Paha Sapa* where Custer had performed a similar act over one hundred years ago. One of the mines planned in the Southern Hills by TVA will pump water from underground aquifers at a rate of some 675 gallons per minute for ten years. Six more TVA mines have received permission to go ahead, and ten others are now planned by other companies.[112]

Moreover, two coal slurry pipelines are planned to run south from the western edge of the Black Hills. The first, undertaken by Energy Transportation Systems, Inc., will mix coal and water, pumping the mixture from Gillette, Wyoming, to Arkansas, in the process using over 20 thousand acre feet of water a year. Water specialists indicate such a plan would affect a large area of South Dakota.[113]

By March of 1979, nine coal mines were either working or being built near Gillette, Wyoming. Six more are planned to be in operation before 1990, along with the power plants themselves.[114] All the residents of Pine Ridge have to look forward to now is pollution, loss of water, an overall damaged environment and dangerous power lines. Indeed, in October of 1980, it was found that water sources in the Black Hills region contained high levels of radiation. These water sources included wells on the Pine Ridge Reservation, towns near Midland, S.D., rivers near Edgemont, S.D., as well as the Rapid Valley areas of Rapid City, S.D.[115]

Overall, the entire Lakota Nation, land guaranteed the Lakota under the 1868 treaty, is being encroached upon by big business, which brings with it ecological and cultural devastation. Figure 3 (page 162) summarizes the plight of the Northern Great Plains tribes.

The movement of the energy corporations is of course not limited to the Black Hills, Pine Ridge, and the Northern Great Plains. Practically every reservation in the Rocky Mountain States and the Four Corners area (Colorado, Utah, Arizona and New Mexico) have energy and waste projects existing, proposed, or under construction on or near Indian land. This includes such things as uranium mines and mills, coal fired power plants, coal strip mines, coal slurry pipelines, coal gasification, oil shale facilities, nuclear waste facilities, nuclear power plants, nuclear power plant parks with 9 or more reactors, and many other disasters.[116] As a result, American Indians on many of these reservations are gearing up for survival and organizing to resist the "final acts of genocide." The battlelines are being drawn for the continuing Indian wars, the energy wars.

However, the American Indian people are not struggling just for their own survival. They are also leading the way for everyone. The depletion of the earth's nonrenewable and renewable resources is reaching crisis proportions. Both the earth's and human survival are at stake this time around, not simply the indigenous people and their land. The redirection of U.S. national energy policies to exploit non-petroleum energy resources under this program will have devastating effects on human existence, unless all join in the struggle.

On 4 April 1981, the Dakota American Indian Movement and its supporters began the process of resettlement in the Black Hills. Dakota-AIM claimed 800 acres of National Forest Service Land, approximately 12 miles southwest of Rapid City. This move by the Lakota people is legal under the 1868 Fort Laramie Treaty, the 1978 Indian Freedom of Religion Act and an 1897 federal law allowing schools and churches to be built in national forests. They plan to build a community, including homes and a church and school, so that their children can learn the traditional cultural and spiritual ways of the Lakota People.[117]

In June 1980, the U.S. Supreme Court ruled on the 1868 Treaty, concluding that the Black Hills region was taken from the Dakota Nation illegally by an 1877 Act of Congress. In the decision, the Court said that the 1877 Act "ignored the stipulation of the Fort Laramie Treaty that any cession of the lands . . . would have to be joined in by three fourths of the adult males." The Lakota people were awarded $105 million, but many have rejected the payment and have asked for an injunction to stop the federal government from paying. They want the land, since it is an ancient spiritual area. As we have seen, their holy land is being destroyed by big oil and other corporations. So it is understandable that they want control returned to them.

The court system has been exhausted and monetary compensation is inadequate. The U.S. government should restore control of these sacred lands to the Lakota people. As the Lakota exclaim, THE BLACK HILLS ARE NOT FOR SALE!

AFTERWARD

As this book is reprinted in 1989, a number of new developments have occurred. As noted earlier, Peltier's attorneys filed a writ of habeas corpus, asking for a new trial for Leonard Peltier. In addition to that, Peltier's attorneys on 3 December 1982 filed a motion of disqualification, asking Judge Paul Benson to remove himself from the case, as well as asking him to sign a subpoena ordering the release of the remaining 6,000 documents. On 30 December 1982, Benson refused both to take himself off the case as well as order the release of the "national security" documents the FBI refuses to give up. The following day, 31 December 1982, he denied Peltier a new trial.

This move on the part of Judge Paul Benson raises important questions once we consider the contents of the motions filed by Peltier's attorneys. We have already discussed somewhat in depth the contents of the writ of habeas corpus. But why did the attorneys ask Benson to remove himself from the case?

FBI documents indicate clearly that the FBI insisted on having a particular Judge, Andrew Bogue, for the grand jury proceedings in the reservation murder case. Moreover, documents also show that the FBI attempted improperly to influence Benson.

Judge Bogue eventually handled the grand jury proceedings, and, as revealed below, acted like a member of the prosecution team. On 17 July 1975 the Assistant Special Agent-in-Charge of the Rapid City office of the FBI informed the Bureau that "the USA [United States Attorney] and the USDJ [United States District Judge] are very sincere in attempting to proceed" with the reservation murders grand jury. In a memorandum dated 20 August 1975, the FBI stated that the "government does not want to have a grand jury sitting in the RESMURS [reservation murders] case unless USDJ Bogue is present." On 16 October 1975 an "urgent" Rapid City FBI teletype informed FBI headquarters that the "prosecution staff and USDC Judge Andrew W. Bogue for the Western District of South Dakota have requested that SAC, Chicago be available for consultation, case preparation and testimony if needed." Nine days later, on 26 October 1975, the FBI headquarters was once again informed by Rapid City of a visit to South Dakota by Special Prosecutor Robert L. Sikma. In that visit "Sikma advised that USDJ Bogue will consider calling the FGJ [Federal Grand Jury] to sit in Rapid City providing Sikma furnishes him with a 'game plan' that would insure there would not be any problems with people either refusing to answer subpoenas or refusing to testify once they were before the FGJ."

On 29 January 1976, Richard Held, Special-Agent-in-Charge, Chicago, informed FBI headquarters that "U.S. District Court Judge Andrew Bogue also wanted to see him when he was in Rapid City" to attend "a conference concerning this case" with Special Prosecutor Sikma. All of this clearly indicates possible collusion with the FBI and prosecution on the part of Judge Bogue.

Judge Bogue would not, however, allow himself to be considered for the trial judge in the case because he owned land in an area claimed by Indian people.[1]

As such, the trial of Leonard Peltier was assigned, as we have seen, to Judge Paul Benson instead of Judge Edward McManus, who had presided over the trial of Dino Butler and Bob Robideau. The FBI was not happy with the performance of McManus. In fact, the FBI concluded that the acquittal of Butler and Robideau was partly the fault of the Judge. As shown in the chart on pages 40-41, the FBI was dissatisfied with Judge McManus' decisions. For example, the Judge, according the FBI study, "forced the government to furnish the defense with all FD-302's prepared by special agents who testified for the prosecution," and the Judge allowed "freedom of questioning of witnesses." Most unfavorable of all, according to the Bureau, was the fact that McManus allowed the defense to introduce "testimony concerning past activities of the FBI." A close examination of the chart on pages 40-41 reveals that during Peltier's trial, Judge Benson ruled in favor of the FBI in almost every case.

Not satisfied with obtaining a Judge that would rule in their favor, the prosecution team planned to provide Judge Benson with information the FBI had on groups that were supporting Native Americans and Leonard Peltier. For example, on 26 January 1977, FBI headquarters was informed by Rapid City that "letter and news release delivered to SAC OTTO by Minnesota Citizens' Review Commission on January 25, 1977, and has been furnished to Special Prosecutor Evan Hultman this date. Special Prosecutor Hultman plans to make this material available to U.S. District Judge Paul Benson who is handling upcoming Peltier trial at Fargo, North Dakota." This material probably would not be allowed into evidence in court and could have, in a number of ways, prejudiced Benson against Peltier.

Most important of all, FBI documents indicate that Special Prosecutor Evan Hultman warned Benson that certain offices of the Old Federal Building in Fargo, as well as his courtroom and chambers, may have been bugged by the defense. As a result, on 6 April 1977, an

FBI memorandum indicates that a "technical security survey" of certain government offices on the second floor of the Old Federal Building had "been approved by U.S. Attorney, Evan Hultman, Special RESMURS Prosecutor, and USDJ Paul Benson...." Moreover, this clearly inflammatory warning aroused such a strong emotion in Judge Benson that he personally requested an electronic sweep⁻ of his courtroom and chambers. According to the above 6 April 1977 FBI document, Judge Benson "sent a personal message to SA [name deleted]. USDJ Benson instructed the FBI to also conduct a technical security survey in the courtroom and judge's chambers on the third floor of the Old Federal Building on the night of 4/7/77. Supervisor [name deleted] advised Judge Benson that the FBI would comply with his instruction."

All of these new developments lead to some interesting unanswered questions. Why was the Peltier trial handled by Judge Benson and not Judge McManus? According to the disqualification motion:

> Based on a telephonic conversation with Chief Judge McManus, on December 2, 1982, counsel can state that he did not recuse [disqualify] himself as trial judge in defendant's case and was prepared to try him after his extradition from Canada. He did not know how the assignment of Judge Benson had been made.

Further, there was no record of a formal motion having been made by federal prosecutors stating the reasons for Peltier's trial to have been removed from Judge McManus. This raised obvious concerns as to exactly who had brought the disastrous change of venue about. Did the Eighth Circuit Court of Appeals control the transfer? If so, at whose request? (It must be remembered that, at the time the case was shifted from McManus to Benson, William Webster was sitting as a judge on the Eighth Circuit, and that Webster oversaw the handling of Peltier's first appeal before going on to be director of the FBI and, more recently, of the CIA.)

Benson's clear stonewall in refusing to recuse himself, to order the release of further RESMURS documents, or to allow a new trial left Peltier's attorneys no alternative but to go back before the Court of Appeals. In April 1984, despite the welter of substantive issues raised by William Kunstler in oral arguments, the Eighth Circuit ordered Benson to conduct an evidentiary hearing, but only on very narrow ballistics matters. This concerned an FBI teletype dated 2 October 1975—among the 12,000 pages of FOIA documents already recovered by Peltier's defense team—which indicates the rifle (a Wichita AR-15) allegedly carried by Peltier on the day of the firefight "contained a different firing pin" than the weapon which killed the agents.

Kunstler argued that this fundamentally undercut the entire federal case presented at Fargo.

During the hearing, reluctantly scheduled by Benson toward the end of October 1984, Kunstler held that the teletype pertained to all AR-15 cartridges found after the firefight. However, Evan Hodge, head of the FBI's ballistics laboratory, testified that the information pertained only to a cluster of seven cartridge casings found in front of the Jumping Bull residences, not those found close to the agents' cars. Asked how this might be, Hodge contended that he had done his ballistics work on the RESMURS case by starting with those "ammunition components" found *furthest* from the agents' bodies and, over time, worked his way in to those cartridge casings found closest to the bodies. In his version of events, the critical evidence against Peltier had yet to be tested at the time the teletype was sent.

When it was pointed out that his alleged procedure of starting with the most remote ammunition components and working his way in to the most proximate represented a complete reversal of standard FBI practice, especially in a case in which on-site Bureau investigators were sending urgent requests on a daily basis calling for examination of ballistics evidence *closest* to the bodies, Hodge groped for a response. The reason for his "anomalous" performance, he said, was because he had "a large volume of work to do" at the time, was "out of town" a lot during the crucial period, and because— due to its "extreme importance"—he handled the RESMURS ballistics work himself.

The last portion of his thin and rather convoluted explanation collapsed almost immediately when Peltier attorneys pointed out that more than only Hodge's handwriting appeared on his lab notes. With that, he altered his testimony to reflect the "fact" that RESMURS ballistics work had been done by himself and *one* lab assistant, Joseph Twardowski. Only he and this single assistant had prepared and made written notations on the ballistics lab notes, Hodge claimed. Upon further review of the documents, the Peltier team moved that the material be submitted for analysis to an independent hand-writing expert insofar as other penmanship seemed to be evidenced, especially on a key worksheet concerning extractor marks on the cartridge casing the prosecution had described as "the most important single piece of evidence" at Peltier's trial. Atypically, despite vociferous federal objections that "this is just another one of their absurdities. They keep grasping at absurdities to keep this case open," Judge Benson granted the motion for handwriting analysis of the FBI's lab notes. He then recessed court for the day.

Approximately one hour after court was adjourned, U.S. Marshals summoned the Peltier team back to the courtroom, where the judge and the prosecution were already assembled. The occasion was that ballistics expert Hodge wished to go back on the stand to admit he'd "mis-spoken." The handwritten notes of a third party *did* appear on the critical worksheet and other documents, Hodge now acknowledged, but he "really had no idea" whose. Hence, not only did the FBI not have a clear evidentiary chain (as is shown on pages 87-93 of this book) concerning who actually found the .223 cartridge casing used to convict Peltier, when it was found, or who controlled it after it supposedly turned up in the trunk of Coler's car, it could no longer claim to show a clear chain of possession within the Bureau's ballistics lab itself. The possibility that the crucial cartridge casing might have been confused with a casing found elsewhere, or that it simply could have been planted at virtually any point along the trail of the FBI's investigation had become plain enough for anyone to see.

Still, Judge Benson could find "no grounds" to order a new trial. This put the matter back before the Eighth Circuit Court. Realizing that its Fargo case had been virtually destroyed by Hodge's eleventh hour admissions, the government now dropped all pretense that it had ever fairly proved Leonard Peltier had killed anyone. "We can't prove who shot those agents," said prosecutor Lynn Crooks, in stark contrast to his summation to the jury at trial.[71] Peltier was nonetheless rightly imprisoned, Crooks continued, because he had been "proven" to have "aided and abetted the murders of the agents." Such contortions generated a marked confusion among the appeals judges, and led to the following exchange between Crooks and Judge Gerald W. Heaney:

Q: Aiding and abetting Robideau and Butler?

A: Aiding and abetting whoever did the final killing. Perhaps aiding and abetting himself. And hopefully the jury would believe that in effect he did it all. But aiding and abetting, nevertheless.[72]

Scratching their heads at this strange turn of events, Heaney, along with judges Donald Ross and John Gibson retired to deliberate on what to do next. In this, they took an inordinately long time. Their problem rested on the fact, as they eventually indicated in the decision they released on 11 September 1986, that Crook's aiding and abetting argument held no merit at all. The prosecutor had, at trial and during the first appeal, vehemently and repeatedly gone on record as contending that Peltier was the principle—the "lone gunman," as it were—in two first degree murders. Accordingly, the jury had convicted Peltier as the murderer, *not* of having aided and abetted murder. Similarly, Peltier's first appeal had been decided on the basis of his guilt as a murderer, not as an "aider and abetter." As Heaney put it:

> ...It seems to me that this would have been an entirely different case, both in terms of the manner in which it was presented to the jury and the sentence the judge imposed, if the only evidence you had was that Leonard Peltier was participating on the periphery of the fire fight and the agents got killed. Now that would have been an entirely different case.[73]

But, without "aiding and abetting," the government had nothing at all. The judges had no real option but to observe that the original federal case presented against Peltier—that he was guilty because the agents had been killed by an AR-15, only one of which weapons was used by AIM during the firefight, and Peltier could be shown to have used it—no longer existed. Instead of one AR-15 having been used by AIM, the court acknowledged the evidence now indicated there had been "several" (what the court did not go into was the fact that documents had long since revealed the FBI was aware of this well before Peltier's trial). Given this, there was really no way of linking Peltier with any specific AR-15, even if the Bureau's by now rather dubious evidence establishing the Wichita rifle as the "murder weapon" was correct. In other words, there was no longer a reasonable basis to consider Leonard Peltier guilty of anything, at least insofar as the material presented by the government to date was concerned. On the face of it, a retrial was clearly called for.[74]

In order to reach any other conclusion, Judges Heaney, Ross and Gibson had to abandon objective considerations altogether, in favor of the purely subjective. This came in the form of their assessment, offered at the end of their opinion, of the likely effects all this additional evidence might have had upon the jury at the original trial. Overall, they "reasoned," such information might "possibly" have led the jury to reach a different verdict. They then held that, in order for a retrial to be warranted, it was necessary that the jury would "probably" have led to a different verdict. No attempt was made to explain how the determination was reached that the absence of *any* real evidence against Peltier—or even the contrived *appearance* of evidence, such as that which was actually used—would "possibly" rather than "probably" have caused the jury to have arrived at different conclusions. Similarly, no effort was made to explain how the judges had decided that probability rather than possibility of acquittal was necessary to warrant retrial insofar as the Ninth Circuit Court of Appeals had already rendered an opinion in another case, stating that a clear possibility was all that was required. In any event, Heaney, Gibson and Ross used the possibility/probability rationale to decline to order a retrial, and allowed Peltier's conviction to stand despite their open admission that there was no concrete evidence with which to support it. A hint as to the judge's motivation in reaching this novel conclusion may be found in a single, almost tangential, sentence of their opinion:

> *We recognize that there is evidence in this record of improper conduct by some FBI agents, but we are reluctant to impute even further improprieties to them* [emphasis added].[75]

Thus, rather than come to grips with the real issues raised by the Peltier case, the judges were willing to leave Leonard Peltier entombed in a maximum security prison cell for double his natural life. The Peltier team immediately protested this outcome, filing a motion for the entire Eighth Circuit Court to review the decision of the three-judge panel which rendered it. Several months later, the court denied this petition on the grounds that it would "demean the dignity" of Ross, Gibson and Heaney. This left an appeal to the Supreme Court as the only avenue of legal recourse open to Peltier. His attorneys filed the necessary paperwork, requesting that the high court decide once and for all whether a retrial need be predicated on a "probability" of acquittal, as the Eighth Circuit insisted, or only on the "possibility," as the Ninth Circuit had already found. On 8 October 1987, the Supreme Court repeated its performance from Peltier's first appeal, refusing to so much as consider the issue. Without bothering to explain its denial of the defendant's right to be heard, the high court simply left him at a dead end of due process, and with the dual standard of justice implied by the possibility/probability matter unresolved and confronting all U.S. citizens.[76]

Meanwhile, in Canada, other processes were at work. Reviewing the Poor Bear affidavits and other items entered before the Canadian courts, Member of Parliament Jim Fulton concluded that:

> [The nature of Peltier's extradition from Canada by the United States] constitutes treaty fraud between our nations and should we sleep on this case there will surely be a repetition in the future...As a nation we should call for the return of Leonard Peltier. He has been fraudulently extradited...[77]

By late 1986, 51 additional members of the Canadian parliament had formally endorsed Fulton's view, a situation which set in motion a lengthy judicial procedure in Canada. As of March 1989, the question is scheduled to go before the Canadian Supreme Court within 30 days. If Canada's high court determines that the United States indeed perpetrated fraud in presenting the evidence leading to Peltier's extradition—as the record indicates they almost have to—Canadian law requires that Canada must formally demand the United States return him to Canadian jurisdiction. A U.S. refusal to comply would constitute a patent treaty violation, could serve to invalidate the extradition agreement between the two countries, and would automatically open the door to UN and/or World Court intervention.

As all this was going on, Spain bestowed upon Peltier its 1986 Human Rights Award on the basis of his service to humanity in "defending the historical and cultural rights of his people against the genocide of his race."[78] By mid-1988, more than 14 million people from around the world had also lent their signatures to demands, filed in Washington, D.C., that the federal government provide Peltier with a new trial.

As Ward Churchill and Jim Vander Wall have observed,

> Meanwhile, the simple fact that Leonard Peltier remains in prison, even after a truly vicious pattern of federal misconduct has been repeatedly demonstrated (and acknowledged by the courts), offers ample testimony to the ongoing power of the FBI to abort the judicial process...They have made of this man a symbol neither he nor they ever intended; the freedom of Leonard Peltier has in many ways become the test of whether the people or the police are ascendant in America.[79]

To this I can add only that one must hope that freedom comes to Peltier, answering the test conclusively in an affirmation of the people rather than the police. It is long past time for this to have occurred.

FOOTNOTES

183

Chapter 1—Introduction

1. Weyler, Rex, "The Story of Leonard Peltier and a Culture Under Siege," *New Age* (December 1980), p. 33.

2. Johansen, Bruce and Robert Maestas, *Wasi'chu: The Continuing Indian Wars* (New York: Monthly Review Press, 1979), p. 79.

3. Hinds, Lennox, *Illusions of Justice: Human Rights Violations in the United States* (University of Iowa, Iowa City, 1978), pp. 270-271.

4. *Ibid.*

5. Tilsen, Ken, "There are Thousands of Political Prisoners in the United States," *Akwasasne Notes* (Summer 1978), p. 18.

6. "Run-off scheduled in Indian Election," *New York Times*, 24 January 1974, p. 25.

7. U.S. Commission on Civil Rights, *Report of Investigation: Oglala Sioux Tribe, General Election* (Washington, D.C.: U.S. Commission on Civil Rights, 1974), p. 1

8. *Ibid.*, pp. 25-27.

9. Johansen and Maestas, *op. cit.*, p. 81

10. See Chapter Four for an elaboration of this issue.

11. Trimble, Al, "Land Use Patterns on the Pine Ridge Reservaton," (Pine Ridge, SD: Bureau of Indian Affairs, 1974), p. 8.

12. *Ibid.*

13. Johansen and Maestas, *op. cit.*, p. 81.

14. See Chapter Five.

15. Vogel, Virgil, *This Country Was Ours* (New York: Harper & Row, 1974) p. 255.

16. U.S. Congress, Joint Economic Committee, *Toward Economic Development for Native American Communities* (Washington, D.C.: U.S. Government Printing Office, 1969), pp. 357-358.

According to *A Statistical Portrait of the American Indian* (DHEW, 1976), which is the last comprehensive *governmental* breakout of data for this population sector, Indians suffer all the classic symptoms of Third World oppression. They lead, far and away, all U.S. population groups in incidence of typhoid, dysentary, diphtheria, infant mortality, malnutrition, death by exposure, smallpox, and cholera. They demonstrate, by far, the highest rates of unemployment and lowest median incomes. Among those who are employed, they exhibit the lowest rate of managerial and professional attainment, as well as an extreme turnover rate. Alcoholism and other forms of substance abuse are endemic. Educational attainment is lowest and drop-out rates highest among all groups nationally at every grade level. Life expectancy is shortest among all U.S. population groups and, indeed, shorter than any other known within the "developed" world. Yet, in theory at least, American Indians possess one of the largest per capita land/resource holdings of any group in the world. Clearly, their tangible wealth—and the potential for alleviating such massive misery—is being syphoned off and utilized for purposes other than underwriting their welfare.

17. "Growing Fight Against Sterilization of Native Women," *Akwesasne Notes* (Late Winter, 1979), p. 29.

18. *Ibid.*

19. Hinds, *op. cit.*, pp. 271-272.

20. Johansen and Maestas, *op. cit.*, p. 80.

21. *Ibid.*, p. 83.

22. *Ibid.*

The following is a partial list of AIM supporters and members murdered at the reservation. The name of each victim is followed by the murder date, a Yes or No according to whether the law enforcement apparatuses have solved the crime and the current legal status of the investigation. Names of individuals marked with an * are, according to the International Indian Treaty Council, known to have been murdered by either the FBI or BIA police.

Frank Clearwater,* 4-27-73, No, No Investigation
Buddy Lamont,* 4-27-73, No, No Investigation
Julius Bad Heart Bull, 7-30-73, Yes, One Man Convicted
Clarence Cross,* 6-73, No, No Investigation
Donald He Crow, 8-27-73, No, No Investigation
Aloysins Long Soldier, 10-5-73, No, No Investigation
Pedro Bisonette,* 10-17-73, No, No Investigation
Philip Little Crow, 11-14-73, No, No Investigation
Allison Little Spotted Horse, 11-23-73, No, No Investigation
Melvin Spider, 9-22-73, No, No Investigation
Verlyn Dale Bad Heart Bull, 2-18-74, No, No Investigation
Edward Standing Soldier, 2-18-74, No, No Investigation
Dennis Le Comple, 9-7-74, Yes, Not Guilty
Jesse Trueblood, 11-17-74, No, No Investigation
Elaine Wagner, 11-30-74, No, No Investigation
Robert Reddy, 9-16-74, No, Under Investigation
William J. Steele, 3-9-75, Yes, One Man Convicted
Stacey Kotier, 3-25-75, Yes, No Man Convicted
Edith Eagle Hawk, 3-21-75, No, No Investigation
Linda Eagle Hawk, 3-21-75, No, No Investigation
Earl W. Janis, Jr., 3-21-75, No, No Investigation
Jeannette M. Bisonette, 3-25-75, No, No Investigation
Roxwood Buffalo, 3-75, No, No Investigation
Joseph Stuntz Kills Right,* 6-25-75, No, No Investigation
Homer Blue Bird, 9-9-75, Yes, One Man Convicted
James Little, 9-10-75, Yes, Three Men Convicted
Janice Black Bear, 10-26-75, Yes, One Man Convicted
Lydia Cut Grass, 1-5-76, Yes, Case Closed, No Conviction

Byron De Sersa, 1-31-76, Yes, One Man Charged, No Conviction
Cleveland Reddest, 3-26-76, No, Case Closed, No Conviction
Anna Mae Aquash, 2-76, No, Open Investigation
Martin Two Two, 5-6-76, No, Under Investigation
Lyle Dean Richards, 7-31-73, No, No Investigation

International Indian Treaty Council, *Violations of American Indian Human Rights by the United States,* reprinted in part in Hinds, *op. cit.,* pp. 287-289.

24. Hinds, *op. cit.,* p. 289.

25. Johansen and Maestas, *op. cit.,* p. 83.

    The murder rate on the reservation is quite close to that in Chile in the early days of Pinochet.

26. Treaty Council Report, *op. cit.,* p. 283.

    The goon squad raid on the Little Bear house in the Fall of 1973 is a case in point. Seven-year-old Mary Ann lost her right eye to an M-16 round. In another raid in 1976 near Porcupine, the goon squad pinned down Charlie Abouresk, son of Senator James Abouresk, for over an hour by armed gunfire.

27. Trial transcript of the proceedings in the case of *United States of America vs. Leonard Peltier,* p. 3894.

28. Johansen and Maestas, *op. cit.,* p. 88.

    Although the FBI "lacked manpower" to investigate major crimes on the Pine Ridge Reservation, during this same period of time they managed to amass some 316,000 separate file classifications *against AIM members* resultant to Wounded Knee.

    By the end of May 1975, the FBI had sixty agents on or near the reservation, including a ten-man SWAT team deployed near Pine Ridge Village.

29. Trial transcript, *op. cit.,* pp. 3584, 3589.

30. *Ibid.,* p. 3813.

31. *Ibid.,* pp. 3804-5.

32. *Ibid.,* p. 3819.

33. *Ibid.,* pp. 1584, 3510, 3969.

34. By "the state" I am referring to the physical and ideological coercive apparatus of society which includes executive and legislative bodies, the military, and most important for our purposes here, the criminal justice system of laws, police, courts, and prison.

Chapter 2—The FBI

1. Belknap, Michael R., "The Mechanics of Repression: J. Edgar Hoover, The Bureau of Investigation and the Radicals, 1917-1925," *Crime and Social Justice* (Spring/Summer, 1972), p. 49.

2. Zinn, Howard, *A Peoples History of the United States* (New York: Harper and Row, 1980), p. 364.

3. Belknap, *op. cit.,* p. 49.

4. Murray, Robert K., *Red Scare: A Study in National Hysteria, 1919-1920*, (New York: McGraw Hill, 1969), p. 193.

5. National Lawyers Guild, *Counterintelligence: A Documentary Look at America's Secret Police*, Vol. I (Chicago: National Lawyers Guild, 1980), p. 1.

6. Cohen, Stanley, *A. Mitchell Palmer: Politician* (New York: Columbia University Press, 1963), p. 207.

7. Preston, William, Jr., *Aliens and Dissenters: Federal Suppression of Radicals, 1903-1933* (Cambridge, MA: Harvard University Press, 1963), p. 221.

8. National Lawyers Guild, *op. cit.*, p. 1.

9. Zinn, *op. cit.*, p. 367.

10. *Ibid.*

11. Belknap, *op. cit.*, pp. 51-52.

12. *Ibid.*, p. 52.

13. *Ibid.*

14. *Ibid.*, pp. 53-55.

15. Zinn, *op. cit.*, pp. 368-376.

16. Belknap, *op. cit.*, p. 56.

17. Zinn, *op. cit.*, pp. 378-397.

18. Whitehead, Don, *The FBI Story: A Report to the People* (New York: Random House, 1956), pp. 159-60.

19. Select Committee to Study Governmental Operations, *Intelligence Activities and the Rights of Americans*, Book II (Washington, D.C.: U.S. Government Printing Office, 1976), p. 30.

20. *Ibid.*, p. 32.

21. *Ibid.*, pp. 36-38.

22. *Ibid.*, p. 48.

23. *Ibid.*, p. 49.

24. *Ibid.*

25. National Lawyers Guild, *op. cit.*, pp. 4-5.

26. *Ibid.*, pp. 1, 6-7.

27. *Ibid.*, pp. 9-10.

28. *Ibid.*, pp. 47, 60, 62.

29. Quoted in *ibid.*, p. 66.

30. *Ibid.*, p. 67.

31. Kunstler, William, "FBI Letters: Writers of the Purple Rage," *Nation*, 30 December 1978, p. 721.

32. Select Committee, *op. cit.*, p. 87.

33. *Ibid.*, p. 88.

34. National Lawyers Guild, *op. cit.*, p. 1.

35. Select Committee, *op. cit.*, p. 89.

36. *Ibid.*, pp. 137-284.

37. Quoted in Nicholas Horrock, "238 Break-Ins Committed by FBI Over 26 Years," *New York Times*, 11 November 1974, p. 15.

38. Editorial, *New York, Times,* 11 November 1974, p. 15.

39. "Using FBI for 'Dirty Tricks'—Behind a Hot Debate," *U.S. News and World Report*, 2 December 1974, p. 38.

40. Michaelson, Martin, "Freedom of Information: Up Against the Stone Wall," *Nation*, 21 May 1977, p. 617.

41. Jackson, Robert L., "FBI Admits It Opened Mail in Eight Cities in Illegal Program Paralleled to that of CIA," *Los Angeles Times*, 2 October 1975, p. 30.

42. Crewdson, John, "Ex-Operative Says He Worked for FBI to Disrupt Political Activities Up to 1974," *New York, Times*, 24 February 1975, p. 36.

43. "FBI Attempts to Break Strike," *Guardian*, 5 July 1978, p. 2.

44. David Helvarg, "NASSCO Spy Takes the Stand," *In These Times*, 20-26 May 1981, p. 4.

45. Crewsdon, John, "FBI is Said to Retain File of Most on Detention List," *New York Times*, 25 October 1975, p. 1.

46. Pogrebin, Letty, C., "The FBI was Watching You," *MS.*, June 1977, pp. 37-44.

47. Hearings Before a Subcommittee of the Committee on Government Operations. House of Representatives. *Access to Records* (Washington, D.C.: U.S. Government Printing Office, 1974), pp. 67-68.

48. Arnold H. Lubasch, "316 Used by FBI in Informer Role," *New York Times*, 5 September 1976, p. 24.

49. Eric Nader, "FBI Can't Keep From Spying," *In These Times*, 20-26 May 1981, p. 4.

50. "Kelly Says FBI is 'Truly Sorry' for Past Abuses," *Washington Post*, 9 May 1976, p. A1; "FBI Break-ins Still Go On, Panel Reports," *Washington Post*, 11 May 1976, pp. 84-85.

51. Select Committee, *op. cit.*, p. 18.

52. Gregory Gordon, "FBI issues guides on use of informants," *Minneapolis Tribune*, 5 December 1980, p. 4B.

53. Parenti, Michael, *Democracy for the Few* (New York: St. Martins Press, 1980), p. 152.

54. Zocchino, Narda, "Ex-FBI Informer Describes Terrorist Role," *Los Angeles Times*, 26 January 1976, p. 24.

55. "Informer Scores FBI on Violence," *New York Times*, 3 December 1975, p. 23. These actions thereby encouraged racial tension and violence, which apparently was the intended aim of such FBI activities.

56. *Ibid.*, p. 3.

57. *Ibid.*

58. Patricia MacKay, "Greensboro Jury Acquits Klan," *In These Times*, 26

November-9 December 1980, p. 7.

59. National Lawyers Guild, *op. cit.,* p. 3.

60. Parenti, *op. cit.,* p. 153 (not a quote).

61. Lichtenstein, William and David Wimhurst, "Red Alert in Puerto Rico," *Nation,* 30 June 1979, pp. 780-82.

62. Johansen, Bruce and Roberto Maestas, *Wasi'chu: The Continuing Indian Wars* (New York: Monthly Review Press, 1979), p. 93; Minnesota Citizens Review Commission on the FBI, *Hearing Board, Report II, General Hearings, 1978* (Minneapolis, MN).

63. Johansen and Maestas, *op. cit.,* p. 88.

64. For example, in the summer of 1967, almost the entire membership of the Revolutionary Action Movement was falsely arrested and jailed in Philadelphia by the FBI and the local police. In 1969, 113 members of the Black Panther Party were arrested in Chicago, resulting, however, in only a handful of convictions. See *Counterintelligence,* p. 49.

65. *Federal Supplement,* Vol. 383 (St. Paul, MN: West Publishing Co., 1975), pp. 393-4.

The charges against Russell Means mentioned in this paragraph were a few of the 40 odd charges, both state and federal, leveled against him—and for which he was tried—during this period. Of the 40, he was ultimately exonerated on 39. His single conviction stemmed from his courtroom performance during one of the clearly harassment-type trials. Hence, it seems arguable that FBI procedures are designed not only to "tie up" targets in judicial quagmires, but to generate frustration leading to outright "criminal" (convictable) conduct. In this sense, if in none other, the FBI may be said to *produce* rather than prevent and detect criminality.

66. *Ibid.,* p. 395; Rex Wyler, "The Story of Leonard Peltier and a Culture Under Siege," *New Age,* December 1980, p. 35.

67. *Federal Supplement, op. cit.,* p. 391.

68. *Ibid.,* pp. 397, 392.

69. "Wounded Knee Jurors Ask Saxbe Not to Appeal Case," *New York Times,* 26 September 1974, p. 55.

70. Kifner, John, "Security Chief for Militant Indian Group Says He was Paid Informer for FBI," *New York Times,* 25 March 1975, p. 31. Quoted in Amnesty International, *Proposal for a Commission of Inquiry Into the Effect of Domestic Intelligence Activities on Criminal Trials in the United States of America* (New York: Amnesty International Publications), pp. 50-51.

71. Subcommittee on Internal Security, U.S. Senate, *Revolutionary Activities Within the United States: The American Indian Movement* (Washington, D.C.: Government Printing Office, 1976), p. 61.

72. National Lawyers Guild, *op. cit.,* p. 31.

73. "FBI Pins Brutal Slaying on AIM," *Guardian,* 1 December 1976, p. 4.

74. Johansen and Maestas, *op. cit.,* p. 118.

75. *Ibid.,* p. 119.

76. "Skyhorse/Mohawk Acquitted," *Akwasasne Notes,* late Spring 1978, p. 22.

77. National Lawyers Guild, *op. cit.,* p. 71.

78. *Ibid.*

79. *Ibid.*

80. Minnesota Citizen's Review Commission on the FBI, *op. cit.*

81. Quoted in *ibid.*

82. Johansen and Maestas, *op. cit.,* p. 93. From a private conversation with defense attorney Ellison, it was learned that the FBI was also training a ten-member BIA SWAT team during this time period.

83. Trial Transcript of the Proceedings in the Case of *United States of America vs. Leonard Peltier,* p. 3629.

84. This warrant was for the theft of a pair of boots.

85. National Lawyers Guild, *op. cit.,* p. 72.

From FBI documents uncovered through the Freedom of Information Act, it seems that the FBI was making preparations for such an event as a firefight. For instance, FBI documents reveal that on 24 April 1975 (two months before the firefight) the FBI was very concerned with its "paramilitary operations" preparedness on Indian land. In a study (same date as above) entitled "The Use of Special Agents of the FBI in a Paramilitary Law Enforcement Operation in the Indian Country," the FBI investigated the following: (1) early history of AIM, (2) jurisdiction of the FBI to investigate within Indian country, (3) background on AIM, (4) history and background concerning the Pine Ridge Indian Reservation of the Oglala Sioux Tribe in South Dakota, (5) a prelude to the occupation of Wounded Knee, (6) the occupation of Wounded Knee by AIM and the use of FBI, U.S. Marshalls and BIA police at Wounded Knee in a paramilitary law enforcement situation.

The study concluded that the FBI response to Wounded Knee was highly inefficient. There was "complete confusion...no coordination...nor was there any advance planning done." The study recommended that if the FBI was to involve itself in a similar incident, it must "insist upon taking charge from the outset"; it is FBI policy in such situations to "get in and out as quickly as possible," to "seize control quickly and take a definite, aggressive stand where necessary."

Thus it seems, only two months prior to the firefight at Pine Ridge, the FBI was highly concerned with making their paramilitary operations work smoothly and quickly. More evidence points to this conclusion. On 5 June 1975 an FBI memorandum entitled "Law Enforcement on Pine Ridge Indian Reservation," set forth the following:

> There are pockets of Indian population which consist almost
> exclusively of American Indian Movement (AIM) members
> and their supporters on the reservation. It is significant in some
> of these AIM centers the residents have built bunkers which

would literally require military assault forces if it were necessary to overcome resistance emanating from the bunkers.

In other words, it would take a paramilitary assault to overcome resistance against the FBI by members and supporters of AIM. (It should be noted that the bunkers referred to here were in fact mounds of earth on the side of a hill.)

The Minneapolis office of the FBI did an inspection of the reservation from 27 May through 6 June 1975 and concluded that there were at least two "bunkers" in the area and that:

the Indians were prepared to use these "bunkers" as a defensive position, and it was believed they were constructed in such a fashion as to defend against a frontal assault. To successfully overcome automatic or semi-automatic fire from such "bunkers," it appeared as though heavy equipment such as an armored personnel carrier would be required.

Succinctly, these documents seem to indicate that the "pockets" of American Indians (and especially AIM members and supporters) were ready to resist a "frontal assault" approximately twenty days prior to the firefight. Moreover, they also suggest that the FBI was highly concerned with the possibility of a successful resistance. So concerned, in fact, that the FBI stated it would "literally" require a military assault force (paramilitary law enforcement operation) to overcome the resistance. Furthermore, just ten days prior to the firefight, the structure of the Rapid City FBI office began to change considerably. On 16 June 1975, it was requested that the Rapid City FBI office (which was at that time a Resident Agency) be designated a "field office" covering North and South Dakota. Six Special Agents were ordered into South Dakota for a *temporary* sixty day period of duty to *supplement* the agents assigned to the Rapid City Resident Agency. This memorandum also highlighted the fact that "pockets" of the population on the Reservation consisted "almost exclusively of American Indian Movement members." Did the FBI prepare for and then eventually engage in a paramilitary assault on the reservation on 26 June 1975?

86. Weir, David and Lowell Bergman, "The Killing of Anna Mae Aquash," *Rolling Stone*, 7 April 1977, p. 52.

87. See the following chapter for a summary of the major differences between the Cedar Rapids trial and the Fargo trial. Evidence came out at the former trial that the FBI substantially contributed to violence and fear on the reservation; therefore, the defendants were acting reasonably in self-defense.

88. Quoted in Weir and Bergman, *op. cit.*, p. 52.

89. Quoted in *ibid.*, p. 52.

90. See *ibid.* for an in-depth account of this story.

91. Quoted in Johansen, Bruce "Leonard Peltier and the Posse: Still Fighting the Indian Wars," *Nation*, 1 October 1977, p. 306.

92. Amnesty International, *op. cit.*, p. 46.

93. Quoted in Weir and Bergman, *op. cit.*, p. 55.

Chapter 3—The Trial

1. Parts of this chapter were written with the help of an unpublished manuscript by Maluca Van den Bergh and Elizabeth Merz. I am indebted to these individuals for allowing me free access to the manuscript. Information on the FBI was taken from the Writ of Habeas Corpus put together by Peltier's attorneys, Bruce Ellison and John Privatera.

2. Trial Transcript of the Proceedings in the case of *United States of America vs. Robert Robideau and Darelle Butler.*

3. A 302 is the report a Special Agent of the FBI is required to write about any event in which he participates while on duty. 302's are usually carefully detailed and written as soon as possible after the event they describe.

4. See page 72 for an explanation of the sacred pipe.

5. Transcripts in the argument before the United States Court of Appeals for the Eighth Circuit for *Leonard Peltier vs. United States of America*, p. 3—5. Cited in Minnesota Citizens' Review Commission on the FBI, *Hearing Board, Report II, General Hearings, 1978.*

6. Amnesty International, *Proposal for a Commission of Inquiry into the Effect of Domestic Intelligence Activities on Criminal Trials in the United States* (New York: Amnesty International Publications, 1981).

7. It is impossible for *anyone* to ballistically determine the origin of a bullet fragment. Of course, it's possible the fragments came from the AR—or one of the other two AR's or one of the other weapons mentioned—on this or another day. Hodge's testimony regarding this is therefore absolutely spurious.

8. None of the weapons, including several M-16s, carried and used by later arriving officers was ever denoted as having been inspected in this connection.

9. Again, this points to discrepancies in the pathologists' reports. At the very least they should have been clear what kind of weapon was used based on the nature of the agents' wounds, the characteristics of which differ according to the basic calibers at issue.

10. Tilsen, Ken, "There are Thousands of Political Prisoners in the United States," *Akwesasne Notes* (Summer 1978), p. 18.

11. *Ibid.*

12. *Ibid.*

13. In 1975, the Minnesota Review Commission on the FBI held hearings, of which some of the testimony concerned the new nominee for FBI Director, William Webster. The Commission concluded the following: "This Hearing Board concludes that William Webster has failed to curb FBI abuses, has not abided by the spirit of the Federal Civil Rights Acts, has not honored basic First Amendment Freedoms, and has allowed abuses of discretion when he was in a position to curb them." See the Commission's *Hearing Board Report II, General Hearings, 1978.*

14. Balbus, Isaac, *The Dialectics of Legal Repression* (New York: Russell Sage Foundation, 1973), Chapter 1.

15. *Ibid.*, p. 3—4.

16. Report to the House Committee on the Judiciary by the Comptroller General, *FBI Domestic Intelligence Operations—Their Purpose and Scope: Issues That Need to be Resolved* (Washington, D.C.: Comptroller General of the U.S., 1976), p. 74.

17. *Ibid.*

18. Select Committee to Study Government Operations, *Intelligence Activities and the Rights of Americans*, Book II (Washington, D.C.: U.S. Government Printing Office, 1976), p. 91.

19. Report to House Committee, *op. cit.*, p. 75.

20. National Lawyers Guild, *Counterintelligence: A Documentary Look at America's Secret Police* (Chicago: National Lawyers Guild, 1980), pp. 56-7.

21. Amnesty International, *op. cit.*, see also *ibid.*

22. *Ibid.*, p. 83.

23. *Ibid.*, pp. 83-4.

24. Jerome Skolnick, "The Police View of Protest and Protesters" in *Policing America*, by Anthony Platt and Lynn Cooper, eds. (Englewood Cliffs NJ: Prentice-Hall, 1974), p. 157.

25. *Ibid.*

26. Quicker, John C. and Janet Schmidt, "A Contribution to the Critique of Bourgeois Criminology: The Case of Criminal Sentencing," *Insurgent Sociologist*, Summer 1977, p. 67.

27. Quoted in *ibid.*

28. Balbus, *op. cit.*, Chapter 1.

29. Freidman, Leon, "Political Power and Legal Legitimacy: A Short History of Political Trials," *The Antioch Review*, 30, Summer 1970, pp. 157, 158.

30. For even more evidence of how either the police, prosecution or the court used criminal techniques in attempting convictions of political activists in other trials, see John Kifner, "Eight Acquitted in Gainesville at G.O.P. Convention Plot," *New York Times*, 1 September 1983, p. 1; "Ellsberg Case: Defendants Freed, Government Convicted," *New York Times*, 13 May 1973, p. E1; Homer Bigart, "Berrigan Case: A Strategy that Failed," *New York Times*, 9 April 1972, p. E2.

Chapter 4—An Assassination Plot

1. "Medical Record of Federal Prisoner in Transit, " for Wilson, Robert H., No. 01499-164, from M.C.C., Chicago IL to U.S.P., Marion IL, 10-29-76.

2. U.S. Penitentiary, Marion IL, "Control Unit Review," for Wilson, Robert H., No. 01499-164, 12-1-76.

3. "Clinical Record" of Wilson, Robert H., 01499-164, 4-13-77, "Medical

Record of Federal Prisoner in Transit," for Wilson, Robert H., 01499-164 from U.S.P. Marion IL to Harris County, Houston TX, 9-28-76 .

4. Sworn Affidavit of Robert Hugh Wilson, 9-4-79, pl.

5. Federal Bureau of Prisons, "Request for Administrative Remedy," Wilson, Robert Hugh, 1499-164, 3-23-78.

6. "Chronological Record of Medical Care" for Wilson, Robert H., 1499-164, 3-29-78.

7. U.S. Penitentiary, Marion IL, "Institution Discipline Committee Report" of Wilson, Robert H., 1499-164, 4-3-78.

8. U.S. Department of Justice Bureau of Prisons, "Inmate Request to Staff Member," to Dr. Plank from Wilson, Robert H., 1499-164, 4-5-78.

9. U.S. Department of Justice Bureau of Prisons, "Inmate Request to Staff Member," to Hospital Administrator Anderson, from Wilson, Robert H., 1499-164, 4-19-78.

10. Sworn Affidavits of Eddie Griffin, 29484; Dennis Giblin, affiant; Stephen M. Kessler, 01707-135.

11. Sworn Affidavit of Wilson, *op. cit.,* p. 1, paragraph 5.

12. "Chronological Record of Medical Care," for Wilson, Robert H. 1499-164, 5-12-78.

13. Clinical Record, "Authorization for Administration of Anesthesia and for Performance of Operations and Other Procedures," U.S. Penitentiary Hospital, Marion IL, 5-15-78.

14. Sworn Affidavit, *op. cit.,* p. 2.

15. Letter from Hayes, Larry D. Sheriff's office, Oklahoma County, Oklahoma City OK to Bonnie L. Streed RCS, Marion Prison, dated 5-24-78.

16. U.S. Department of Justice Bureau of Prisons, U.S. Penitentiary, Marion Il, "Comply with Request to Remove Detainer," 6-1-78.

17. U.S. Department of Justice Bureau of Prisons, "Inmate Request to Staff Member" to Dr. McMillan and Administrator Anderson, from Wilson, Robert H. 1499-164, 6-17-78.

18. Sworn Affidavit, *op. cit.,* p. 2.

19. "Membership Roster of Native American Spiritual and Cultural Society," 5-13-78 and 9-5-78.

20. Federal Bureau of Prisons, "Request for Administrative Remedy" from Wilson, Robert H., 9-28-78. Federal Bureau of Prisons, Regional Appeal "Response for Administrative Remedy Request" from Wilson, Robert H., 11-27-78. Letter to Regional Director, Bureau of Prisons from Wilson, Robert H., 10-20-78, "Minutes of regular meeting—Native American Cultural Society," 10-23-78. "Memorandum from the Chairman of the Native American Cultural Society."

21. U.S. Penitentiary Marion Illinois "Memorandum" from Bonnie Streed, Manager Records Office to CB Faulkner, Regional Legal Council, 9-15-78.

22. Sworn Affidavit, *op. cit.*, p. 2.

23. *Ibid.*, pp. 2-3.

24. "Movement Summary" for Wilson, Robert H. 1499-164, 12-21-78.

25. U.S. Department of Justice Bureau of Prisons, "Incident Report" for Robert H. Wilson, 12-25-78.

26. *Ibid.*

27. "Daily Transfer Sheet" for Leavenworth Prison, 2-8-80.

28. Sworn Affidavit, *op. cit.*, p. 3.

29. "Motions to Dismiss" seven felony counts. Filed 5 June 1975, dismissed 12 April 1979. State of Oklahoma vs. Robert H. Wilson, District Court, Oklahoma County.

30. Federal Bureau of Investigation, memorandum by SA Daniel M. Payne, Lompoc CA 7-31-79.

31. This figure is based on a communication from L. G. Grossman, Regional Director, Bureau of Prisons, 8 November 1979.

32. U.S. Department of Justice Bureau of Prisons, "Extra Good Time Recommendation" for Wilson, Robert H. 1499-164, 25 June 1979.

33. Daily Transit Sheet, U.S.P. Leavenworth, 20 July 1979.

34. See the Select Committee to Study Governmental Operations, *Intelligence Activities and the Rights of American,* Book II (Washington, D.C.: U.S. Government Printing Office, 1976), pp. 219-23.

35. *New Times,* 18 February 1977, p. 20. The mothers of Fred Hampton and Mark Clark and survivors of the raid, in June 1970, filed a civil rights action suit against city and state officials. By April of 1977, the judge overseeing the case had dismissed charges against all defendants except for seven raiders who admitted firing into the apartment. On 16 June 1977, the jury deliberated as to the raiders' liability for their actions during the raid. The defendants were acquitted, and the judge ordered the plaintiffs—the mothers of two slain men and the survivors—to pay court costs of $100,000. See *Minnesota Review Commission,* cited in note 4.

Chapter 5—Corporate Expansion & Indian Survival

1. Barnet, Richard, *The Lean Years* (New York: Simon and Schuster, 1980) pp. 21, 36.

2. "World Report," *Oil and Gas Journal,* 29 December 1975.

3. "World Report," *Oil and Gas Journal,* 27 December 1976.

4. Brown, Lester, *The Twenty-Ninth Day* (New York, W.W. Norton, 1978), pp. 104-5.

5. Barnet, *op. cit.,* p. 37.

6. Schipper, Lee, "Energy: Global Prospects 1985-2000," *Bulletin of the Atomic Scientists,* March 1978, p. 58.

7. Garitty, Michael, "The U.S. Colonial Empire is as Close as the Nearest Reservation: The Pending Energy Wars," in *Trilateralism: The Trilateral*

Commission and Elite Planning for World Management, edited by Holly Sklar (Boston: South End Press, 1980), p. 241.

8. Quoted in "World Oil Shortage is Called Inevitable," *New York Times*, 17 May 1977.

9. Sklar, Holly, "Trilateralism: Managing Dependence and Democracy—An Overview," in *Trilateralism, op. cit.*, p. 2.

10. Rowen, Hobart, "Oil Supply Adequate, Possibly to 1990s, Trilateral Commission Study Concludes," *The Washington Post*, 14 June 1978.

11. Cluster, Dick and Nancy Rutter, *Shrinking Dollars, Vanishing Jobs* (Boston: Beacon Press, 1980), pp. 89-97.

12. Barnet, *op. cit.*, pp. 30, 31.

13. *Ibid.*, p. 37.

14. Rifkin, Jeremy with Ted Howard, *The Emerging Order* (New York, G.P. Putnam Sons, 1979), p. 85.

15. Garitty, *op. cit.*, pp. 241-2.

16. *Ibid.*, p. 242.

17. *Ibid.*, p. 267, and Jorgensen, Joseph G., "A Century of Political Economic Effects on American Indian Society, 1880-1980," *Journal of Ethnic Studies*, 6, 3 (1978), p. 51. It is also estimated that American Indians control ten percent of oil and gas reserves.

18. Garitty, *op. cit.*, p. 255.

19. Jorgensen, *op. cit.*, p. 51.

20. Garitty, *op. cit.*, p. 240.

21. *Engineering and Mining Journal*, November 1978, p. 128.

22. See "Union Carbide is on Welfare," Black Hills Alliance Research Center, Rapid City, SD.

23. Washburn, Wilcomb E., *The Indian and the White Man* (Garden City: Doubleday, 1964).

24. Meyer, William, *Native Americans* (New York: International Pub., 1977), p. 27.

25. Washburn, *op. cit.*, p. 203; Meyer, *op. cit.*, p. 27.

26. Meyer, *op. cit.*, p. 30.

27. *Ibid.*, p. 31; Washburn, *op. cit.*, p. 204.

28. Meyer, *op. cit.*, p. 36.

29. Garitty, *op. cit.*, p. 262.

30. Johansen, Bruce and Roberto Maestas, *Wasi'chu: The Continuing Indian Wars* (New York: Monthly Review Press, 1979), p. 125.

31. Garitty, *op. cit.*, p. 263.

32. Johansen and Maestas, *op. cit.*, p. 29.

33. Garitty, *op. cit.*, p. 29.

34. Ortiz, Roxanne Dunbar, *The Great Sioux Nation* (Berkeley, CA: Moon Books, 1977), p. 92.

35. Dowd, Douglas, *The Twisted Dream: Capitalist Development in the United States Since 1776* (Cambridge, MA: Winthrop, Pub., 1977), p. 63.

36. Huberman, Leo, *We The People* (New York: Monthly Review Press, 1960), pp. 190-1.

37. Miner, H. Craig, *The Corporation and the Indian* (Columbia, MO: University of Missouri Press, 1976), pp. 5, 6, 9.

38. *Ibid.*, p. 9.

39. *Ibid.*, p. 14.

40. Williams, William A., *The Contours of American History* (Cleveland: The World Publishing Co., 1961), p. 261.

41. Huberman, *op. cit.*, p. 192.

42. Josephson, Matthew, *The Robber Barons: The Great American Capitalists* (New York: Harcourt, Brace and Co., 1934). Dickenson, James R., "How the Scandals of History Left Mud on the White House Step" in Jack Douglas and John Johnson's (eds) *Official Deviance* (Philadelphia: Lippincott, 1977), p. 37.

43. Shannon, Fred A., *The Farmers Last Frontier: Agriculture, 1860-1897* (New York: Holt, Rinehart and Winston, 1961), p. 65.

44. *Ibid.*, p. 64.

45. Josephson, *op. cit.*, pp. 89-90.

46. *Ibid.*, p. 29.

47. Kolko, Gabriel, *Railroads and Regulation: 1877-1916* (Princeton: Princeton University Press, 1965), p. 1.

48. Sandoz, Mari, *The Buffalo Hunters* (Norman: University of Oklahoma, 1954), p. xii.

49. Brown, Dee, *Bury My Heart at Wounded Knee* (New York: Bantam, 1978), p. 254.

50. Clark, Ira G., *Then Came the Railroads* (Norman: University of Oklahoma Press, 1958), p. 101.

51. Gibson, A.M., *The American Indian* (Lexington, MA: D.C. Heath and Co., 1980), p. 415.

52. Jacobs, Paul et al., *To Serve the Devil, Vol. I: Natives and Slaves* (New York: Vintage Books, 1971), p. 34.

53. Clark, *op. cit.*, p. 168.

54. Miner, *op. cit.*, pp. 65-76.

55. Clark, *op. cit.*, p. 168.

56. *Ibid.*, p. 169.

57. Aldrich, Gene, "A History of the Coal Industry in Oklahoma to 1907," unpublished PhD dissertation, University of Oklahoma, 1952, p. 18.

58. Clark, *op. cit.*, p. 105.

59. See Johoda, Gloria, *The Trail of Tears* (New York: Holt, Rinehart and Winston, 1975), for the removal policies set down by Congress, which forced hundreds of American Indians to move west of the Mississippi in order to make their land available to big business.

60. Miner, *op. cit.*, p. 119.

61. *Ibid.*, p. 97.

62. Williams, *op. cit.*, p. 303.

63. Josephson, *op. cit.*, p. 114; Williams, *op. cit.*, p. 303.

64. Josephson, *op. cit.*, p. 118.

65. *Ibid.*, pp. 230, 266, 272, 396, 403; Kolko, Gabriel, *Main Currents in Modern American History* (New York: Harper and Row, 1976), p. 6.

66. Miner, *op. cit.*, pp. 157, 174, 183-4.

67. Quoted in Washburn, *op. cit.*, p. 234.

68. Miner, *op. cit.*, pp. 79, 56.

69. See Otis, D.S., *The Dawes Act and the Allotment of Indian Lands* (Norman: University of Oklahoma Press, 1973), p. 23.

70. Kickingbird, Kirke and Karen Duchencaux, *One Hundred Million Acres* (New York: MacMillan Publishing Co., 1973), p. 20.

71. Miner, *op. cit.*, pp. 192-3.

72. Both quoted in Washburn, *op. cit.*, p. 242.

73. Deloria, Vine, *Behind the Trail of Broken Treaties* (New York: Dela Pub. Co., 1974), p. 205.

74. Washburn, *op. cit.*, p. 243; Washburn, Wilcomb, *Red Man's Land/White Man's Law* (New York: Charles Schribner & Son, 1971), p. 145.

75. Garitty, Michael, "The Pending Energy Wars: America's Final Act of Genocide," *Akwesasne Notes*, vol. II, no. 5 (Winter 1980), p. 16.

76. Both quoted in Washburn, *op. cit.*, p. 208.

77. Garitty, *op. cit.*, p. 264.

78. Brown, *op. cit.*, p. 415.

79. Johansen and Maestas, *op. cit.*, p. 31.

80. *North Central Power Study, Vol. I: Study of Mine-Mouth Thermal Power Plants with Extra-High Voltage Transmission for Delivery to Load Centers* (Billings, MT: Bureau of Reclamation, October 1971), p. 75.

81. Toole, K. Ross, *The Rape of the Great Plains* (Boston: Little, Brown & Co., 1976), pp. 3-4.

82. Gyorgy, Anna and Friends, *No Nukes: Everyone's Guide to Nuclear Power* (Boston: South End Press, 1979), p. 244; see Toole, *op. cit.*, Chapter 7.

83. NCPS, *op. cit.*, p. 11.

84. Toole, *op. cit.*, p. 4.

85. Joseph J. Devaney, "Physics—related problems of coal fired power plant pollution," *The Physics Teacher* (September 1978), pp. 358-66.

86. National Academy of Sciences, *Energy and Climate* (Washington, D.C.: National Academy of Sciences, 1977), p. 2.

87. Rifkin, *op. cit.*, p. 50.

88. NCPS, *op. cit.*, pp. 16-17.

89. Garitty, *op. cit.*

90. NCPS, *op. cit.,* pp. 19-20.

91. Toole, *op. cit.,* pp. 6, 2.

92. Wibert, Wendy, "Powerline Health and Safety," *Northern Sun News,* March 1980, p. 5.

93. Toole, *op. cit.,* p. 7.

94. Amelia, Irvin, "The Black Hills 'National Sacrifice Area': A Study in U.S. Colonialism," *Minority Notes,* Vol. 1, Nos. 3-4 (Fall-Winter 1980), p. 8.

95. Raymond, W.H., et al., *Status of Mineral Resource Information for the Pine Ridge Indian Reservation, South Dakota* (U.S. Geological Survey; U.S. Bureau of Mines; Bureau of Indian Affairs, 1976), pp. 1, 36, 72.

96. Fischman, Louise, "Every Dose is an Overdose: Effects of Uranium Mining" (Rapid City, SD: Black Hills Alliance, 1980).

97. Gyorgy, *op. cit.,* p. 47.

98. Garitty, *op. cit.,* p. 256.

99. Fischman, *op. cit.*

100. *Memorandum of Agreement Between the Oglala Sioux Tribe of South Dakota and the National Park Service of the Department of the Interior to Facilitate Establishment, Development, Administration and Public Use of the Oglala Sioux Tribal Lands, Badlands National Monument,* 2 January 1976.

101. See National Park Service, *Master Plan Badlands National Monument* (Rocky Mountain Region: National Park Service, 1978), p. 28.

102. Bureau of Reclamation, *Water for Energy,* Final Environmental Impact Statement, U.S. Department of Interior, 1 December 1977, p. i.

103. *Ibid.,* p. 5—1.

104. *Ibid.,* p. 5—2.

105. *Ibid.,* p. 5—3.

106. *Ibid.* .

107. *Ibid.,* p. 5—4.

108. *Ibid.,* p. 5—5.

109. *Ibid.,* p. 3—119.

110. Johansen and Maestas: *op. cit.,* p. 130.

111. Fischman, *op. cit.*

112. "Water and Energy," publication of the Black Hills Alliance, p. 7 (Box 2508, Rapid City, SD 57709).

113. *Ibid.,* p. 4. An acre foot of water is the amount of water needed to cover an acre of land one foot deep.

114. *Ibid.,* p. 5.

115. "Radioactive Water Contamination in Rapid Valley," Lilras Jones, Black Hills Alliance.

116. For an extensive review of these see in particular Garitty, *op. cit.,* and Johansen and Maestas, *op. cit.,* pp. 123-197.

117. See Ward Churchill, "The Extralegal Implications of Yellow Thunder Tiospaye: Misadventure or Watershed Action?" *Policy Perspectives*, vol. 2, no. 2, September 1982, Rutgers University, Newark, pp. 322-326, for details.

Afterward

1. *United States v. Leonard Peltier,* 731 F2d. 550, (8th Cir. 1984), p. 18.

2. *Ibid.*

3. Heaney's statement was made in an interchange with Crooks, 15 October 1985.

4. *United States v. Leonard Peltier,* No. 95-5192.

5. *Ibid.*

6. "Court refuses Peltier appeal," *Rapid City Journal,* 6 October 1987.

7. "External Affairs: Canada-U.S. Extradition Treaty—Case of Leonard Peltier, Statement of Mr. James Fulton, *House of Commons Debate, Canada,* Vol. 128, No. 129, 1st Session, 33rd Parliament, Official Report, Thursday, 17 April 1986.

8. "Peltier back in Penitentiary, wins prize in Spain," *Rapid City Journal,* 12 December 1986.

9. Churchill, Ward, and Jim Vander Wall, *Agents of Repression: The FBI's Secret Wars Against the Black Panther Party and the American Indian Movement* (South End Press, Boston, 1988), p. 327.